W9-BEC-360

LEARNING LIMITS

LEARNING LIMITS

College Women, Drugs, and Relationships

Kimberly M. Williams

BERGIN & GARVEY
Westport, Connecticut • London

Library of Congress Cataloging-in-Publication Data

Williams, Kimberly M., 1968–
     Learning limits : college women, drugs, and relationships /
     Kimberly M. Williams.
          p.   cm.
     Includes bibliographical references and index.
     ISBN 0–89789–556–8 (alk. paper)—ISBN 0–89789–741–2 (pbk.)
     1. Women college students—Drug use—United States.
     2. Interpersonal relations—United States.   3. Man–woman
     relationships—United States.   I. Title.
     HV5824.W6W55   1998
     362.29'082'0973—dc21   97–31520

British Library Cataloguing in Publication Data is available.

Library of Congress Catalog Card Number: 97–31520
ISBN: 0–89789–741–2 (pbk.)

First published in 1998

Bergin & Garvey, 88 Post Road West, Westport, CT 06881
An imprint of Greenwood Publishing Group, Inc.
www.greenwood.com

Printed in the United States of America

The paper used in this book complies with the
Permanent Paper Standard issued by the National
Information Standards Organization (Z39.48–1984).

10 9 8 7 6 5 4 3 2 1

Contents

Preface

WHY QUALITATIVE FEMINIST RESEARCH IS NEEDED

One consistency among social science research studies on drug use and abuse is that quantitative methods examining differences between and among groups (i.e., gender differences, race differences, social class differences) have been the methods of choice. Gender-differences research continues to further separate the categories of men and women by demonstrating statistically that college women use drugs *essentially* one way and college men use drugs *essentially another* way. Because the way that men have been found to use drugs generally has been portrayed as a more threatening and harmful way (i.e., associated with more aggressive behavior and harm to self or others), treatment options have tended to target men's needs, and women's drug and drug-related problems have been downplayed or ignored (Nechas & Foley, 1994; Sandmaier, 1980).

Race-differences drug research has reinforced existing racial labels, categories, and stereotypes, suggesting that various racial groups use drugs in certain ways and White people use them in other ways. Some drug research has looked at social class differences, and many have reported that the poor use drugs one way and the wealthy use drugs in a different way. Drugs used more often by the poor and people of color have been constructed as more dangerous, and use of these drugs is more likely to be criminalized than the drugs of choice of White, wealthy people. For example, smoking cocaine in the form of crack (popular in urban ghettos where there are high percentages of nonwhites) is penalized one hundred times more severely than snorting the same amount of powdered cocaine (popular among wealthy Whites) (*United States of America v. Booker*, 1995).

Sexual orientation and power position of the researched have seemed to be assumed in drug research to be heterosexual and of equal power and rarely made problematic. However, projects need to be carried out to examine these two (and other) aspects of social location.

In my project, I wanted to make aspects of women's social locations more complicated than previous research literature on college drug use had. To accomplish this objective, I analyzed the words a group of women from various backgrounds used to construct their social locations (including gender, race, social class, sexual preference, religion, and geographical location) as they described the role of drugs in their lives. Historically, the literature has not examined women's words but has statistically examined gender differences (referred to in the literature as "sex differences"), race differences, and social class differences when studying drug use and abuse.

Gender-Differences Drug Research and the Implications

Around the same time that feminism's second wave began, in the 1960s, women began to use alcohol and other drugs more openly in society; alcohol and other drug abuse, which had previously been closeted, started to become slightly more overt in mainstream society (Sandmaier, 1980). However, the literature tended to downplay women's experiences with substances and substance abuse, providing evidence that men's problems with substances were more common and significant.

Gender-differences research during the 1970s. Many research reports throughout the 1970s focused on the differences between men and women and their licit and illicit drug use. Gender differences were reported in nearly every quantitative study performed on college drug use. Many studies found that women showed increases in cigarette smoking, while men demonstrated increased use of illicit drugs and alcohol (Fago & Sedlacek, 1973; Girdano & Girdano, 1976; Hanson, 1975). Most studies reported gender differences claiming that significantly more men than women used drugs (including alcohol) (e.g., Fago & Sedlacek, 1973; Rebstock & Young, 1978). However, some conflicting studies reported that women's use of marijuana, alcohol, and speed approached the same levels as men's (e.g., Fidler & Bucy, 1976).

During the 1970s, studies emerged linking college women's drug (including alcohol) use and their sexual behaviors and attitudes. Studies of this nature were not typically conducted with college men. For example, in 1973, a survey conducted exclusively with college women reported that women who used drugs (specifically marijuana or hallucinogens) were more likely than nonusers to have "liberal attitudes" about premarital sex and were more likely to have engaged in sexual intercourse (67% of the "drug-using" group reported having engaged in sexual intercourse in contrast to only 18% of the nondrug-using group) (Arafat & Yorburg, 1973). Studies like this one, common during this decade, served to perpetuate the stereotype of the college woman drug user as one who was sexually promiscuous without critically analyzing the sexual mores of the college culture as experienced by the students in the culture.

College women's alcohol and other substance use, in the rare instances when it was the focus of a research question, often centered around issues of a woman's sexuality (i.e., attitudes about sex, sexual involvement, arousal-seeking tendencies, etc.) and her personality (i.e., self-esteem, self-concept, learned-helplessness, etc.). One such example portrayed college women as using alcohol to gain attention and affection, and using alcohol and other drugs as a means of gaining greater sexual prowess (through lowered inhibitions) (e.g., Jessor, 1968). A couple of drug studies that focused on college women examined "daydreaming styles" and "organization of needs" (Huba, 1977a, 1977b). Studies attempting to link "learned helplessness" and "self-concept" to alcohol use were conducted exclusively with college women without discussions of similar studies for men. One such study argued that women with lower ratings in self-esteem/self-concept drank more and used more drugs than women with higher self-esteem ratings (Segal, 1975). Men, on the other hand, in the popular gender-differences paradigm, as described in studies such as Kreutzer's (1980), were frequently portrayed as using alcohol to become more aggressive (socially and sexually).

Gender-differences research in the 1980s. Lester (1983) conducted a research project comparing male and female students across many different variables over a ten-year period. The study explored such variables as illicit drug and alcohol use and sexual behavior. Lester concluded that the significant differences that existed between college men and women in 1973 had disappeared ten years later. This study marked the beginning of the period when research attempted to provide evidence for the disappearance of gender differences suggesting that women and men were beginning (for the first time in American history) to use psychoactive substances at similar rates. Another study that argued that the gap between college men's and college women's drug use was closing or had already closed was Traub's (1983) survey of male and female undergraduates. He demonstrated that female (like male) substance users used drugs quite often, associated with many friends who used and abused drugs, and tended to graduate to "stronger drugs" after using marijuana.

Johnson (1988) reexamined some popular personality characteristics that have historically shown a significant relationship to college women's drinking: social desirability, internal/external locus of control, fear of failure, and sensation seeking. The relative importance of these factors was compared for "heavy drinkers" and "light drinkers." Johnson found significant differences between heavy and light drinkers for the variables "sensation seeking" and "fear of failure," with heavy drinkers rating higher on each. This study, like many others, attempted to study gender differences by focusing specifically on the behaviors of college women and on stereotypical aspects of a gendered personality.

Gender-differences research in the 1990s. Throughout the 1980s and into the 1990s, many gender stereotypes persisted, and the gender-differences approach continued to dominate the literature on college student substance use and abuse, with few if any explanations as to why these differences exist. For example, a frequently cited survey analysis, called "insightful" by Hanson and Venturelli (1995), which compared male and female drug abuse patterns between 1975 and

1993, demonstrated the following statistically, but without comment or explanation as to why these differences might be so: Male college students reported higher usage rates for all illicit drugs, particularly heroin, inhalants, LSD (and hallucinogens in general), and marijuana; similarities were found for stimulants, narcotics other than heroin, barbiturates and other depressants; and men were found to have significantly higher rates of "intense" (everyday) use (the only exception was cigarettes, which women were found to use more and more intensely) (Johnston, O'Malley, & Bachman, 1993).

Lex (1990) provided a comprehensive twenty-year overview of the literature on substance abuse problems in research journals. Frequently cited gender differences between males and females listed for clinically identified subgroups with alcohol dependence have included: a difference in women and men's socialization (i.e., women tended to be less assertive and had a greater reliance on and need for support systems); women tended to become involved with drugs as a result of their relationships with men who abuse drugs (husbands, fathers, boyfriends, etc.); women addicts were more likely to have been sexually abused; women tended to have more medical problems (and were taken less seriously when they sought medical attention) (Lex, 1990). While this article did not focus specifically on college women, it dealt with other issues relevant for college women such as the aforementioned gender differences as well as the relationship of stress and major life events on women's substance use and abuse. Lex connected stressful life events with social class by writing that research supported the idea that "the closest association between stressful life events and the onset of alcohol abuse was found in the lowest social class, with the smallest association found for women in the higher social classes" (p. 181). The study also marked the beginning of descriptive summaries that included a discussion of significant physiological differences between men and women and the impact of these differences on alcohol metabolism and health risks.

Heritage and West (1993) summarized the results of campuswide surveys conducted at Middle Tennessee State University in 1977, 1983, 1987, and 1992. They reported that gender differences in drug use, which seemed to be quite significant in 1977, were not as significant in 1992, and they argued that differences would continue to become less significant in the future. In 1993, feminist researcher Jacqueline White wrote that the research would likely continue to move away from documenting gender differences and would focus more on the processes that make gender a significant feature in social interactions. However, drug research since 1993 has failed to focus on these processes.

The gender-differences approach has also tended to ignore categories within gender such as class and race by examining them separately or attempting to *control* for these *variables*. Some studies have attempted to show (quantitatively) the differences among diverse groups in their drug use. For example, Johnson and Gallo-Treacy (1993) conducted a rare study examining both ethnicity and gender. They linked aspects of cultural identity, ethnicity, and gender by examining the drinking behaviors of forty-five college women—fifteen Irish, fifteen Italian, and fifteen Hispanic. The Irish women reported higher drinking rates than the other groups. Irish women were also significantly more likely to attribute more positive expectations to alcohol use (i.e., assertiveness, social enhancement, and disinhibition) than the Hispanic or Italian women. This article summarized other research on ethnic differences but failed to address the role of gender.   Johnson and Gallo-Treacy made some dangerously stereotypical assumptions about ethnic identities, particularly the Irish, while ignoring other issues such as social class. Since all were women, this study suggests that disempowerment through alcohol as experienced by some women is a cultural artifact and that the differing effects of alcohol and other drugs by gender may be socially constructed.   This article also failed to discuss the context of the college environment and the role that this factor might have played in influencing or maintaining these stereotypes.

The information from the Core drug and alcohol survey of students at the university. The student affairs office at the university where I conducted this project administered a thirty-nine-question survey in February and March 1996. The U. S. Department of Education funded this survey which was developed by the Core Institute. Of the 1,210 randomly selected students, 406 (35%) returned a completed questionnaire. Survey results indicated that women drank alcohol less than men, fewer women (43%) reported binge drinking (five or more drinks in a sitting) than men (64%), students of color drank less than White students, and sophomores and juniors drank less than seniors and first-year students. The percentages for different drugs will be discussed in Chapter 7. The findings of the Core Institute's survey were similar to the national averages at other campuses (Bushman, 1996). Although these statistics were useful, they tell only a limited part of the story of college women's drug use. For more detailed information about the Core Survey data, see Appendix A.

Implications of Gender Differences in Research Literature

Gender-differences research demonstrating consistently that men's drug use is more problematic than women's has had some troubling implications. Lott (1988) wrote that "the perception of polarized and opposing gender attributes (separate spheres) has serious social ramifications for personal growth opportunities and access to resources for women" (p. 55). For example, one possible result of college women's separation from college men in the literature on college student drug abuse has been that women (not just college women but all women) have historically been underrepresented in alcohol and substance abuse treatment programs. This is not due to women's lack of significant problems with substance abuse, but to the belief that substance abuse is a man's problem. As a result, treatment programs (resources and opportunities for rehabilitation) have seemed less available to women than to men. Nechas and Foley (1994, p. 156) stated that "Traditionally, substance abuse has been regarded almost entirely as a male affliction, an unfortunate assumption that has compounded the invisibility problem for addicted women."

Lott (1988, p. 56) argued that "gender differences exist for certain behaviors at certain ages and in some situations, but that behaviors are better understood in context, not by gender alone." Despite the concerns raised such as Lott's, research in the area of women's alcohol and other drug use has not headed in a direction where the context or environment is analyzed critically from the perspective of women living within it. One important way of understanding the role that drugs play in college culture for women is to gain a deeper understanding of the nature of the words women use to describe drugs in their lives and the themes that emerge around the use of psychoactive substances. A deeper level of understanding of the context in which different substances are used on college campuses from the perspective of women will improve our understanding of the nature of substance abuse problems prevalent on college campuses.

The limited qualitative literature on women and drugs: The addicts. Qualitative methods such as ethnographies, in-depth interviewing, and participant observations have been absent from the literature on college students' drug usage. In the mid-1980s and into the 1990s, ethnographies involving college students (but not about their drug use) such as Weis's (1985), Moffatt's (1989), and Holland and Eisenhart's (1990) were published. In addition, in the 1980s, ethnographic studies about alcoholic women such as Sandmaier's (1980) *Invisible Alcoholics*, Stammer's (1991) book *Women and Alcohol*, and Hafner's (1991) *Nice Girls Don't Drink* emerged to bring the hidden problems of female alcoholics to public attention.

These studies show a shift toward an increased awareness of women's alcohol problems in the literature since 1980. Alcohol abuse among adolescent and college-aged women also seems to be coming to the attention of scholars. However, qualitative studies about women and drugs have focused on women considered "deviant" or as having drug "problems" instead of focusing on how women in a particular environment where drugs are prevalent make sense of drugs in their daily lives.

Race, Social Class, and Drug Use in the Literature

Feminist Methodology and Perspectives from Underrepresented Groups. DeVault (1996) in her article "Talking Back to Sociology" wrote: "it is ironic that writing on feminist methodology has so rarely incorporated the perspectives of women from underrepresented groups and nations (and their male allies), even as these writers have become more central to feminist theory. . . contributions of women from underrepresented groups have too often been ignored or appropriated. Women from these groups continue to mount pointed challenges to emerging orthodoxies that ignore their perspectives" (p. 17). Palmer (in Takaki, 1994, p. 186) observed that White feminists have a tendency to downplay or ignore race and class because they are "unexperienced elements in their oppression." Palmer (p. 168) wrote: "often treating race and class as secondary factors in social organization, feminist theorists write from experiences in which race and class are not felt as oppressive elements in their lives." In social science drug research, feminist scholarship has been absent, and existing quantitative research has often ignored historically underrepresented groups and their experiences with drugs. In my feminist analysis, I attempted to include the often forgotten issues of race, social class, and power. I wanted to demonstrate how women in my project took up race, class, and power as they described their experiences and decisions about drug use. No other social science research on drug use has done this.

Deconstructing racial and ethnic labels. The topic of college student drug use and abuse has used existing racial categories in an attempt to simplify and make generalizations about race and class. This strategy has often failed to acknowledge the complexities of race and social class. Granted, race is very difficult to define. Different theorists have different ideas about what is meant by race or how race is socially constructed. The common perception in American culture is that of a binary: majority or minority. The "minority" label is often applied to African-Americans, Hispanics, Native Americans, and Asian-Americans. The term lumps these groups together, despite the fact that these groups are diverse in their goals, customs, and beliefs. Goldberg (1997, p. 114) believed that "any discussion of drinking patterns among Hispanics is complicated by their cultural diversity. Among the numerous Hispanic groups are Mexicans, Puerto Ricans, and Cubans." Asian-Americans are sometimes considered "minorities," and Goldberg reported significant differences in drinking patterns between the "Asian-American subgroups" Korean, Japanese, Chinese, and Filipino. In addition, Goldberg (1997, p. 114) wrote: "to generalize about drinking patterns of American Indians is difficult because of tribal diversity. Some tribes have a high incidence of alcohol abuse, and others are primarily abstinent." Clearly, racial categories and labels are insufficient, and generalizations based on race are inappropriate.

Heath (1990) suggested that we deconstruct the labels associated with categories of race and ethnicity. He acknowledged that "valuable insights have been made in understanding sociocultural systems and alcohol through studies using ethnicity as a variable, but since neither ethnic categories nor alcohol use are static, new models should be applied" (p. 607). Cheung (1990) pointed out that her review of the literature demonstrated methodological and theoretical problems in research on ethnicity and drug use. "Explanations of variation in drug use due to ethnicity have been confounded by the confusion between ethnicity and race." Cheung suggested that we need to examine "cultural and structural aspects of ethnicity at both the individual (e.g., ethnic culture retention and ethnic socialization) and the collective (e.g., ethnic community involvement)" to help solve some of the past problems in the literature (p. 602).

As Cheung (1993, p. 1209) argued, "because ethnicity is a multidimensional concept, the use of only one dimension, as is the case in many alcohol/drug use studies, is inadequate. Studies of ethnicity and substance use also often fail to recognize the presence of subcultural differences within an ethnic group." Research on substance use and abuse has typically looked at race and ethnicity in a unidimensional way without regard for context or subcultures. Drug research needs to focus on race and how race is experienced, as well as how these experiences may influence an individual's decisions about drug use.

Race differences in the drug research literature. In the literature on drug use and college students, race has typically been discussed as a variable that is statistically "controlled for" and race is the independent variable. For example, in the 1970s a large study surveyed 24,475 college and university students in the United States. African-American students had the lowest reported rates of alcohol, marijuana, stimulants, and hallucinogen use followed by Asian-Americans and Whites. Native Americans reported the highest use rates, and no data were reported for Hispanic students (Strimbu, Schoenfeldt, Sims, & Suthern, 1973). A more recent example, a study by O'Hare (1990), found in a random sample of 606 undergraduates at Rutgers University that 81.5% of the sample drank and 18.8% were heavy drinkers. He argued that although half as many women as men reported being heavy drinkers, they had an equal number (proportionately) of alcohol-related problems. This study statistically controlled for race and found that White students drank more alcohol than nonwhite students, reinforcing the notion of a racial binary without complicating race.

Another recent example, building on the popular tradition of statistically controlling for race by Winslow and Gay (1993), involving 1,035 undergraduates at a large western university, found that "members of minority and low-income groups tend to be less deviant than their more affluent, White classmates, at least in regard to acts of low-consensus deviance, that is, pertaining to traditional morality, including sexual activity, alcohol consumption and drug usage" (p. 17). They argued further that having not been exposed to law enforcement was perhaps a better predictor of serious deviance than income or race, suggesting that the negative experiences of "inner-city" youth with law enforcement in their culture was likely to deter students of color from using drugs. However, these students were never asked how (or even if) their experiences with law enforcement influenced their decisions about drug use.

Black adolescents have been shown to drink less, start drinking when they are older, and are less likely to drink heavily than Whites (Johnstone, 1994). Recent reports have found that more black men and women abstain from drug and alcohol use than Whites. For example, Caetano and Kaskutas (1995) found that 29% of Black men abstained versus 23% of White men, and 46% of Black women abstained versus 34% of White women. Herd (1989) found that more Whites were heavy drinkers than Blacks within the 18-to-29 age group, and that Blacks within this age group were more likely to be abstainers. However, more Black and Latino men die as a direct or indirect result of alcohol than White and Asian-American men (Goldberg, 1997). Herd argued that Black men have had more alcohol-related problems than White men, not because of the alcohol, but because of poverty, higher unemployment, discrimination, poor living conditions, and lack of health care. These studies show a recent interest in combining *variables* such as race, class, and gender by quantifying and controlling them, and the tendency of researchers to report race as Black and White.

One of the rare qualitative studies examining how students in an urban community college made meaning of their lives as college students was conducted in the mid-1980s. Weis's (1985) book entitled *Between Two Worlds* devoted only a brief section to the role of drugs among this population and failed to address gender. However, she did discuss how race and social class were experienced for a group of mostly Black community college students. Weis's goal with this work was to "fill a significant void in the literature on education and cultural and economic reproduction" (p. 10). She wrote: "while students do not spend all their time engaged in drug use at college (although some do just that), drugs are part and parcel of day-to-day existence within the institution. Drug use serves to maintain the collectivity (it is not, for the most part, an individual act), and also serves to distance students from the process that is education." She likened student drug use to that which Paul Willis in his famous ethnography *Learning to Labor*, referred to as a "lived contradiction" (Willis in Weis, 1995, p. 10). Working class students touted the importance of attending class and doing well in school, but in contradiction to this ideal they engaged in activities such as excessive drug use. These behaviors contributed to social class reproduction. That is, the working-class students did poorly in school (perhaps partly because of their drug use), and as a result did not get better jobs than their parents, and remained working-class. More work needs to be done to examine the role of social class in drug-use choices.

Acculturation level and drug use. Recent studies have examined one's drug use relative to how acculturated one has become into American society. For example, Neff and Hoppe (1992), in their study of 412 Whites, 239 Blacks, and 635 Mexican Americans, found that "though it was hypothesized, in an acculturation stress model of alcohol use, that more alcohol would be consumed to alleviate stress associated with the attainment of high or upper-medium acculturation, the data supported the opposite case: the lowest acculturation group exhibited slightly higher quantity and frequency of drinking." They acknowledged that their yardstick for measuring "acculturation level" (i.e., generations in America) is "inadequate" and recommend that other ways of measuring acculturation be considered. Marin, Posner, and Kinyon (1993, p. 373) wrote about the notion of "acculturation" that the "more acculturated Hispanics tended to respond in a manner similar to non-Hispanic Whites." These studies suggest that it is still unclear what influence (if any) one's "acculturation level" has on a person's decisions about drinking and other drug use.

The Relationships between Race, Social Class, and Drug Use

Social class is another important aspect of one's social location that has been overlooked in the literature on adolescent or college-aged drug use. When research examines the drug use of "inner-city youth" from different racial groups, the importance of social class is sometimes assumed, downplayed, or ignored. Inner-city youth are often stereotyped as being more likely to abuse illicit drugs than their wealthier and White counterparts. For example, a comprehensive literature review by Padilla, Duran, and Nobles (1995) concluded that "inner-city youth and young adults are at high risk for substance abuse, which further lessens their chances for educational and occupational advancement" (p. 411).

The popular media frequently portray inner-city poor youth of color as drug dealers and drug abusers. Statistical analyses examining race frequently ignore social class or take it for granted. Statistical analyses have been made at the university where I conducted my project, and racial differences in attitudes and use patterns were evident. In contrast to many stereotypes that exist about people of color using drugs more often than Whites, White students at the university where I conducted my project were found to use drugs more frequently and more excessively than Black, Hispanic, and Asian-American students, according to unpublished survey data collected for the United States Department of Education (U.S. Department of Education, 1996). This statistical analysis did not include an examination of social class background and drug use.

Some drug studies have focused exclusively on social class, and other studies have centered on race and social class. Social class has been demonstrated in the literature to have some influence on one's decisions about alcohol and other substance use and abuse. For example, McGee (1992) hypothesized that the influence of parents and peers varied by social class. Using regression analyses to determine the statistical significance of different predictors, she found that among the middle class, peer influence was significant and parental influence was insignificant in predicting adolescent drug use. Among the upper and lower classes, the influence of parents and peers was not found to be a statistically significant indicator of drug use.

An example of a large-scale, quantitative project examining the impact of race and social class on adolescent drug use involved 77,500 high school seniors in forty-eight states from various racial, ethnic, social class, and family backgrounds. This study found that "controlling for [family] background [i.e., single or two-parent families] alone does not account for most racial/ethnic differences in drug use. In fact, if black youth were as likely as whites to live in two-parent households and have highly educated parents, their drug use might have even been lower than reported" (Wallace & Bachman, 1991, p. 352). These authors found that when they controlled for social class and family background, "many of the racial/ethnic differences in drug use [were] considerably reduced" (p. 350).

Drugs that have been constructed as abused primarily by the poor and people of color have been socially constructed as "worse" than drugs used by Whites (e.g., crack and heroin). These "worse drugs" frequently result in stiffer penalties and fewer treatment options than the drugs that have been constructed as White drugs (e.g., alcohol, nicotine, and marijuana). More about this will be described in Part III.

I wanted my project to begin to fill a void in the literature about college student drug use that traditionally has statistically examined gender, race, and social class differences. I could not find any research literature that seemed to problematize the drug-related experiences of college women. None of the literature described adequately my own experiences as a college woman or what I had heard other college women describe. The research articles and books about college drug use were very simple, and my drug experiences and the drug experiences of other college women were very complicated.

After reading many studies on college student drug use, completing a quantitative study about college students' problems with drinking, and teaching for several semesters a course about drugs to college students, I knew that the voices of students living in the college culture were missing from the research literature. I had heard stories in the classroom, read detailed narratives of what it was like to live in an environment where drug abuse was prevalent and expected by many, and I reflected on my own experiences around drugs. I thought these experiences were much more meaningful and complicated than the statistical "truth" presented in nearly every drug study about college students. In addition, I realized that the experiences of women in the quantitative research literature were absent from or lumped together, ignoring such aspects of one's social location as race, social class, sexual orientation, power position, geographic location, and privilege in much of the biological (emphasizing physiological explanations for drug use and abuse), psychological (emphasizing reinforcement and individual personality traits in explanations for drug use and abuse), and sociological (emphasizing the social forces, subcultures, and social interactions in explanations for drug use and abuse) theory created about drug use from the volumes of quantitative research.

I locate this research project within feminist methodology given my own commitment to the challenging, yet critical, goals that DeVault (1996, p. 5) described. First, "feminists seek a methodology that will do the work of 'excavation,' shifting the focus of standard practice from men's in order to reveal the locations and perspectives of (all) women." Second, "feminists seek a science that minimizes harm and control in the research process." Third, "feminists seek a methodology that will support research of value to women, leading to social change or action beneficial to women." DeVault (1996, p. 7) continued that "together these criteria for feminist methodology provide the outline for a possible alternative to the distanced, distorting, and dispassionately objective procedures of much social research." In my project, I sought to provide an alternative to the existing objective and quantitative measures used in social science drug research by using DeVault's criteria as my guide.

In this project, I sought to analyze critically the meaning women attached to the role of drugs in their lives in college. The focus was on a particular group of college women, *their* perspectives, and the words *they* used to describe the role of drugs in *their* lives, and more specifically the role of drugs in *their* interpersonal relationships. This has not been done before.

THE PROJECT

Undergraduate women enrolled in the course that I taught entitled "Drug Education for Teachers" at some time during the Fall 1995 semester through the Fall 1996 semester at a large, private, research university participated in my project. The seven-week course was offered twice each semester. The average class size was eighteen with the smallest ten and the largest twenty-five. At the time of my project, this was a mandatory course for all students in the Elementary and Special Education Inclusive Program. Most of the students were matriculated in the School of Education. However, non-Education majors also could and did enroll in the course. At the time I began this project, I had been teaching the course for two years.

Within my teacher role, I attempted to downplay my position of power by having students voice their experiences in class and in journals, and by having each student assume the teacher role, teaching part of the course. I showed respect for all ideas presented in the classroom and gave students the choice to write about whatever they felt comfortable in their journals. I thought I had successfully created a safe classroom environment that fostered open and honest discussion among students in the classroom (and outside the classroom) where students felt that their opinions and experiences were heard and mattered. I viewed myself as a peer, a colleague, and a fellow researcher of education.

Throughout my project, I was committed to downplaying my power position as much as I could. I did not want to take on a "view from above," which Mies (1983, p. 124) considered popular among researchers. Rather, I wanted to take a view from below where I was seeking help and information from these women. I tried to communicate this perspective throughout the project, and to further emphasize it, I did not grade the journals, and conducted interviews after they had completed the course.

I have since realized that I cannot deny the power *inherent* in my role. Rather, I must accept it and try to determine how my role as "teacher" may have influenced my relationships with these women, as well as the nature of the information they provided me. I believe that although teachers still initially have the power over their students, they also have the power to decide how to use it, just as the researcher has the power to decide how to gather data from informants.

The project involved multiple parts. In addition to making observations from my vantage point as "teacher" in the classroom, I also asked students to keep a journal of drug-related behavior and conducted in-depth interviews with students who were more involved with drugs—either directly or indirectly.

The Journal Assignment

Men and women in the course wrote one journal entry each week during the seven-week course about the role of drugs in their lives and the lives of those around them. The assignment read as follows:

Observations of drug use within your social setting. Students should include their personal exposure to substance use. The personal observation/use section will not be graded for specific content, but credit will be given. Please include your personal use, to the extent that you feel comfortable, as well as the use of those around you. Include your reactions to the drugs being used in your "society" (i.e., the college and home environment), and make observations of your social and cultural settings—the residence halls, off campus apartments, parties, bars, etc. Observations should be made weekly. Observations will be confidential.

Students asked questions about this assignment in class. At that time I emphasized that I would prefer that students focus on their own experiences rather than on those of others and give honest descriptions of these experiences. At this time, I also explained to them the nature of my project and assured them that their names would not be used.

Only the narratives of women who were full-time, matriculated undergraduates residing in University housing were used in my project. Seventy-two women met these criteria, and each of their journals was analyzed: Forty-three first-year, seventeen second-year, ten third-year, and two fourth-year students. Sixty of the women were enrolled in the School of Education, seven were in the College of Arts and Sciences, one was in the College of Visual and Performing Arts, one was in the School of Management, and three were in the College for Human Development. Sixty-one of the women were White, three were Asian, two were Latina, and six were Black (including Jamaican and African-American).

As I read the journals, I began to think more critically about issues of gender, race, and class. I have become increasingly aware of, and wanted to avoid, what Spellman (1988) described as the problem of "false universalization" where differences among women are ignored (i.e. race, sexual orientation, religion, class, ethnicity, etc.). Much as Bannerji (1995) argued that race, ethnicity, gender, and nationality are part of any social act and that any feminist research must take these differences into account, I sought to examine how aspects of social location were taken up in discussions and written descriptions of drug use. As Bell and Yalom (1990, p. 7) wrote in their edited book *Revealing Lives: Autobiography, Biography and Gender,* "individuals writing about themselves have traditionally been prone to take their gender as a given, usually conflating it with sex, and to reflect upon it less than they do their race, class, religious or political affiliation, which have appeared to them as more idiosyncratic." They argued further that often "men rarely make an issue of their gender because the generic masculine has been the norm in Western society for at least three millennia, with woman conceptualized as derivative from and secondary to man" (p. 7). Although Bell and Yalom did not address the issue of race in writing autobiographical material, I began to notice as I read through the women's narratives that "Whiteness" was taken for granted, as was gender.

The Interviews

At the end of the seven-week course, I asked the women whether they would be willing to be involved in an in-depth interview with me about the nature of their drug use. If so, they were asked to include a telephone number and e-mail address on the informed consent form when they submitted their journals to me. Each of the seventy-two women signed an informed consent form (Appendix B) to allow me to use their journal entries in this research, and twenty-five women gave me their phone numbers, indicating that they would be willing to be interviewed. Based on their responses in the journals, I selected thirteen women who seemed to be exposed to or directly involved in groups of fairly regular drug users (i.e., daily to weekly use of illicit drugs or alcohol). As it turned out, women who wrote about their involvement with drugs more openly seemed more likely to be willing to be interviewed. I surmised, based on informal discussions with women who did not wish to be interviewed, that some of them might have felt, as one woman put it, that "I would have nothing to say because I don't use drugs and I really don't see them." However, some women who did not use or see drugs volunteered to be interviewed.

The thirteen women I selected were interviewed for approximately ninety minutes about their experiences with drugs in college. Ten of the women were White, and the other three were Asian-American, African-American, and Latina. I interviewed each of the women of color who volunteered. Four were sophomores and nine were first-year students. All except one were students in the School of Education with aspirations of becoming a teacher. Pseudonyms were used for the names of the women involved as well as the individuals mentioned in the journal entries and interviews.

In Graham's (1984, p. 112) words, "the use of semi-structured interviews has become the principal means by which feminists have sought to achieve active involvement of their respondents in the construction of data about their lives." Reinharz (1992, p. 19) wrote that "interviewing offers researchers access to people's ideas, thoughts, and memories in their own words rather than in the words of the researcher." My goal was for the interview to follow what Reinharz (1983, p. 77) called "phenomenological interviewing," that is, "an interviewee-guided investigation of a lived experience." I had also hoped that phenomenological interviewing would yield rich narratives about the role of drugs in everyday life.

I had hoped that, through the use of phenomenological interviewing following written journal reports after seven weeks of rapport-building in the classroom, these women would feel safe in talking about the role of psychoactive substances in their lives. Oakley (1981, p. 58) described why building rapport and trust is essential to the interviewer–interviewee relationship: "If [feminist research in social science] requires, further, that the mythology of 'hygienic' research with its accompanying mystification of the researcher and the researched as objective instruments of data production be replaced by the recognition that personal involvement is more than dangerous bias—it is the condition under which people come to know each other and to admit others into their lives."

Despite my initial concerns about building "enough" rapport with these women for them to feel comfortable sharing with me the nature of their involvement in illegal activities around drug use, they were remarkably candid about their drug-related experiences. Not all of the women were immediately open about their illicit involvement in the interviews; some were quite guarded initially before they opened up and shared with me some alarming information. I use the term *alarming* because I was surprised that they trusted me enough to share some of the stories (which I will describe later).

Women were asked at the start of the interview if they would be willing to be audiotaped. Each of the women was willing, and interviews were audiotaped and transcribed as soon after as possible. I attempted to follow DeVault's (1990, p. 101) advice to be aware that "the words available often do not fit, women learn to 'translate' when they talk about their experiences. As they do so, parts of their lives disappear because they are not included in the language of the account. In order to 'recover' these parts of women's lives, researchers must develop methods for listening around and beyond words." To do this, DeVault (1990, p. 101) argued that we need to "ground our interviewing in accounts of everyday activity." Reinharz (1992, p. 24) suggested that one possible way to achieve this is the "interviewee-guided interview" that "requires great attentiveness on the part of the interviewer during an interview and a kind of trust that the interviewee will lead the interviewer in fruitful directions."

These thirteen women were asked to discuss the role alcohol and other drugs played in their everyday lives and the lives of those around them. Interviewees were asked broad open-ended questions such as "Describe what you do when you're not doing school-related activities" or "what do you do for fun in college?" and "what role do drugs play in this?" Because the term *drugs* is often interpreted to mean illicit drugs, specific questions about alcohol and cigarette smoking were also asked. The questions I asked after a woman's response to the initial question varied dramatically because I wanted them to talk about all aspects of their lives related to drugs and drug use. In most cases, the discussion centered around the women and their various relationships. This emerged as a central theme to be described in the chapters.

As I read the narratives of these women and began to conduct interviews with some of them, I realized, as Taylor, Gilligan, and Sullivan (1995, p. 14) observed in their interview study of teenage girls about race: "A narrative account is produced interactively, depending not only on the questions of the interviewer and the experiences of the narrator, but also on the 'social location' of both. Hence, any telling of a 'story' may be affected by race, ethnicity, gender, class, age, sexual orientation, religious background, personal history, character—an infinite list of possible factors that form the scaffolding of relationships between people." I became more aware of issues of race and class (and other aspects of one's social location) as I began to read the narratives of women of color, and this critical reading forced me to question my own social location and biases.

In addition to reading and hearing the narratives of women about how they made meaning of the role of drugs in their lives as college students, I also wanted to find out how a particular group of women made meaning of their complex social locations within a culture where drug use seemed to be tightly integrated into the social life. I wanted to examine how a group of women socially constructed the role of drugs within their relationships, and I wanted to determine some of the issues for these women that have not previously been identified in the literature.

Data Analysis

Within the field of symbolic interactionism, a basic tenet exists, which as Ritzer (1996, p. 349) wrote: "individuals learn the meanings of objects during the socialization process. . . . People learn symbols as well as meanings in social interaction." Blumer (1969, p. 11) wrote: "the nature of an object. . . consists of the meaning that it has for the person for whom it is an object." The objects that I was interested in for my project were various psychoactive drugs. These drugs had different meaning for different women, and these meanings were socially constructed in various ways.

My analysis sought to improve our understanding of how college women socially constructed meaning about drugs in their everyday worlds. Women were asked to begin by describing their everyday activities (using classroom observations, phenomenological interviewing, and written narratives), and the role drugs played in these everyday experiences and social activities. I examined how notions about drug use within college were socially constructed.

Data analysis was ongoing throughout the course of this project. Through the use of observer comments and analytical memos throughout the period of data collection, I analyzed the meanings women were taking from their experiences with and around drugs and examined specific leads or possible categories and themes that seemed to be emerging. At the conclusion of data collection, transcribed materials were carefully organized and analyzed. All interviews and journals were transcribed and analyzed critically. I have left words and phrases unchanged. That is, I have not corrected grammar, spelling and punctuation in the women's written words, or their grammar in their spoken words. Occasionally, I denote misspellings with a *[sic]*, but grammatical and punctuation errors are not noted. I wanted to keep the women's words as true as possible.

Coding categories were developed based on recurring ideas (words, phrases, activities) that emerged. I engaged in in-depth interpretive textual analysis of the written words that the women used. I paid careful attention to the particular sites where drug use seemed to intersect with these college women's lives, the discourses women used to construct meaning based on their experiences within these sites, and the ways relationships shaped how these women made meaning of drugs in their lives.

Throughout my data analysis, I was concerned about analyzing and writing about race and class as well as about the ways I represented the women in this project. I struggled with the issues of speaking for others and making generalizations about groups of women. Linda Alcoff's (1994) chapter entitled "The Problem of Speaking for Others" proved helpful as I thought about this issue. Alcoff (p. 286) wrote: "There is a strong, albeit contested, current within feminism that holds that speaking for others—even for other women—is arrogant, vain, unethical, and politically illegitimate. Feminist scholarship has a liberatory agenda that almost requires that women scholars speak on behalf of other women, and yet the dangers of speaking across differences of race, culture, sexuality, and power are becoming increasingly clear to all."

I battled with the notion of "speaking across" the differences Alcoff mentioned throughout my data analysis. I wanted to avoid what Alcoff described as "the practice of privileged persons speaking for or on behalf of less privileged persons [that] has actually resulted (in many cases) in increasing or reinforcing the oppression of the group spoken for" (p. 287). To avoid this practice, I thought critically, and sometimes painfully, about race, class, sexuality, and power.

Having read the journals of women of color from the "city" who mentioned race and their experiences, I realized that my White, middle-class background was influencing my interpretation of these women's experiences. I had previously thought about race and class as concepts but had not realized how these influenced one's experiences, which in turn influenced one's decisions about drug use while in college. I had not problematized Whiteness until I "heard" how Whiteness was taken up in the narratives of women of color.

I began to examine the White women's narratives more critically for more subtle writings about race and class. Although race was never directly mentioned in the White women's narratives, when questioned in the interviews women were able to speak about race as if it was something about which they had each thought (although not something that most of them could articulate easily). I observed, like Chase (1995), that for most of these women race was a "relatively unsettled. . . ideological discursive realm." According to Chase, talking about issues of inequality in interviews "constrains our talk in ways that make us self-conscious about what we are saying." When I raised race as an issue, the words seemed difficult for me as well as for my informants. I was uneasy about labels such as Black, White, Latina, and Hispanic. The women in the interviews also seemed to struggle with these racial labels, tending toward more formal and "politically correct" labels like African-American and Caucasian, particularly when describing races other than their own, and less formal or less politically correct labels, like Blacks or minorities, or Whites when describing their own race.

The White women also did not (or perhaps could not) speak at length about racial differences in drug use or even differences in "partying," perhaps because they did not know what to say or did not have the words available to say what they wanted. This also may have been because they did not see students of color at their parties and did not go to parties where students of color predominated. The only two White women who had attended such parties noticed that there were separate party cultures that were segregated by race and quite different in the focus of the "partying" and the drugs necessary to have a "party."

I began to follow Fine's advice presented in Taylor et al. (1995, p. 16) to "interrupt the dominant cultural taboo on speaking directly about race by bringing. . . questions about race into. . . interviews." When asked directly, the White women were aware of the racial segregation on campus; in some cases they seemed concerned, but they felt helpless about it. Segregation simply was a fact of life. For example, Jude, who was White (when asked about race in her interview), said: "I had lots of Black friends in high school, and it's like now [in college], they won't even talk to me because I'm White."

Race and social class were identified for some of the Black, Asian-American, and Latina women as a critical feature when they wrote about or spoke about the role of drugs in their lives. Regardless of their race, most of the women indicated that race and social class influenced their choices about their social circles (i.e., their decisions about their friends), although the White women tended to be less aware of this influence (or at least they tended to articulate this difference less than women of color).

My work as a counselor provided valuable insight into the racial segregation on campus. Although the overwhelming majority of women in this project were White, and the White women did not address race in their journals or in their interviews (until I started asking them about it), I suspected that there were differences for women of color around drug use on campus. Most of my suspicions originated in my work as a counselor working primarily with "disadvantaged" students, federally defined as low-income, first-generation and barely academically eligible for college. The majority of these students were students of color from the poorer sections of New York City. I had heard from many about the segregated nature of the campus where I worked—that is, that White students associated with White students, African-American students associated with African-American students and sometimes Hispanic students, and Asian-American students with Asian-American students. I use the term *associated* here because students of color and White students often did not speak with one another unless they needed to in connection with a class project that was assigned by the teacher. In my drug class, students were allowed to choose their own groups for cooperative assignments. The two Asian women paired up, two of the Latina women paired up, and three of the African-American women made a group. These racial groupings happened consistently every semester.

In my counseling role, students of color with whom I worked would frequently tell me about their experiences with their race at this predominantly

White university. The few students of color who did associate with Whites, as one of my African-American male students told me, were called "Oreos" by the other students of color (Black on the outside, White on the inside). Students of color with whom I worked would tell me that White students would not say "hello" to them and that they would not say "hello" to White students, but they would say "hello" to a student of color (Asian-Americans excluded), even if a stranger. One student with whom I worked said that Asian-Americans can hang out with Whites or with Blacks and Hispanics, but mostly, he said, "Asian students tended to hang out together." Some of the students I counseled mentioned that it seemed that Asian students from "the City" (New York City) tended to "hang out" more with African-American and Hispanic students, while Asians from more rural areas or the "suburbs" tended to associate with Whites.

These comments (and many others throughout the years of working with this population) about the racial division on campus, combined with some comments in class, in journals, and in interviews made by women of color and a couple of White women, made me aware that differences existed between the experiences of White women and women of color. Thus, any study involving a group of college women, particularly on this racially segregated campus, needed to include perspectives from women of different races.

Concerns about "Speaking for": A Return to Feminist Methodologists

Having read the feminist literature and debates about feminist research and speaking for others, I was apprehensive about speaking for these women. I was concerned about reporting racial differences for fear of sounding as though I were reinforcing existing racial stereotypes or creating new ones. I was worried that these women's words would be used to make generalizations about *all* women. Then I started to analyze the root of my concerns and to question my right to make any assertions at all. Who was I to speak for these women? Alcoff (1994) tackled this complex issue: "In the practice of speaking for as well as the practice of speaking about others, I am engaging in the act of representing the other's needs, goals, situation, and in fact, who they are. I am representing them as such and such, or in post-structuralist terms, I am participating in the construction of their subject positions" (p. 289).

Representing others is a very scary undertaking. What if I misrepresented these women's positions? I began to accept the idea that this project was not only about this particular group of women but also about me and my interpretations of their experiences. I thought about how I was representing myself in this work and how guarded I was about what I would share of myself and my experiences, in much the same way that the women in this project were guarded about how they represented themselves in their journals and in their interviews. Thinking about representing myself in this way helped me deal with the idea of representing others. Alcoff (1994, p. 289) wrote:

In speaking for myself, I am also representing my self in a certain way, as occupying a specific subject position, having certain characteristics and not others, and so on. In speaking for myself, I (momentarily) create myself—just as much as when I speak for others, I create their selves—in the sense that I create a public, discursive self, a self which is much more unified than any subjective experience can support. . . . The point is that a kind of representation occurs in all cases of speaking for, whether I am speaking for myself or others, that this representation is never a simple act of discovery.

Telling my own story (representing myself) when describing how I came to this research was not a "simple act of discovery," but a very challenging task, as was representing these women. I began to feel more comfortable about the issue of representation, as I recognized that meanings drawn from these representations were "plural and shifting" (Alcoff, 1994, p. 291). I was still concerned about generating theory because I was afraid that the plural and shifting nature of the meanings I had drawn from these representations would be forgotten, or simply interpreted as "true" or "the way it is."

Trinh Minh-ha wrote of theoretical or academic writing or jargon that "to many men's ears, . . [it] is synonymous with 'profound,' serious,' 'substantial,' 'scientific,' 'consequential,' 'thoughtful,' or 'thought-engaging'" (1989, p. 41). I felt torn between the academic push to create grounded theory and the desire to allow women to speak for themselves without analysis or representation. I selected a safe middle ground.

I decided that I would engage in some analysis, such as looking at similar themes, points of contention, and points of contradiction. I feared the power of my words as I created my arguments because language is powerful. Trinh Minh-ha (1989, p. 49) captured the power of language by quoting a "wise Dogon man" from a "remote village of Africa" who: "used to say 'to be naked is to be speechless.' Power, as unveiled by numerous contemporary writings, has always inscribed itself in language. . . . And language is one of the most complex forms of subjugation." Recognizing the power of language to "subjugate" women, I challenged every assertion I made in my analysis and questioned what right I had to make it. This should be part of all research where one is representing or speaking for another.

CONCLUSIONS

The predominant reporting method in social science drug research has been a quantitative approach that has often statistically controlled for and essentialized aspects of one's complex social location such as gender, race, and social class by examining the differences among groups and making generalizations from these findings that frequently reinforce existing stereotypes. One way to break down the existing race, gender, and social class stereotypes that continue to be reinforced in the quantitative research literature is to listen to many diverse voices about how gender, race, and class are experienced in drug use and how aspects of social location are taken up by people when they construct meaning about drugs. Aspects of social location such as power, social class, and race were problematic in this project, making representation challenging but necessary. Feminist methodologists as well as the women in my project helped me rise to this challenge by thinking critically about representation and my own complex and shifting social location.

Feminist methods allowed me to hear and analyze women's words about drugs in ways that quantitative paradigms would not. Using the work of feminist methodologists as a guide, I selected a variety of methods (interviewing, narrative analysis, and classroom observations) that allowed me access to these women's words about a topic that many young people tend to avoid talking to people in authority about because they fear getting in trouble (with the law, their parents, school officials).

Reflections on my own experiences, reading and listening to the words of other college women, and a thorough analysis of the literature convinced me of the clear need for projects using qualitative, feminist methodologies that will take into account women's complex, multiple, and shifting social locations to help explain college drug use from the perspective of the women involved in it. In the words of Dorothy Smith (1987): "A sociology for women preserves the presence of subjects as knowers and actors. . . . Its methods of thinking and its analytic procedures must preserve the presence of the active and experiencing subject" (pp. 105–106).

The literature on college women's substance use has to date failed to include the subjective experiences of women *as active and experiencing subjects* in their social worlds. As a direct result of this omission, the role of drugs on college campuses from a woman's perspective has yet to be depicted. My project begins to fill a void in the literature by describing how a particular group of women made meaning of drugs in their lives as college students. I also describe how this particular group of college women took up issues of gender, race, and social class when writing about and talking about their experience around drug use in college. Nevertheless, more needs to be done to include a more diverse array of voices from those who have been marginalized in the literature on college drug use. In addition, more needs to be done to examine other aspects of individuals' complex and shifting social locations such as sexual orientation, geographic location, age, and privilege.

Acknowledgments

This work would not have been completed had it not been for the support of the many loved ones with whom I have been blessed. I would like to thank, first and foremost, my loving and supportive husband Jon Denison, without whom I would certainly never have finished this work (or would be living in squalor and insanity). Thank you for knowing when to help and when to take a step back and when to hold my hand to remind me that I could write this book. I also want to thank my entire family, especially my loving parents Walt and Mary Williams who supported me throughout my entire educational journey. Thank you for the twelve-hour "Mommy calls" reminding me about what really matters and for the fatherly editorial comments keeping me focused and thinking critically.

I would also like to thank my dear friends who, despite being tired of hearing about this project, indulged me, listened to my thoughts, and entertained me when I needed it. Especially, I would like to thank my dear friend Josh Webb who taught me what really matters in life (love, hope, strength, and courage) as he fought the odds for more time on this earth with us.

I also want to thank my colleagues/friends who picked up the slack for me when I was completely overwhelmed with this project, and my students who were patient with me.

I would like to thank my advisor and chair, Joan Burstyn, who worked above and beyond the call of duty to help me complete this work, and Ednita Wright and Sari Biklen for their helpful comments and support.

Finally, I would like to thank the women who trusted me enough to share their stories that made this project possible.

Introduction:
The College Drug Tales of
Seventy-Three Women

I have spent most of my life reading about, thinking about, observing, and experiencing drug use. As a professional teaching and researching in the field of drugs, I began to reflect critically on my own college experiences because college was the time in my life when drugs were the most prevalent and, for me, the most problematic. As I reflected, I realized that my experiences as a college woman negotiating drug use were missing from the research literature on drug use. Research that attempted to capture the complexities of my experiences as a White, middle-class college woman had been simplified and essentialized, reducing my experiences to percentages, correlations, and regressions. I felt that my experiences and those of other college women were important and needed to be considered among the research literature.

Drug use has been and continues to be prevalent and problematic on college campuses. In one week at the university where I conducted this study in February 1997, the headlines of the student newspaper were filled with drug-related problems. A woman was found naked and passed out drunk on a loading dock and alleged she was raped during a drunken blackout. A first-year student jumped to his death from a fourth floor residence hall room when the police arrived outside his room. His friends said he had taken two hits of LSD. Another young woman had been killed in a drunk driving accident.

Individuals involved in studying higher education have spent a great deal of time, energy, and money attempting to determine why substance abuse continues to be prevalent on college campuses. Although alcohol has received more attention than any other psychoactive drug in the literature on drug use and college students, this project did not focus exclusively on alcohol. Instead, it examined how a particular group of women, living in the environment of a large, northeastern, private university, made meaning of *all* psychoactive substances available to them. For this project, I used Ray and Ksir's (1993, p. 4) definition of a drug as "any substance, natural or artificial, other than food, that by its chemical nature alters structure or function in the living organism." The drugs that women mentioned included both licit and illicit drugs: nicotine, caffeine, over-the-counter and prescription psychoactive substances (Vivarin, Robitussen, Clonopin, Codeine, Ritilin), alcohol, cocaine, heroin, Ketamine (Special K), the psychedelic drugs (MDMA/Ecstasy, Psilocybin mushrooms, LSD), marijuana, and hashish. It is important to mention that I asked these women specifically about drugs such as nicotine, caffeine, and alcohol because they typically did not consider these "drugs."

I locate this project in the tradition of feminist research, which draws upon several approaches to examine the meaning women make about their social reality, "including any study that incorporates or develops the insights of feminism" (DeVault, 1996, p. 3) and recognizes the important role of the researcher in the research process. DeVault (1996, p. 14) believes that "the feminist sociologist, in her formulation, must refuse to put aside her experience and, indeed, must make her bodily existence and activity a 'starting point' for inquiry." Because my experiences provided the *starting point* for this *tale of seventy-three women,* I included myself in the number. I began this research journey several years ago as a young woman in high school, and then in college, observing, experiencing, analyzing, and theorizing the role of drugs in my own experiences with friends and boyfriends who were regular users and abusers of drugs. My experiences shaped how I think about drug use among college students; they have provided a "starting point" for my inquiry and are interwoven throughout my analysis.

I have been touched by drugs throughout my life both positively and negatively. The ways people with whom I had intimate relationships (family, close friends, and boyfriends) constructed meaning about drugs, and the ways drugs affected my relationships with them, profoundly influenced my constructions of various drugs. As a very young girl, my life was saved by chemotherapy, and psychoactive painkilling drugs allowed physicians to perform surgery and reduce my pain. At that time, the messages my parents and my doctors sent me were that certain drugs (in the hospital context) were "good." As an early adolescent, I remember being frightened by drugs (including cigarettes and alcohol) when I saw them on television or heard about friends or people I knew using drugs because my parents and teachers (people whose approval I sought) sent powerful messages that drugs were "bad." In high school and college I remember spending a great deal of time concerned about my friends' and boyfriends' drug use—trying to "help" them when their problems with drugs surfaced. Even though my boyfriends thought that most drugs were "great," I thought that certain drugs were "bad" for them because I thought these drugs caused problems in our relationships. However, within the context of "partying" with my college friends, I thought certain drugs (mostly alcohol and sometimes marijuana) were "good" when used in moderation because in these settings, these drugs were "fun."

For this book, I wanted to focus on how women constructed meaning about various drugs within their *college* relationships. This should not suggest that experiences and relationships prior to college were not important in these women's lives and how they derived meaning about drugs—they surely were. However, I wanted to narrow my focus to their time in college, and how these experiences shaped the meaning they constructed about drugs. I narrowed my scope further to examine how these women made meaning of drugs within their relationships in college. Therefore, I did not address the issue of how drug use intersected with their academic and career goals unless relevant within their discussions of drugs within their college relationships.

UNDERSTANDING COLLEGE CULTURE: A HISTORICAL SKETCH

Drug use has been part of the American college culture for several decades. Horowitz's (1986) book *Campus Life* presented a historical analysis of college experiences, and she touched briefly on the role of drinking and other drug use in the 1950s, 1960s, and 1970s among college students. In the 1950s college students' attitudes (which, for the most part had been antidrug) were beginning to shift. Horowitz (p. 169) wrote: "By the late 1950s undergraduates uncomfortable with conformist pressures began to gather on campus to listen to Beat poetry and to sing folk music. Struggling to find their authentic selves, they questioned their parents' compromises about sex and drugs and began to experiment. Although the media still focused on either the conformity of American college students or their academic striving, apparent to a few were the increasing numbers of undergraduates who felt alienated from the society and its central values."

In the 1960s, "alienation" and rebellion continued, as did experimentation with drugs (particularly the "mind-expanding" hallucinogenic drugs like LSD and Psilocybin mushrooms and marijuana). Horowitz described this phenomenon (p. 228) as "many young people coming of age in the 1960s, with access to the Pill, demanded complete sexual freedom. Sex could be casual, divorced from commitment, out in the open, and initiated by women. Drugs began to edge out alcohol as the mind-altering substance of choice." Sex and drugs began to become more closely connected (a trend that seems to be continuing today).

During the 1970s, Horowitz argued, drinking and drug use were somewhat less than in the previous decade:

Despite the popularity of *Animal House*, social life appeared on the decline. In some places formal dating (though certainly not coupling) had largely stopped in the 1960s, replaced by informal group partying and movie going. When undergraduates stopped hanging out together in the 1970s in quite the same mass way, many young people found themselves studying on Saturday night. . . . Drugs and sex remained, and drinking resumed with a new vengeance, but more cautious collegians felt threatened and withdrew (p. 260).

Horowitz argued that this picture changed somewhat during the decade as there was a return to Greek life (i.e., fraternities and sororities) and organized athletics.

As I thought about my project and its particular historical location, I began to think about my more memorable drug-related college experiences and relationships during the 1980s. For example, during my first year of college I remember the contempt and anger I felt toward one young woman who would drink herself into a stupor every night and come home and pull the fire alarm at 3:00 a.m. I remember the different men leaving her room the "morning after" and watching her do the "walk of shame" from some young man's room. She always had money, and she always had drugs (she supplied our hall with LSD, cocaine, marijuana, and Psilocybin mushrooms that she obtained from her "connections in New York City"). She always had men (she had sex with more men than any woman I had ever met), and she never struck me then as an insecure, depressed, drug-addicted woman trying to navigate the college culture as she does now as I write this. One of my most shocking reactions to her occurred when I learned that she had passed out on a pool table at a fraternity house and different men "fucked" her. My reaction was not one of outrage or pity over the fact that she had been gang-raped, but that she *deserved* it. She *asked* for it. She *wanted* it. She never did seem too terribly upset about it, but then again, she rarely showed any emotions because they were dulled by her chronic substance abuse. However, to me and most everyone else she was a slut, a whore. At the same time, we did not consider the guys on my hall who would sleep with many different partners sluts, and if they ever had an opportunity to sleep with more than one woman at a time, other men considered them heroes and the women thought the women involved were sluts. Despite this label, this woman from my first-year residence hall was still somewhat respected and revered by many because she could "hold her own" (meaning she could party and use drugs at the same rate as, or more than, most of the college men).

Also during my first year in college, my then long-time boyfriend lived in a fraternity house at a neighboring college. I would visit him almost daily and nightly, and I witnessed a cycle of drug abuse—drinking into a coma state, sleeping through classes, smoking marijuana all day long, bingeing hard on the weekends with "special drugs" like cocaine and LSD. I witnessed "power-nose-booting contests" where the brothers would drink so much that they would vomit as hard as they could out their nose. I knew the "secret rituals," and I became (as much as I possibly could) "one of the guys." They trusted me upstairs when they engaged in these rituals. I was frequently the only woman in the house. They kept little, if anything from me, and as drunk or as high as they got, I always felt safe.

By the end of my first year in college, I grew tired of my boyfriend's neglect when the drugs and "hanging out with the guys" became more important than being with me. Nevertheless, I did not break up with him until I met back up with a former boyfriend from high school who had been to drug rehabilitation and was drug-free at the time. He and I were together throughout the rest of college and a few years after college. He was in and out of "recovery," (i.e., he would start drinking and using drugs periodically). I thought our relationship terrible when he was using drugs but good when he was not. I stood by him throughout many bad times because I thought I was his savior—that was the message that he and others sent me, and I truly thought I could save him from his drug dependency. Eventually, I learned that I was powerless over his drug use—a difficult lesson indeed.

My relationship with him affected my relationships with my college friends because I often avoided sites where drugs (including alcohol) were being used, and part of what seemed to bring and keep friends together was drinking and using other drugs. I drifted from my friends because I could not share in the laughs about the party the night before, or the giddy mocking of girlfriends who were drunk and "fooled around" with a guy who we thought was a "loser." I sacrificed some of my college friends for my boyfriend in an attempt to create a place where there would be few temptations for him to use drugs.

When I began this project, I wondered how other college women constructed meaning about drugs, in various college settings and within different intimate relationships in the 1990s. Initially, I wanted to find out generally what drugs these women observed in their college setting and how they would describe their experiences around drugs. Fascination with the power of their intimate, interpersonal relationships emerged later as I read these women's journals and spoke with them in their interviews and in class. I became even more curious about how their relationships with friends and loved ones influenced their social constructions about drugs. I also wanted to find out how these women's relationships were affected by drugs and drug use.

On the campus where my project was completed nearly a decade (1995–1996) after my own college experiences, there were some similarities to what Horowitz described of college culture as well as similarities to my own experiences. For example, coupling was popular but formal dating was not. The Greek system (fraternities and sororities) was popular among students, and some of the alcohol and other drug use was done at White fraternities and sororities. However, the Greek system on the campus where my project was conducted was racially segregated into Black/Latino/a and predominantly White fraternities and sororities. Organized athletics were somewhat popular, and teams tended to stay away from illicit drugs but "partied" with teammates using alcohol. Academics and "partying" were viewed oppositionally, and the two spheres rarely intersected. Fridays, Saturdays, and often Thursdays were reserved for "partying" (drug use) and rarely academics.

Informing my understanding of this particular college culture were seventy-two women who agreed to be part of this project by sharing their personal drug experiences through their written narratives and class participation. They described their college culture and the role of drugs within it, some in great detail. I was introduced to all of the women (with the exception of Paula) as their teacher for the "Drug Education for Teachers" course. I got to know each of them through classroom experiences and journal entries. Thirteen of these

women shared more of their drug experiences with me during in-depth interviews. At this point, I would like to introduce the reader to these key informants
and point out some of the issues that they focused on in their narratives and
during their interviews. Information from other women's journals will be used,
and these women will be described in appropriate chapters.

Maggie. Maggie was a White woman and a sophomore in the School of
Education at the time of the interview and journal entries. She was in my class
during the semester when there were only eleven people in it, so most of the
students in that class seemed to feel comfortable enough with one another and
with me to share their personal experiences about their illegal drug use both in
class and in the journals. Maggie was from the Midwest. She may have come
from a wealthy family because she described fairly extensive traveling and attending a private high school. Much of her journal and interview focused on her
relationships, mostly those with men. She volunteered to be interviewed, so I
selected her because, based on information from her journals, she seemed to be
involved in a subculture where drug use was a significant part of her college
experience.

Jude. Jude, also a White woman, was a sophomore in the School of Education at the time of her interview and journal writing. She was quiet in the
classroom, but the class size that semester was large—over twenty-five people.
She grew up in a wealthy family and attended a private high school. Like
Maggie, she was involved in a subculture where different drugs were "all
around her," and she too devoted quite a bit of time talking about and writing
about her relationships, but with both men and women.

Hers, my second interview for this project, made me stop and think about
race more critically. Her comment about a "Black man" with a gun who held
her friends at gunpoint over a drug deal that had gone bad made me think about
how race is constructed for White women. I then began to question her (and
others) about race and how she (and other women I interviewed) saw the role of
race in drug use on campus.

Hetty. Hetty was a White woman and a junior in the College of Visual and
Performing Arts, and was taking this course as an elective because she was interested in finding out more about drugs. She was in the smaller class with
Maggie, and they sat next to one another. She had gone to a public, suburban
high school. She did not give any indication about her social class, nor did she
describe her family. She shared her stories about her friends who used different
drugs and asked many questions about what different drugs did to a person and
why. She was very concerned about confidentiality both during the class and in
the interview. She seemed to have a fascination with the topic of drugs and with
trying different drugs. She also tended to speak and write more "globally" about
more sociological types of issues (i.e., laws, deviance, education, etc.) than
about her own personal use.

Zoie. Zoie, a dark-skinned Latina, was a first-year student in the School of
Education from New York City. She came from a poor family where she lived

with her alcoholic uncle and her mother. (Her uncle died from alcoholism while she was taking the course.) She went to a large urban public high school. She shared some very personal information about herself regarding drugs and her relationships with her family and community in her journals. Although she did not use drugs herself, she had come from an environment where drugs were prevalent. She agreed to be interviewed and spoke at length about her perceptions of the different worlds on campus between what she referred to with me, a White woman interviewer, as "Caucasian students" and students of color. In the interview, she spoke at length about her relationships with her family and her boyfriends.

Alana. Alana was an African-American woman who was also in her first year at the university in the School of Education for the purpose of becoming a teacher. She was from the same poor borough of New York City as Zoie was. The first day of class she told the class that her father was a Rastafarian and that she was surprised when she asked her mother if they smoked marijuana and she said "yes." Alana had no desire to try it. She lived with both parents and went to an all-girls, private high school. Since she had Federal Work Study and discussed her struggles financing her college education after breaking up with her drug-dealing boyfriend who helped finance her education, I suspected that her family was poor. Although she did not use illicit drugs, she did drink occasionally, but only to "get nice" and did not see any reason to "get drunk." Alana agreed to be interviewed. Her interview tended to focus on the racial segregation on campus, her relationships with her family, and her boyfriends.

Richy. Richy was an Asian-American woman from New York City. She attended a large urban high school and admitted that she was "really, really poor." She was a 21-year-old first-year student in the School of Education. She had postponed her education so that she could work for a few years to save money for school. Her journals were highly detailed narratives of her experiences with alcohol and the "bar-scene" and her experiences within this culture of romance. She tended to "hang out" with mostly White women and men, although she said that in high school she had "hung out" with mostly the "Black and Hispanic" students. She was excited about being interviewed and came up to me after class to say "anytime" I wanted I could call and schedule an interview. Throughout her narrative and her interview, Richy was very focused on "romance" and her sexuality.

Mara. Mara was an Italian-American woman who was fairly dark-skinned. When I first saw her in class, I thought she was Latina. She was a first-year student in the School of Education. It was difficult to determine what her social class status was, but she attended a large, urban high school. She did not write much in her journals about herself, but she wanted to be interviewed. She spoke at length in the interview about race and her experiences as a White woman on a racially segregated campus with a boyfriend "from home" who was "half Puerto Rican, half Black." As a White woman, she had difficulty gaining access to the cliques of students of color. She discussed her navigation of these two distinctly different worlds on campus and her desire to "hang out" with the students of color because they didn't "party like the White students."

Paula. Paula, a White woman from an urban high school, was a first-year student in the School of Education. She was the only woman who had attended the Summer Institute program (SI), a six-week, intensive, pre-college Summer program that was a significant part of my position as academic counselor. The Summer program was mandatory for students who were considered academically "at-risk" because they had lower SAT scores and high school grades than the majority of incoming first-year students. The majority of students in this program (there had been between 120 and 200 students in this program every Summer) were students of color, many from some of the poorest areas of New York City. Since I was Paula's counselor in SI, she and I had already built a rapport before the class started. Although as a White woman, she was a "minority," she said she was "used to it" because that was how her high school was. Paula observed both worlds, and while she was allowed to "cross over" during SI, she found that she could not continue doing so as easily during the academic year. She did still enjoy drinking malt liquor (what the Black and Hispanic students tended to drink, but the White students did not), and listening to hip-hop and rap music (what the Black and Hispanic students said that they listened to). She would go to hip-hop night on the rare occasion that a local bar would have one, and remarked that she would be one of the few White women there. She was very enthusiastic about being interviewed and talked at length about race and drug use on campus.

Lee. Lee was a White woman and a sophomore in the School of Education at the time of the narrative assignment and interview. She was not in Jude's class, but as I came to find out in the interview she was friends with Jude and was going to live with her and five other women in the following semester. She was open about her drug use, but seemed to talk and write more about other people's use. She grew up in a wealthy family and attended a private high school for two years because her parents thought she was "getting into trouble because of drugs." She had tried every drug on the acceptability ranking (see Appendix C and Chapter 8) except that she had never "injected" heroin (although she thought she may have had something cut with it before). She had extensive experiences with different drugs prior to and during her college experience. In the interview, I thought that she might have even been high from smoking marijuana because she seemed "spacey" and her eyes were bloodshot.

Kelly. Kelly, a White woman and first-year student in the School of Education at the time of the narrative assignment, had just finished her first year at the time of the interview. She was so quiet in class that I wasn't quite sure who she was until she came in for her interview. I remember being surprised at her experiences with different illicit drugs in her journal and in her interview because I had thought she was very academically focused. She seemed uncomfortable throughout most of the interview. She did not give any indication of her social class or her high school background.

Cathy. Cathy was a White woman who was a first-year student in the School of Education when she was taking the course; she had just completed her first year at the time of the interview. She described herself as "middle-class" from a public high school where most of the students were "preppie." She wrote volumes about every detail concerning any drug or drinking. She tended to write about her relationships, but she also spent a fair amount of time talking about and writing about herself, and her experiences both prior to college in her very large family with an alcoholic father and in college.

Sally. Sally was a White woman and a first-year student in the School of Education when she completed the journal assignment and had just completed her first year at the time of the interview. She was self-described as "middle class" and she went to a public, suburban high school. Her narratives and her interview centered on her boyfriend's abuse of different substances and her role as caretaker in that relationship. She also talked a little bit about the issue of race when asked and a bit about growing up in an alcoholic family.

Christine. Christine, a White woman who had just completed her first year in the School of Education, described herself as "middle class." She went to a local, suburban high school. Her journal was explicit about her experiences with her cocaine-addicted boyfriend and about her involvement in this culture in order to get closer to him. She wrote at length about this experience in her journals and volunteered to be interviewed. Christine was the only interviewee who seemed very nervous (playing with her keys, stammering, and nervously giggling) until after about forty-five minutes. At the end of the interview, however, she said, "this was actually really nice to have someone to talk to about this."

WOMEN'S WORDS: SOME OF THE NUMBERS
AND GENERAL THEMES

My project tells a limited tale, located in a particular historical period, but one that is somewhat more animated and complicated than the tale of numbers. I have transcribed this tale about what a particular group of women told me about the role drugs played in their lives at college. I was reluctant to create labels or groups (e.g., "binge drinkers," "regular drug users") because I wanted to examine how each woman made meaning of her own drug use and that of the people around her. However, I felt it necessary to indicate some of the proportions. For example, of the seventy-two women who participated in this project, ten did not use alcohol or other illicit drugs (one was interviewed), and the remaining sixty-two used alcohol at least occasionally (only four said or wrote that they were 21 or older). Thirty-seven smoked marijuana, but it was difficult to determine how regular this use was. Of these thirty-seven, eight were interviewed. Only fifteen of the seventy-two had used illicit drugs in addition to marijuana (six of the interviewees fell into this group).

Numbers tell only a small part of the story. College drug use is a social event and an important part of relationships with others (although more important for some than for others). It is critical that we find out how individuals living within this culture, experiencing these social events, and building intimate relationships with others make meaning of drugs within these events.

Relationships were of primary importance to these women, and decisions to use or abstain from using certain drugs were often viewed as important in finding, keeping, and ending relationships. My central argument is that these women socially constructed drugs in traditional ways (i.e., using discourses of morality, legality, health, and safety), drawing upon experiences within their relationships with friends and boyfriends. Relationships were influenced by aspects of one's social location, particularly race and social class. Based on experiences within their relationships, women formed and modified what I labeled a "drug acceptability ranking," which simplified the often complex decisions about drug use and helped women set their own personal limits. Women were not only learning their limits for each new drug they encountered (e.g., how much alcohol they could drink and still be "in control"), but were also setting their limits for what drugs they would use (e.g., women would often decide to use alcohol and marijuana but not the hallucinogens). These personal acceptability rankings were constantly modified and/or validated as each woman obtained new information through a personal drug experience or through intimate involvement with another's drug experience.

The book is organized around these themes. Part I focuses on how these women described the role of drugs in finding friends (through sorority, athletic, and residence hall involvement), keeping friends (through sharing drug experiences and taking care of one another in these situations), and separating from their college friends. Part II illustrates the ways these women described the role of drugs in finding boyfriends (including the importance placed on being thin and attractive as well as the sexual violence that sometimes accompanied the process of coupling when heavy drinking was involved), keeping boyfriends (including caretaking in what some traditions might label "codependent" relationships), and losing or separating from their boyfriends. Part III demonstrates how women's personal experiences with drugs and their relationships with friends' and boyfriends' drug use helped them socially construct meaning about drugs. Women seemed to create what I termed an "individualized drug acceptability ranking" according to their perception of a drug's legality, morality, or the likelihood of causing immediate physiological or psychological harm. The drug acceptability ranking was modified as new experiences and new information about drugs were encountered within the context of their important interpersonal relationships. Finally, the conclusion chapter focuses on some of the implications of these women's words and makes some recommendations for education, research, and policy.

PART I

RELATIONSHIPS WITH OTHER WOMEN

Chapter 1
Drug Use and Finding Like-Using
Female Friends

Most of the women in this project gave a great deal of importance to their college friendships. These women described how drug use intersected with their friendships with other women in college. Each of these women wrote and spoke, many at great length, about their relationships with friends in college and the role of drugs in these relationships.

Women sought female friends with similar attitudes about a variety of subjects—including drug use. Women found friends with attitudes like their own, who tended to use drugs at comparable levels, through organized groups such as the Summer Institute, the multicultural weekend, athletic teams, sororities, and the residence halls. Some of these organized sites contributed to a culture that was racially segregated. "Partying" (typically involving drug use) was segregated as well, and women tended to make and keep friends who were culturally similar. Friendships with other women sometimes influenced the choices and meaning women made about their own drug use including their personal limits.

THE CAMPUS COMMUNITY DIVIDED: RACIAL POLARIZATION ON CAMPUS

The seeking of culturally similar peers (who shared values on a variety of topics including drug use) led to a racially segregated community of students where Black and Latina/Latino students were on one side, White students on the other, and Asian-Americans were forced to choose one or the other or to form a third side. All of the women who spoke directly about race relations on campus acknowledged that the campus was racially segregated and that the two worlds were distinctly different in their socializing. White women acknowledged, for the most part, that students of color were absent from the bars and White fraternity parties. The women and men of color in the class and the students of color with whom I have worked as their academic counselor had a perception of White students as sitting around drinking until they were drunk and "causing a ruckus and vomiting," smoking a lot of weed, and using other psychedelic drugs such as LSD and mushrooms. One male student of color said of cocaine, "it's the rich White students who use cocaine, because they're the only ones who can afford it."

The Black and Latina women tended to socialize with other Black and Latin women and men. I suspected that the same was true for many of the White women (although they never explicitly stated that). The three Asian-American women socialized with White women and men, and their drug-use patterns, particularly regarding drinking, were similar to the White women's.

Several themes emerged from these women's words around race and class, not only based on information collected in interviews and journals of the women of color, but also from White women, a couple of whom (Paula and Mara) had an opportunity to witness two different worlds on campus. Paula had this opportunity through the Summer Institute (referred to as SI). Mara described breaking into the SI clique and her experiences as a White woman wanting to "hang out" with students of color.

How Relationships Formed Down Racial Lines: Perceptions of the Summer Institute

Paula was the only woman in my project who had been through the Summer Institute program. She was White, and she worked directly with me during the Summer program, and we had built a good rapport. She was open with me about topics that are often difficult—drugs, race, sex—perhaps because we already knew each other fairly well from our relationship in the Summer. Paula described the SI's racial composition as similar to that of her high school, but when the SI was over she was surprised to find that the majority of students were White and wealthy, and that the campus was racially segregated:

My high school was like SI was. Where the White people were the minority and the Black people were like the majority. . . . I felt like I was back at [her high school] or whatever, and it was like the Black kids would all go to the parties with us this summer. But now, it is like 90% White and like everybody is rich. Really rich. If I had known that [her residence hall known for having mostly White, wealthy, first-year students living in it] was the way it was I would not have chosen to live there. I would have been down in [the residence hall that was known for having more of the students of color].

Paula was experienced in multicultural living when she arrived in the SI but inexperienced in the overwhelming "Whiteness" and wealth that existed at the university when the entire student body arrived on campus. For Paula, social class became an issue in her adjustment to life in her residence hall in the Fall semester (after the SI) with students who were far wealthier than she was. It seemed that she was able to fit in with these wealthier students at least somewhat because she was White and a fun "partier" (i.e., she drank a lot and had fun when she did).

The SI was perceived as the site where most of the relationships among students of color began and where many bonds were formed. Many students of color with whom I have spoken informally (and the women in the interviews) perceived that a very tight-knit "clique" was formed during the SI. Because I had been a full-time counselor with the SI program for four years at the time of the interviews, I had watched cliques form down racial lines, but I had never heard about these cliques from other students of color who had not attended the SI. Alana, Zoie, and Mara each mentioned that it was difficult to break into the "clique" of SI students.

I think that Alana and Zoie were more open with me about some difficult subjects in their interviews because they knew that I had already worked closely with some of their friends who had been through the SI; this may have made them willing to trust me. Both Alana and Zoie examined the photographs on the walls of my office and pointed out their friends (other first-year students, mostly students of color with whom I had worked in the previous SI). The photographs and discussions of the students in them seemed to work well as an ice-breaker for the interviews.

In my four years working for Summer Institute, I observed that students tended to group into cliques based on race. After the SI, the Black and Hispanic students tended to remain together in a clique, often with Black and Hispanic sophomores, juniors, and seniors (many of whom had attended former sessions of the SI). White students from the SI, like Paula, tended to remain friends with other students of color from there, but rarely "hung out" or "partied" with them when the academic year started. Mara was Italian and somewhat dark-skinned, and she gained entrée into the SI clique of mostly Black and Hispanic students through her friend, who was friends with people from the SI. Mara sought people who didn't drink to drunkenness or party like the "White students." She found friendships among the students of color who enjoyed the same music as she did and didn't drink to excess.

Paula did not accept racial segregation as willingly as Zoie and Mara and others who spoke about it as a normal part of life. Paula noticed the differences in the bars and parties frequented by White students whom she knew (i.e., that they did not play the music she and other students of color reported that they liked). In her interview, when I asked about her friends from the SI once the school year started, Paula did discuss these different partying styles:

If you are at Summer Institute then you are accepted. Still. It is kind of different now than it was at Summer Institute because, it was cool being Summer Institute because there was only 117 of us so we had to be friends. But now it is like, "oh well now Paula hangs out with her little rich White friends you know." They are different towards me now than they were during the summer. It is like they still say hi to me like in the dining hall but it is not like, "hi what's up, how is writing, you know." Like Speedy is the same and Charlie is the same but certain people I don't seem to talk to any more. So even though I knew you during the summer, I am going to hang with my kind, you hang with yours.

Paula acknowledged that, as a White woman, she was the "minority" in the SI but that she was "used to it" since her high school had been diverse. She felt comfortable in a multicultural environment and struggled with the fact that when she returned in the Fall the campus seemed overwhelmingly White. Now she felt somewhat alienated from those of her friends from the SI who were students of color. She also felt that having Black friends and listening to rap music was not acceptable to her new White peers who tended to be from wealthier families and communities. She was able to maintain her close ties with the White students she met in the SI (I only know they are White because I know the people she mentioned in her journal and her interview). She still went to the bars on hip-hop night because she "liked the music," but only a few other White people were there.

Self-segregation: Choosing to party with one's "own kind." For some students, racial segregation began before they officially began their first year of college—during the SI. For others it began with the university's "multicultural weekend" during which students of color hosted other students of color from high school (seniors) who were interested in applying to the university. For still others this separation began when they arrived on campus. Zoie described how she met friends because of "the color of [her] skin." Zoie described how this happened:

Well, the thing is that like I remember sitting in the [student center] my first week and every person of color was like "hey, whassup?" How you doing? I'm fine. . . so eventually you start talking or whatever, and then the girl who hosted me for the multicultural weekend 'cuz she hosted me, she knows like the whole school, and when we walked down the hall with her it's like hi, hi, hi, so she helped me like, she introduced me to a lot of people and then like some classes, and I also know a lot of people in SAS [Student African Society]. . . usually you have to go to the right parties to meet these people.

Zoie, like Mara, Alana, and others, was not opposed to the segregation that happened on campus. As Zoie said in her interview about the segregated nature of campus:

It's not like I hate segregation 'cause I mean. . . minority and Caucasians. . . when it comes down to it people hang out with who [sic] they want to hang out with. . . everybody goes to their own little group. . . . I think it has to do with the music. . . . Like Caucasians or White people or whatever, I know they listen to like. . . . I don't want to generalize, but most of the people that I know listen to alternative and rock music, well all us minorities like to listen to R and B and hip hop. . . and up here it's hard to come by that kind of music. So we all get together so if somebody has a tape we are all like "oh yeah, come on."

Segregation seemed understandable to some of the women of color, who stated, as Zoie did, that people from different cultures and backgrounds had different tastes in music and different ideas of what constituted a "fun party." Parties, bars, and dances were segregated, and the term *party* meant different things for the different groups. Different parties, bars, and dances had various ways of using different drugs. For example, Zoie spoke about parties being focused on dancing and listening to music (hip-hop, rap, R&B), and observed that since the local bars did not play the music she and her friends liked, and nobody danced, they had their own parties—separate from those of the White students. According to Zoie, Mara, and Alana, alcohol was not necessary for a party. Zoie gave an example of a party where they drank Kool-Aid and ate grilled cheese sandwiches at someone's campus apartment while they danced and listened to new music someone had recently gotten: "Well, we would go to like somebody's room, or if not we'd go down to south campus, we chill there, you know we drink like Kool-aid, everybody likes Kool-aid."

I asked her if she meant "actual Kool-aid" the sweet soft drink, and she said, "yes." Drinking alcohol was unnecessary for a party, she said, but good music was absolutely necessary. Parties at the student center with disc jockeys who played hip-hop and rap were mostly attended by students of color. There would be no food there and usually only water to drink. For most White women alcohol and often other drugs were essential to "party."

Choosing not to party with one's own "kind." Both Mara and Paula described their struggles to "hang out" with students from cultural backgrounds different from their own. Mara talked about trying to "break in" to the SI "clique" of Black and Latina/Latino students. She found breaking in a bit difficult at first because she was White, but she earned respect from students in this group when they found out or met her boyfriend from home who was "half Black and half Puerto Rican." She said that at first it was difficult to break into the clique as a White woman because: "when we first came to college every race stuck to themselves. And I guess that's fine because people feel more comfortable that way."

Others, as well as Mara, accepted self-segregation as "fine" or "normal." In Mara's case acceptance seemed somewhat contradictory given that she was White and wanted to be accepted by a group, most of whom were students of color. She admitted that the group with whom she "hung out" was "pretty much a closed circle. And the thing is it's like whenever we would go to a party like everyone that you know is there. And you know, pretty much, there's really no new people, I guess cause there's only a small number of minorities on the campus. . . and it seems like everyone knows who you are and who everyone else is."

Richy, who was Asian-American, discussed her race, and the guilt and embarrassment she felt denying her cultural identity because she chose to not "hang out" with other students of color including Asian-American students in college. She described why she tended to associate and party more with White students than with other Asian-American students:

Most of the places I moved there weren't really that many Asians, I would love for more Asian friends, basically because I kind of feel I am betraying my own culture and stuff like that because like I love the food, but I don't really know anything about the history or culture and stuff. That is one of the reasons I don't want to hang out with the Asian people, because some of them that I have, like Matt, they make me feel so sad because I can't speak the language, but I can understand it, you know. But that doesn't count as much. I feel like I betrayed them you know, like I betrayed my own kind or something. I do have one close Asian friend.

Richy touched on what I described earlier about the racial polarization on campus, and how Asian-American students felt forced to choose the tightly knit cliques of Black and Hispanic students, or to associate with other Asian-American students, or to deny their cultural identity or "minority" identity entirely by "hanging out" or "partying" with the White students. In Richy's case, she felt unwelcome among the African-American and Latino/Latina students on campus. She also described her amazement to find White students as the primary drug users when in her previous experiences in her racially diverse high school, she felt that the Black and Hispanic students were the ones who used illicit drugs, not the White students.

Richy, like most of the women when asked directly in their interviews about race on campus, noticed marked differences in the ways that students of color and White students used drugs. This was the dichotomy used by each of the women—White students and students of color (which generally meant Black and Hispanic)—and even by Richy who was not a member of any of these racial groups.

Yeh, and that just totally like shocked me you know [coming to college and finding many White students using drugs]. Because like the Black and Hispanic kids are supposed to do that [different illegal drugs], not Whites. . . . None of them [the White students in her high school] really did it [illegal drugs] as far as I knew. Maybe a couple of them smoked cigarettes. One might have drank beer or whatever but nothing illegal. . . . [At college], I have friends who are like Black, or Hispanics but I don't really hang out with them. I mean, most of them pretty much keep to themselves. . . . As far as I know it is like they do less [fewer drugs than White students], far less than the Whites that I know.

Richy would occasionally make these racial distinctions in her interview when I asked her about race. Most of the Black and Latina women, who rarely saw drug use within their friendship groups, focused their journal writing on observations of White students, comparing this drug use, as Richy did, to the drug use they saw in their communities at home and among their peers at college. White women made no such observations of cultural or racial differences of drug use in their journals.

The Residence Hall Experience

When women arrived on campus, they sought peers with common values and beliefs about many things, including drug use. These commonalties helped draw women to their social groups, and often these resulting social groups tended to reformulate the group's views on various drugs. As Maggie said about finding like-using peers when she first arrived at college: "It's just comforting to find people who like to do the same drugs you have and have had similar experiences and stuff." However, women with strong antidrug convictions tended to maintain these convictions, although a few did experiment with alcohol.

Zoie described how students of color found out before choosing their residence halls that some of the residence halls were more White than others and that there was more racism in them and should be avoided. During the Fall semester of 1996, the student newspaper did a front-page story about the racial segregation in the residence halls. Some of the students of color struggled as the minority in the halls that were comprised of mostly White students, and some tried to move to the residence halls where their peers (other students of color) were. Zoie described her friend who was in such a hall: "I have a guy friend there and he hates it. . . it's horrible, [He said] 'I always get picked on because I'm Black.' And sometimes I'm like well maybe that might not be true, but once they get it in their heads it's hard to get it out."

At the university where I conducted my project, the majority of students lived in the residence halls their first year, and many moved to university-owned apartments near campus in their sophomore year. Many of the women found like-using friends who lived in their residence halls during their first semester. Sometimes finding like-using friends was as easy as having a roommate who shared similar attitudes about drugs, and sometimes women knew friends from home (high school) who used drugs at similar levels who went to this university. (Or as in Zoie's and Richy's cases, they chose their roommates because they were friends from home.) Sometimes like-using peers were down the hall, and sometimes women had to search for them. Lee provided an example in her interview of how she formed her friendships at least partly based on similar attitudes about drugs and similar drug-use patterns. She described in her interview how she became friends with her current group of friends (she was a sophomore at the time of the interview) when she arrived in her first-year residence hall: "I met Dani 'cause me and Betty, that's one of my roommates now, I used to buy weed from Dani and that's how I met Jude . . . we had friends that had met her and then one night we were looking for a bag and they were like, there's a girl down in 305, you should go down there, and like we were all drunk."

Lee, who was in the second semester of her sophomore year, said they had "been friends ever since," and she and her group of female friends were going to move into a big house together the following semester. She said "a lot of the first few people I met I still hang out with like all the time. In fact my roommate now is like the first girl I met up here."

Maggie described seeking others with similar drug experiences and attitudes about drugs because she was very uncomfortable when she first arrived. She described her first-year residence hall:

It's like Long Island, you know what I mean. I'm from the Midwest, and I've never seen anything like that before in my life. . . . so I found some people, you know, that were like me, and had tried different things [illegal drugs]. . . . My roommate now [her sophomore year] was friends with all these people last year, and she introduced me to them. . . . She was in one of my classes, and I just started talking to her. . . . I really didn't know who I was, and so I just kind of followed them all. And I just did that and this and that was like fun. I'll just do that for a while.

Maggie's frequency of illicit drug use increased dramatically after she moved in with this friend who was friends with a group of people who "partied every night." Once she started living with her friend and "hanging out" with a group of people who used drugs regularly, she said, "I've never partied that much in my life." Maggie had positive associations with drugs before coming to college. She had smoked marijuana regularly and had experimented with LSD, but within this group she experimented with snorting Ritilin, smoking opium, and taking Ecstasy.

Richy described meeting her friend Megan who introduced her to smoking cigarettes (she was a pack-a-day smoker at the time of the interview two semesters after having met Megan), drinking, and experimenting with marijuana:

Megan who lives just like downstairs from me, and she was in my class, and she met me and she introduced me to one of her friends and then basically I met most of my friends through Megan. . . . She introduced me to so many people, but she basically she has also introduced me to you know like drinking and smoking. I mean she warned me from the beginning that, like I just took a couple of puffs from her in the beginning and I said, I don't even really like it, and now it is like, I am out of cigarettes, could I have a couple, I will pay you later or something like that.

Perhaps it was just happenstance that women tended to be placed next to one another in the residence hall, became friends, and began to "party" together. As Richy suggested, she did not smoke or drink before she met Megan, and then she began to regularly. However, Megan and Richy had dissimilar drug-use patterns (Megan tended to be a fairly regular illicit drug user), and this led the two of them to "constantly get into fights" (described later). Richy also suggested that Megan had another group of more regular drug-using friends who were "totally drugged out. I think drug dealers are friends of hers."

In several cases, if a woman was placed with a roommate or was friends with a group of friends initially but later did not get along with them (sometimes because of dramatically different drug usage patterns), eventually she would move in with a woman who used drugs at a similar level or she would find another group of friends. The latter was far more difficult the longer a woman had been "hanging out" with a group. If a woman thought she could not move out immediately, she would sometimes elect to live a "separate life" (i.e., went to different parties, had different friends, etc.) from her roommate. Once a woman thought she could change her roommate situation, she would choose other women (or men) who "partied" at similar levels with whom to live.

Lee described her relationship with her first roommate, and even though they got along well together, their drug-using patterns were very different and they had separate social lives, but they coexisted better than most women with roommates with different use patterns. However, Lee's roommate ended up transferring to another university at the end of the first semester:

We were complete opposites. She was from Long Island. We got along really well though . . . the only thing we had in common is that. . . we got here late. . . . At the end of the night we'd hang out and smoke a cigarette and be like, hey, and I'd tell her what was going on with me and she'd tell me what was going on with her, you know but we never really hung out, every once in a while she'd get really drunk like with her friends, and she'd come by and say, "Lee, let's smoke," and that's it. It was really funny.

If roommates used at different levels, and this was a problem, often women moved in with someone who used drugs at the same levels, but this was not the case with Lee. In a couple of examples where use patterns were different (particularly if one drank heavily and the other one did not), this resulted in regular caretaking (a theme that emerged for many women, which will be described in detail later in the chapter). This was the case with Alana and her roommate who drank excessively during her first semester:

She went drinking from like 5 o'clock, she was drunk or whatever, so she went to bed, and then I heard her make like a big bump, okay and then uh, uh, uh, and she's vomiting in her sleep. I got up to turn her over. It was so gross. I was so like disgusted, and that was before we had gotten tight. . . . And like I'm a clean freak. . . . Like she was really messy and I changed her. I cleaned her up. I took the sheets off. I had my Lysol disinfectant. . . . She was just like in a daze. She was just in a daze. She got up, and like one of her friends came, and she stayed in her friend's room, 'cause I think she was really embarrassed. 'Cause the next morning she apologized or whatever.

Even in her drunken stupor, Alana's roommate sought her like-using friends. Alana and her roommate led separate lives, and ultimately they each found and moved in with other people who had similar "partying styles." Moving was a fairly common occurrence when women were placed with other women who used at dramatically different levels, particularly if one was very academically focused and the other was into partying or drug use.

Sometimes roommates who were placed together as strangers initially exerted significant influence on each other's use, particularly if they shared somewhat similar attitudes about drugs prior to their living together. Some of the White women came to college with positive feelings about most drugs and were open to experimenting. These women seemed to be influenced by roommates who were regular or more experienced users to experiment with new substances or use some drugs more frequently than in the past. Generally, the abstainers exerted little influence over regular users and vice versa. Women who came to college strongly opposed to drug use or experimenting were not influenced by their roommate's use. They either found different friends and led separate lives from their roommate or they moved out (separating from them entirely).

Their roommates were the primary people with whom Laren, Maggie, Lee, and Jude used different drugs. Each came to college already having experimented with marijuana, and Maggie, Lee, and Jude had also experimented with other illicit drugs before college. They all had fairly open and positive views about experimenting with different drugs. Laren tried Psilocybin mushrooms for the first time with her roommate. Her "roomie" was a more experienced drug user, who eventually was using drugs more frequently than Laren felt comfortable with, so she moved out. Jude used drugs regularly with her roommate, and she described one of many examples succinctly in her journal: "My roommate and I did have a late night (late night session—2 am) [smoking marijuana] to celebrate the complecion [sic] of both of our take home mid-terms."

Drug use was an important part of what friends did together for some of the women, particularly the women for whom drug use was a significant part of their daily life. Dara described some of the different drug-using groups with whom she had associated, and how different groups of her friends had different drugs of choice: "I've hung out with the heads [Grateful Deadheads], the freaks [Speed freaks], the yuppies, the ravers [those who go to Raves], all kinds of kids. In each group there is usually one drug that dominates. Pretty much everyone is a polydrug user. You learn new tricks and types of drugs each day. Drugs are always around you if you're down, you can't go back. It's not like you can wake up and think about having one complete [sic] sober day."

Dara was excited about using different drugs and sought peers who were equally excited about drugs. She was different from most of the regular users who tended to be drawn toward one of these groups based on similar attitudes about drugs and drugs of choice. Dara mentioned several groups. For example, the "heads," I suspect, are the Grateful Deadheads who tend mostly to smoke marijuana and use hallucinogens. The "freaks," I believe, are the speed freaks who are known for using stimulants such as cocaine, amphetamine, and some of the hallucinogens. The ravers are those who tend to go to Rave parties (Rave parties will be described in more detail in Chapter 7), and drugs like Ecstasy, heroin, cocaine, and other hallucinogens tend to predominate at these parties. The yuppies generally tend to use more alcohol and marijuana; occasionally, they might snort cocaine. Different groups tended to have drugs of choice, but as Dara wrote they were "polydrug users."

Women who used different drugs tended to find and "hang out" or "party" with friends who used similar drugs at similar levels (most of the heavier users tended to associate with more men than women), and those who did not use illicit drugs or alcohol sought friends who did not use illicit drugs or alcohol. The latter seemed to be more difficult to find within this particular college environment, particularly if one did not drink alcohol and wanted friends who did not drink. The perception of many of the White women was that "everybody drinks." Nikky was the only informant who reported living on the "wellness floor" of her residence hall. She made it very clear to her friends that she didn't want to engage in the "typical college" behavior. She thought that everyone in college drank and used other drugs excessively until she discovered the wellness floor. On this floor students signed contracts to lead healthy, drug-free lives. The organizers in residence life had a budget to provide other drug-free alternatives to this population of students. Nikky described what living on this floor (and finally finding peers who did not use drugs) meant to her:

From my experiences last year I assumed that most everyone at [the University] drank and it was the only thing to do. I was very disappointed; I knew alcohol was big at college but I didn't realize the extent.
A friend of mine lived on the [wellness] floor. As soon as she told me about it I knew it would be perfect for me. The [wellness] floor is geared to people who are interested in emotional, physical, spiritual, and occupational growth. It offers special programs such as problem-solving or stress-management. The people participate in activities other than drinking such as going to plays, movies, dances, etc. I see now that there are other things to do here as well as people who enjoy other things. There are people who do go out and drink on the [wellness] floor, but it is not their life as it is for many college students.

The wellness floor was a site where Nikky could feel good about being drug-free and surround herself with others who constructed drugs in similar ways. The wellness floor offered alternatives to drug use. However, it was difficult to determine the "other things to do here" that Nikky mentioned. Richy mentioned that her roommate, with whom she had been friends in high school, did not use any drugs, and described what her roommate (who Richy said was "Jamaican-Indian") and her nondrug-using friends would do for fun: "They'll go to the movies or the mall or something like that. My roommate is like 16 years old, she doesn't drink. Like three or four other people from my floor that don't drink, so like every Thursday, Friday, Saturday they would have their own little get-together in my room. So it is cool—I like that. It seems like some part of it, part of it sometimes seems like they had more fun staying in my room than me going out . . . . I admire them that they can have fun without beer or cigarettes."

Richy and her roommate had quite different drug-using patterns, resulting in "fights" between them. Roommates with different drug-use patterns will be described in more detail later in the chapter.

Differences in fear of getting in trouble with friends in the residence hall. Zoie and Alana mentioned that they feared getting in trouble in the residence hall and that students of color would get in more trouble for the same offense than a White student. Few of the White women said they feared getting in trouble, even when they engaged in illegal drug-using activities. Zoie described why she thought that her friends (other students of color) did not use illegal drugs at school, even though some of them used drugs on occasion at home: "I think that's kind of weird [i.e., that some of the other students of color with whom she partied did not smoke marijuana at school but did so at home]. I guess 'cause they don't want to get caught. Most of them are on scholarships or whatever and they are on their best behavior."

Richy admitted that she tried smoking marijuana, but she didn't like it because it "scared her." She said, "it's bad, I know that cigarettes are really, really bad for you but it's legal." She admitted that she tried smoking marijuana at college when she discovered that her friends (most of whom were White) were doing it, but she said to her friends: "I was like, I want to be like you guys, and I tried it and didn't like it, so I just was like, you guys can keep doing it, I just don't want to get caught and get thrown off campus."

There was a pervasive fear among the women of color that they would be treated differently and more harshly than White students for the same offense. This fear was not limited to drug use. I think it had serious implications for many of the students of color and affected their decisions about drug use and the risks involved. Both Zoie and Alana voiced their perception that students of color were treated differently than Whites, and Zoie wrote that her friends stayed away from drugs because they felt that they would get in more trouble than Whites for the same offense. When I asked Zoie why she thought so, she said that she had seen it just with her music. When she would play her music, which is "in Spanish so people don't know it or understand it," at the same volume as the White students in her hall, she would be told to turn it down or she would be written up [a more formal warning in the residence hall] for having her music too loud. Also, she said that she'd been at parties with mostly students of color that had been broken up for being too loud. Women of color and some of their friends felt that they would be risking their college education if they got caught with illicit drugs.

Zoie, like Alana and a couple of other students of color with whom I had spoken informally, felt they would be treated differently: "I think another thing is that most people our age are White and some people have like this complex that oh if the RAs [Resident Advisors] busted me, it'll be different if he busted so and so down the hall. . . like I mean there's always times where you get in trouble for something small like pumping your music really loud and you might get in trouble more than like somebody else, like somebody playing alternative music or something like that."

In contrast to the women of color who thought they would be treated differently and more harshly than White students for the same offense, many of the White women felt that if *they* got caught smoking marijuana, they would only receive a slap on the wrist. In fact, Emma, who was White, wrote: "My floor [located in the predominantly White first-year residence hall] is known for its marijuana problem. I would say that over half of the people on my floor smoke pot on a regular basis. A few weeks ago, Lt. Williams called a floor meeting. He told us that our floor was known for drugs and he wanted it stopped. Most of my floormates who smoke, are chronic smokers—they smoke everyday. I don't think that the lecture by Lt. Williams made any effect on them."

Mara, who was also White but associated more with students of color than with White students, had a perception of getting in trouble that was similar to her friends (who were Black and Latino/Latina). She expressed her concerns about getting caught smoking marijuana, even though she did smoke on occasion: "I just don't want to get in trouble. 'Cause I feel like it's such a big thing. It seems like if you get in trouble for it would be so stupid. I mean it would be just so stupid. 'Cause it seems like it's weird how people get caught for it, 'cause everyone has it, you know what I mean, like not everyone but the majority of people like have it or can get it. It's very accessible, you know. And it seems like there's like if you're the one who is going to get in trouble for it."

The fear of getting in trouble for illicit drug use was expressed more often by the women of color than the White women. Alana, Zoie, Alana, Jesse, and Richy, in particular, felt that students of color would be treated more harshly and less fairly than Whites if they were "caught" with illicit drugs or alcohol. In Richy's and Mara's case, this fear was enough to make them stay away from marijuana and to be careful about their drinking in the residence halls, but it was less clear how this fear influenced Jesse's, Zoie's, and Alana's decisions. It seemed as though their minds were already made up before they arrived on campus.

Most of the women in the project were drawn to friends in their residence halls or in other organizations with similar attitudes about drugs, sex, school, and families. Some women found these friends shortly after they arrived at college by going to parties and bars, and some knew other women before they arrived (from high school, multicultural weekend, or the Summer Institute). Some women met others based on "the color of their skin," and others found friends with similar interests by participating in more structured activities such as athletics and sororities. Often in these more "structured" groupings, women found other female friends with similar attitudes about drugs.

Athletics as a Site for Finding Like-Using Peers

Volumes have recently been written about female college athletes. Birrell's (1987) literature review entitled "The Woman Athlete's College Experiences: Knowns and Unknowns" found that "the life of a female college athlete differs little from that of her nonathletic counterpart, though much more research needs to be done regarding the impact of athletic performance on self-esteem, academic performance, social life, drug use, and post-college adjustment" (p. 92). Without conducting a study exclusively on female college athletes, I found that among the few college athletes, there were some similarities in attitudes about drugs.

Spreitzer (1993) conducted a longitudinal study of 18-to-24-year-olds to determine if participation in athletics during adolescence affected their development into adulthood. He examined differences in gender, social class background, grade point average, and self-esteem. The only significant gender difference reported was that females were more likely than males to drop out of athletics by their senior year. Disadvantaged youth were also more likely to quit their participation in athletics by their senior year than adolescents from wealthier backgrounds. Spreitzer also found that athletic participation was not a good predictor of later alcohol abuse or one's self-esteem, but educational attainment tended to be higher for athletes than for nonathletes.

Many studies since Birrell (1987) and Spreitzer (1993) have examined female athletes and their drug use. For example, Shields (1995) found that adolescent student athletes tended to use drugs less than the nonstudent athletes. He wrote that "in virtually every comparison of student-athletes with their peers in the general student body, the drug problem was found to be less for student-athletes, and in some cases, dramatically less" (p. 858). My project found that female student-athletes tended to use drugs less than nonstudent-athletes, but these experiences were different for different women.

Ten women in this project identified themselves as Division I college athletes. Not all of these women were necessarily scholarship athletes. Only Maria as far as I know was receiving an athletic scholarship. Athletic teams provided a circle of female friends who typically did not engage in any illicit drug use, mostly out of fear of being caught in a drug test or out of concern for their body's athletic performance suffering from drug use. The athletes seemed to appreciate their bodies as machines that needed to be taken care of for maximum performance. However, some of the athletes, particularly nonscholarship athletes, felt that they were "missing out" because they were unable to smoke marijuana with their friends—a couple mentioned how unfair they thought the National Collegiate Athletic Association's drug-testing policies were, and that they felt that they should be able to drink or "party" during their sport's "season." One woman athlete who did attempt to smoke marijuana a couple of times described her fears about being drug-tested: "A [team] friend of mine had been smoking pot lately also. The two of us became very worried about this. We felt trapped. We soon learned from people ways to get around it. Well, the next thing I knew the two of us were stowaways on the train to the Mall. We were headed towards GNC. We found it sitting in a glass cabinet in the store. These pills we were supposed to take which would clean out our systems. We each bought a bottle and we popped between four and six pills."

During the season, the women who considered themselves competitive athletes tended to stay away from drugs altogether, including drinking alcohol, and even avoided the places where they were likely to see them (bars, parties). Their network of contacts during "the season" consisted of their female teammates, who also tended to be drug-free.

When the female athletes did drink, they tended to drink together, sometimes with male athletes. Their teammates were on the same schedules and also tended to be more aware of their bodies and the impact of alcohol and other drugs on their bodies, particularly when they were training. Maria who was a senior on the basketball team, and on a full-athletic scholarship, stayed away from illicit drugs, and reported that she only drank "maybe 20 times" in college. Dani wrote about her experiences as a swimmer. She drank, one time excessively which she discussed in her journal, but she did not use any illicit drugs or smoke cigarettes except once when she was pressured by her teammates. This example illustrated some of the influence teammates had on one another's drug use (more often in the "off-season"): "Last night I was at a party with a bunch of teammates where there was a lot of smoking. One of my teammates was smoking and kept asking me to try and French inhale. It was really stupid. I never smoke. Of course, I gave into peer pressure after a few drinks and the first inhale I couldn't stop coughing. It was disgusting. I got so dizzy. I know smoking will not be something I'll ever get into the habit of doing, I know the only reason I did it Saturday was because I was drunk and being stupid. I guess you learn from your mistakes."

Dani smoked because of the pressure of her friend and teammate, but she blamed her "stupidity" on being drunk. Renae described the drug use for athletes during the season versus that in the "off-season." Her words reinforced the notion that Birrell (1987, p. 93) found in her twenty-year literature review of female college athletes that "the life of the female college athlete differs little from that of her nonathletic counterpart, though much more work needs to be done regarding the impact of athletic performance on self-esteem, academic performance, social life, drug use and post-college adjustment, particularly for minority athletes." Renae described a couple of somewhat excessive drinking experiences in her journal, and she wrote this note at the end:

I would like to just sum up these experiences by noting to you (for your research) that all the people that I have been partying with are division I athletes. The sports are soccer, tennis, lax, field hockey, wrestling, etc. No sports team is perfect! I think that people try to separate athletes from regular students, but we too are students first, and athletes second! We like to have our fun as much as other students! The thing to note is that our season was over for most of these nights [in many of which she described some excessive drinking] and after the season is over, people like to let loose, relax and just have some fun cause *[sic]* during season, there is no time to go out because we are away most weekends! It probably sounds like I'm trying to make excuses for our drunkenness, but I thought a little explanation would help show you that this kind of behavior doesn't occur during the season!

This passage contains a tone of defensiveness, but perhaps it was due to the defending that athletes were forced to do if they engaged in any drug-using behavior (except alcohol which is not tested for). Athletes were repeatedly drug-tested. Renae said that she was tested three times in one semester. The university and the NCAA had strict rules and regulations that athletes must remain free of illegal substances. The policy stated that if an athlete tested positive once, his or her parents would be notified and he or she must attend drug counseling and rehabilitation sessions. A second positive test resulted in the athlete being removed from the team. He or she would not be allowed to practice or compete. The third positive test resulted in removal of all athletic-related financial aid. Many of the athletes viewed being on the team as more important than using drugs and so did not want to risk testing positive even once.

For the most part, athletic teams were sites where women could be "drug-free" and be respected for it most of the time. Some female athletes did drink excessively at times in the off-season, but use of illicit substances was only mentioned twice (smoking marijuana). Renae's journal, which started when her season was over, described her experiences at parties with other sports teams. Alcohol was prevalent and abused at some team parties, but marijuana was only mentioned once, and no other illicit drugs were mentioned in the athlete's journals. Renae described a Saturday during the off-season:

This weekend was a crazy one. Well, we were going to pre-party before the football game, so we started drinking (w/my team) a couple of hours before kick-off. Game time came around and we weren't quite ready to go, so we continued to drink. About a 1/2 hour went by and some of our teammates wanted to go to the game, and we had 2 recruits. One wanted to go to the game and the other one didn't. We dropped off about 1/2 our friends at the game, went on a beer run and kept drinking at the apartment with one of the recruits. After the game was over, our friends came back and we were all loaded! We had been funneling and shotgunning beers and also doing shots. Later we went to a [male team] party. It was their "freshman initiation" night! I personally don't remember being there, most of my friends threw up or passed out. We had a sober friend who made sure that we all got home, but everyone was extremely hung over the next day.

The drinking Renae described on this evening was similar to many of the nonathletes' descriptions of a heavy-drinking night. The only difference was that most of the people involved were Division I athletes. Teammates partied together and with other teams, not unlike the sororities who partied with other Greek houses. Sororities, similar to the various sport teams, used various drugs at different levels and had varied reputations for drug use; as Renae wrote, "no team is perfect." Female athletic teams had male athletic teams that they partied with, much like sororities had fraternities with whom they "partied."

Sororities as a Site for Finding Like-Using Peers

Lo and Globetti (1993), in their 1991 survey of 493 college students from a medium-sized state university and a small, predominantly black university in Alabama, found that 46.5% of students who did not drink in their senior year of high school started to drink in college. Based on regression analyses, the most significant predictor of whether or not one would begin drinking in college was if they "were affiliated with a fraternity or sorority" (p. 715). Lo and Globetti found that students who were involved with Greek life were "three times more likely to become drinkers in college" than students who were not in fraternities or sororities. Fraternity and sorority life has consistently been associated with heavy drinking and illegal drug use. However, more research has been done on fraternities and alcohol and other drug use than on sororities.

Handler (1995), in her ethnographic study of twenty-six White sorority women, argued that "young women use sororities as a strategy for dealing with the complexities of gender(ed) relations—both among women and between women and men. . . . Employing a language of sisterhood, sororities encourage strong bonds between members; still, they fail to resolve tensions between the collective interests of the sororities and the individualistic strategies of members in the romantic marketplace. . . while sororities can be seen as a collective response to male domination, they are not a challenge to it" (p. 236). Handler also emphasized the sorority's role in perpetuating the culture where romance is emphasized. Romance was emphasized among the women in my project and will be described in Part II.

Women in my project could find similar drug-using female peers in sororities. I did not read any mention of sorority membership or pledging until the second set of journals in the Spring semester of 1996. I suspected that this was because the overwhelming majority of the women in this study were first-year students and most of the pledging for them occurred in the Spring of their first year. Women who rushed and ultimately pledged looked for other women who were like themselves.

Sororities varied in their drugs of choice. For some it was alcohol, for some of the wealthier ones (although none of the women who mentioned that admitted to being in one of these sororities) it was cocaine apparently, and for others it was marijuana. There were Black and Latina sororities on campus, but none of the women mentioned these. Alcohol was overwhelmingly the drug of choice. Much of the socializing in sororities centered around drinking, and alcohol was most typically used to facilitate romance (this will be elaborated in the next chapter) at date parties and parties with fraternities.

Sally did not pledge. She admitted that she and her roommate were the only "girls" on her residence hall floor who did not. She thought that many of the women were influenced by their boyfriends (if they were in fraternities) to join sororities. She described the drug use and the drugs that the various sororities were known for:

Like she's not in [sorority] , that's where all the rich girls are, and I know they do a lot of coke. I think she was talking about taking marijuana and cocaine. She's like a strong person, so I don't think she would really get into something like cocaine cause it made her feel uncomfortable. She has the composure and she's always like drinking and it's very seldom that she allows herself to get drunk to the point where she's not in control of herself, and like one or two times and she went straight to bed. Like her boy friend was in a fraternity as well so like I think that contributed a lot to her decision to pledge.

Similar drug-using behaviors were not the only factor considered when determining which sorority to pledge. For example, Paula described how religious beliefs were taken into consideration when rushing and pledging:

I always go to church. It is just one of those things. Like if you brush your teeth in the morning, you go to church. As one of the only Catholic people up in [residence hall], it is kind of like. . . . I remember during rush, I almost got a bid to [sorority] the biggest like Jewish House, and I guess they didn't know that I wasn't Jewish. I am talking with this girl, and she was pointing things out about the house to me like, "Oh my God. . . this and that" and then she is talking about her brother's bar mitzvah. And I went "Oh I have never been to one." And she just kind of looked at me, "You've NEVER been to a bar mitzvah? "NO I haven't. There weren't that many Jewish people back in [her state]." So I did not get a bid from there but that was okay.

Decisions that the women made about which sorority to pledge were based in part on their perceptions about the general drug-use patterns of a given sorority and whether these use patterns were comparable to their own. However, there needed to be some other similarities as well (e.g., religious beliefs, cultural identity, attitudes about femininity), as Jude described: "I don't like sororities or fraternities. I was going to rush, but I didn't. I found a house I liked, but I just couldn't do it. The whole system is so. . . what are you wearing, how do you look, who do you know. . . I don't know, I just didn't agree with that and so I didn't [pledge]."

Cathy mentioned her decision not to pledge a sorority and her perceptions about the role of drinking in her "best friend's" sorority. When I asked her whether she had pledged, she said:

No I'm pledging next semester. It was a financial reason and I wanted to see my friends do it first because I wanted to see. . . . I wanted to be able to tell my parents that it wasn't all drinking. And my best friend had me convinced in the beginning that there wasn't a lot of events around alcohol, and then I saw her go through it. They don't have to drink. There's no hazing in her sorority at all. Like any point in time she could say, 'I don't want to drink.' Her friends have done it you know, she likes to drink so she does   . . . you know she'll drink. You don't have to go to every activity, when you go you don't have to drink. Like a lot of girls will go on school nights but they don't drink.

Cathy's descriptions here were not true of other women's described experiences pledging sororities. Many of the relationships with other women in the sororities centered around regular and sometimes excessive alcohol use, and it was difficult to say "no." Alcohol use was promoted heavily during the pledging ritual, and usually to drunkenness. Alcohol use (and sometimes illicit drug use) seemed to be controlled by sisters, and the pledges in many instances were told when and how much to drink. In her journal, Dell mentioned being the "designated driver" as a way to "get out" of heavy drinking that was strongly encouraged by her sorority sisters. However, not all of the women were as successful in "getting out of drinking" even when they intended not to drink. Melissa described trying to get out of drinking the week after drinking to the point that she blacked out. She, like many of the women, swore off excessive drinking after a blackout, but she did not keep this promise to herself because of the pressure to drink. She also described some of what will be discussed in Part II, the emphasis on romance and how the sororities promoted this with such events like "grab a date" parties.

This past week I was still sworn away from drinking, after what happened to me the week before. I was very scared to even go near alcohol because the smell and even the thought of it made my stomach turn. I spent most of this week catching up on my work because I fell behind due to the fact that I was out of commission after that terrible night that I had. I am pledging a sorority house right now so my time has been very consumed not allowing me to go out as much as I would have liked to therefore I have cut back on the amounts that I have been drinking. Thursday night we had a grab a date party, this is where you are told about the party at the last minute and you have to get a date in about a half an hour. It was very hectic but I was very excited to go out because of this past week I was relaxing and staying home. When I got down to the bar I drank a little bit but I was perfectly sober. Then one of my friends bought me a shot, that was not bad except for the fact that one shot turned into two, then three, and then four. By this time I was intoxicated but I was in complete control of myself and realized that I was at my limit and began to refuse drinks. After the party ended I went back to one of my friends house for after hours. I promised myself that I would not drink, so instead I smoked. Between five of us we had three blunts circling. I was really high and I refused to have any more because I realized that if I kept on going I would have ended up like I was the week before, and I would not let that happen to me again. I had a really good time that night and I was glad that I kept control of myself.

Melissa described here the importance and emphasized how critical it was within this environment to "know one's limits" and to "stay in control." It seemed that she did learn a lesson from her blackout the week before, but despite her initial plans of not using drugs, abstaining was not an option within this setting. She chose these friends, though, at least in part because they "partied" (used drugs) the way she wanted.

Marijuana was sometimes used with sorority sisters, but marijuana smoking was simply a part of going out and getting drunk—before, during, and after the bar/party scene. Marijuana did not seem to be as heavily pushed as alcohol (partly due to the strength of the norm of individual morality around illicit drugs described in Chapter 8), but all of the women who were pledging had the perception that marijuana smoking was the norm. Darlene wrote: "Its not that big of a deal for me to smoke at school because everybody does it and there is probably minimal chance of me getting caught and being penalized for it."

During their initiation and pledging process, most of the women reported drinking, and in some cases smoking marijuana. Erin, for example, described her initiation week: "I was at the sisters [sic] mercy therefore I did not go out much at all that week. They took us to the bars twice and bought us whatever we wanted to drink. It was very nice to get out after being in the house for so many days."

Most of the women who were pledging wrote more about social events like dances and mixers and "Mom's" weekend or "Dad's" weekend or formal parties and the role drinking, smoking, and smoking marijuana played in these events than they wrote about actual pledging practices. Nevertheless, as Erin described, pledges were often at the sisters' mercy. Dara described the not-so-subtle pressure to drink—even when she did not want to: "Many of my sisters drank and got drunk, but for some reason I was not in the mood, so I didn't drink. And I have to say it is hard to not drink when everybody else is. And it's not peer pressure because none of my friends would ever pressure me into drinking, but when everybody else is and they are laughing about things that if you are not intoxicated, you are just not going to think are funny. So it can be hard."

Many of the women, not just those involved in sororities, denied that peer pressure ever played a role in their decisions to use certain drugs. Peer pressure was viewed as a sign of weakness or an inability to take control of one's life. However, many of the women who pledged reported using drugs (usually drinking) at times when they did not want to, but they did so because their sisters were.

By the end of pledging, many of these women were exhausted, and I could see the tired looks on their faces in class on the last day. The same women who mentioned in their journals that they were pledging also tended to miss class, or they would come to class and have difficulty staying awake, or they were physically ill. For many, it seemed that by the end, they were drinking and using other drugs because it was part of the ritual and it was expected of them, despite the fact that their bodies were physically exhausted. Dell summed it up well in her final journal entry during the final week of the Spring semester: "I honestly can't wait to go home and keep all of these substances out of my body."

Deciding about Drug Use Before College

I do not mean to suggest here that all the women came to college with completely formed ideas of the kind of "partying" (translated for most of the White women this meant smoking cigarettes, marijuana smoking, drinking alcohol, and in some cases other illicit drugs) they wanted to do, although some did. Lee, Jude, Hetty, Laren, and Maggie came to college already having experimented extensively in high school, and their use escalated during their first year of college. However, Sally, Dell, Caren and Kelly and quite a few women in the narratives began most of their experimentation with marijuana and regular (sometimes excessive) alcohol use after they arrived at college. They tended to be more drawn toward people who were already experimenting (or seemed willing to experiment) with different drugs, and they enjoyed drinking on weekends.

There were also a few women like Zoie, Mara, and Alana who came to college seeking peers who did not use illicit drugs or drink to excess. Women of color from poor, urban communities constructed college and drug use oppositionally. College was a way to get out of the ghetto, and drugs were part of the world they were escaping. Among their culturally similar peers from similar environments, these women were able to remain drug-free within an environment where abstinence or at most infrequent use was the norm.

What the women in my project demonstrated was that women with strong convictions against drinking tended to remain abstinent, avoided settings like sororities that were known for excessive drinking, and gravitated toward peers who shared these attitudes (or at least "respected" these attitudes). White women often needed to look harder to find drug-free peers within these sites than women of color. Women of color from urban ghettos tended to find others with similar antidrug sentiments without difficulty. Athletes also seemed to be able to find drug-free peers fairly easily.

Women who enjoyed drinking and experimenting with other drugs sought sites where they found others who felt similarly about drugs. These women often found these friends in their residence halls and in sororities. Finding drug-using friends was not difficult; however, a greater number of the more regular and heavier users tended to have more male friends than female friends (described in Part II).

Chapter 2
Drug Use and Keeping
Female Friends

Women who were regular drinkers or illicit drug users often described "partying" together (which frequently meant using drugs) as part of the glue that held their relationships together. Within these friendships, caretaking after excessive drug use (especially heavy drinking) was a common expectation. Most of the women played a caretaking role in a drug-using situation at some point during the project. Some played this role more often than others.

The role of caretaking in drug-using situations has not been described in the literature. However, care and caretaking emerged as a critical theme for the women in my project when they wrote and spoke about their experiences with drugs. Many have written extensively on the issue of care and caring. For example, Noddings (1992) in her book *The Challenge to Care in Schools* wrote of caring and caring relations as "in its most basic form, a connection or encounter between two human beings—a carer and a recipient of care or cared-for" (p. 14). She summarized Heidegger's definition of care as "the very Being of human life . . . the deepest existential longings, fleeting moments of concern, and all the burdens and woes that belong to human life. From his perspective we are immersed in care; it is the ultimate reality of life" (p. 15). As Noddings (p. 16) wrote: "My description of a caring relation does not entail that carer and cared-for are permanent labels for individuals. Mature relationships are characterized by mutuality. They are made up of strings of encounters in which the parties exchange places; both members are carers and cared-fors as opportunities arise." Most of the women in my project described taking care of friends and boyfriends in drug-using situations. Perhaps not unrelated, the majority of these women had selected the occupation (at least most of them at this certain point in their academic lives) of teacher in elementary and special education, an occupation that tends to be very "care" focused.

Gilligan's work described an "ethic of care" arguing against Kohlberg's "ethic of justice" (Nunner-Winkler, 1984 in Noddings, 1992). Nunner-Winkler (in Noddings, 1992, p. 143) offered a succinct description contrasting the two approaches:

Gilligan has recently claimed that there are two contrasting approaches to morality: an ethic of care and responsibility and an ethic of justice and rights. . . . The first approach, more typical for females, corresponds to the experience of the self as part of relationships, as "connected self"; moral judgments consider specific details of concrete situations and are guided by an interest in minimizing the overall harm done. The justice orientation, more characteristic of males, on the other hand, is an expression of autonomous, independent, "individuated" self; moral judgments follow principles defining rights and duties without "due" consideration of specific circumstances and costs implied. Gilligan accuses Kohlberg of stating the justice orientation as the only valid moral orientation, thus neglecting the contribution of the other approach to morality.

Both Noddings and Gilligan had somewhat essentialized views about care; that is, women take a different approach to caring than men do, an approach that is somehow part of the female identity. Nevertheless, some of Gilligan's (1993) findings were helpful in framing some of the themes that emerged in my project. For example, Gilligan argued that women placed a great deal of emphasis on interpersonal relationships when making moral and caretaking decisions: "Women not only define themselves in a context of human relationship but also judge themselves in terms of their ability to care. Women's place in the man's life cycle has been that of nurturer, caretaker, and helpmate, the weaver of those networks of relationships on which she in turn relies. But while women have thus taken care of men, men have, in their theories of psychological development, as in their economic relationships, tended to assume or devalue that care" (Gilligan, 1993, p. 17). I noticed similarities in the way women in my project thought of their roles as caregivers and nurturers as they described the role of drugs in their relationships, as will be described later in the chapter.

I used DeVault's (1991) strategy for examining care. DeVault took a different approach to the question of the role of gender in caring relationships in her book *Feeding the Family* than did Noddings and Gilligan. DeVault (1991, p. 11) wrote: "I do not assume, as do the difference theorists, that wishing or choosing to care is necessarily part of womanly character or identity; rather, I emphasize the ways in which caring is constructed as women's work, and the power of this social construction." My analysis began from a similar position as I critically analyzed the themes that emerged around drug use and how caretaking was constructed within discourses of drug use for the women in this project.

Many of the women in my project were regular caretakers. Some took official positions that placed them in caretaking roles (e.g., the resident advisor), and others took unofficial positions that placed them in caretaking roles (e.g., the designated driver). The light users or nonusers seemed to be placed in situations where they played the caretaker very often—even when this was not their choice.

PARTYING TOGETHER AND TAKING CARE OF EACH OTHER

Most of these women tended to find and keep friends who used drugs at similar levels. Many frequent drug users surrounded themselves with like-using friends and seemed honestly shocked to find that others did not use drugs. Maggie described her surprise to find out about her classmates' drug use (or lack thereof). She said: "There weren't very many in our class [the Drug class] that were participants of the drug scene. . . you know what I mean. And it was really shocking to me because I don't associate with anyone like that. . . . Like everyone I know is into drugs basically."

Drugs played a complex role in relationships with female friends regardless of whether or not one was a self-proclaimed abstainer or infrequent drinker. When women in this project described the drug use they observed or personally experienced, many of their stories about their female friends involved partying together or taking care of one another after excessive use.

The Role of the Resident Advisor, Designated Driver, and "Regular" Caretakers

Excessive drinking often resulted in women being in dangerous situations. Women took care of one another in these instances, although usually a heavier burden to do so was placed on the light users and abstainers. Caretaking was a great deal of responsibility, as the women who played this role on a regular basis were keenly aware.

Candy and Gilly were the only two women who wrote about their responsibilities as resident advisors. They both tended to write about the "residents" as if they were somehow distant, nonpeers whom they were charged with caring for and protecting (sometimes from themselves). However, enforcing the rules around alcohol and other drug policies was difficult at times, as Candy described on a particular night when she was on duty:

They opened the door and there were two guys who didn't go to school here, one guy who does, and two of my residents in the room. A few of them were smoking and it stank in the room. I could see one beer bottle in sight. I stated the policy and told them they were in violation of it and that I knew they knew the policy. Behind the door was a case of empty bottles and some other hard liquor bottles, half full. It was clear that these had been drunk the night before. They were cooperative and helped me dump everything and I documented their names and IDs. I walked away from that room and went to the bathroom in the other hallway. One of my residents who is a friend of mine, had her door open and I walked up to the door to say hi. My resident and two of her friends were sitting on the floor with two bottles of hard liquor and a shot glass. I just looked at my friend sadly and said that I wished she had not put me in that situation. They were very nice and cooperative. It meant more because she was my friend. But it felt like a crazy night because of two documentations in one night.

Gilly and Candy both mentioned some concerns about being perceived as "dorky" or "nerdy" or leading a "sheltered" life because they did not use drugs, and they played this role of enforcing often unpopular rules around drugs. In both

Candy's and Gilly's case, they felt the need to justify why they chose the path of the resident advisor and to be "drug-free." Gilly wrote: "I am proud that I am a leader and I don't fall into the follower category. I may look like a dork to a lot of people, but I have found people who respect me and care for me, and those people I want to be with. Not the people who think I am a creep for not trying something that I know will have a negative effect on my body."

Resident advisors were viewed differently by different women. Many of the women who lived in the residence halls described their resident advisors. For the women who tended not to use any drugs (and did not break the rules), "good" RAs were those who "did their job" and enforced the rules. For those who drank and used illicit drugs, a "good" RA was one who left them alone (or even "partied" with them).

In her interview, Mara described getting "written up" (receive a formal written warning) by her resident advisor within the first week of school for bringing alcohol into her residence hall:

The RAs caught us. So we got written up for that. . . I was really scared, like me and my other friend who's a really good friend of mine now, like we were paranoid. . . this is not good, I didn't want to be written up and stuff like that. . . I wasn't even drinking it but they [the RAs] were like "it's still in your room you still have to get the consequences" blah, blah, blah. So all we had to do was like have a meeting with the director and then he was pretty much like okay well you know that's fine. . . . But I mean a lot of people, like a few weeks after that like a lot of people smoke weed in their room all the time, they put like a towel under their door, the wet towel, and open up the window and use their airfreshener, stuff like that, and I've seen a few people get caught with that.

For more regular drinkers and illicit drug users, avoiding the wrath of the resident advisor, or figuring out how to sneak around and use their drugs of choice without being "written up," was important. Some were successful, and some were unsuccessful. Some would go to other places to use substances if they were afraid of getting caught. Paula described her feelings about the RAs in her mostly White first-year residence hall: "A few weeks ago the RAs in [her residence hall] organized a drug awareness evening where they set up all kinds of tables with literature and flyers about alcohol abuse and gave them to the drunks as we all staggered in. It was the funniest thing because here we were already toasted and they're trying to give us pamphlets about where to go for help."

Some of the women took the resident advisors seriously, but others like Paula saw them as a nuisance or as people who were generally good-intentioned but to be avoided if one really wanted to have fun.

While some of the resident advisors were known as being strict when enforcing the antidrug/antidrinking rules, some were less strict. Laren described the latter and what some of her friends would do to avoid getting caught by the RA: "A few days ago two rooms on my floor were written up by RAs for marijuana. There was lots of smoke in the hall and the smell was extremely strong, I was surprised that it took so long for them to get written up because the RA passes by the rooms many times. There are many people living in the dorms who deal marijuana and there is always a lot of traffic coming and going from their rooms. People come and go at all hours of the day and night."

Many of the women knew the strategies used to keep from getting in trouble by the resident advisors for illicit drug use or drinking. Although the resident advisors (Gilly and Candy) saw themselves in a caretaker role, most of the women saw their role as one that was primarily punitive, and not helpful.

The "regular" caretakers as the most "in control." Eden described the role she played as a nondrinker. Like Gilly and Candy who had responsibilities in their resident advisor positions, Eden took on additional responsibility for her peers' welfare when they engaged in drug use as well: "Until second semester last year, I had never drank *[sic]* alcohol for the purpose of drinking. I told people I was the 'designated walker,' and my friends were counting on me to get them back to the dorm safely. They would just laugh, and that would be the end of it."

When asked to write about and speak about drugs, most of these women described a feeling of responsibility to take care of people who needed it. This responsibility took on many forms for these women and surfaced in many ways. Sometimes, some of the women were the "cared for," and sometimes they were the "carers." But at one point or another, each woman described being in one of these two roles (or both) around drug use. For example, Lizzy wrote of her role as caretaker that she was expected to play because she was the most "in control": "The one person we were with that really *never* drinks did 10 shots of vodka and threw up. And I, being the most 'in control,' was designated to sit in the bathroom with her and make sure she was okay. The next morning my other friend got sick and I was in there again I never want to drink that much. It's not worth it."

The person who was deemed the most "in control" became responsible for caring for the most "out of control." In many cases, this meant sitting in the bathroom, cleaning up vomit, calling security, walking or driving the person home, or in a few cases going to the hospital while they pumped the other person's stomach: "A half an hour later she began vomiting blood, so we called the hospital. I rode in the ambulance with Kelly and stayed in the hospital with her until the next morning when she was released. Kelly had alcohol poisoning! The next day she could not remember anything from the night before. She said that the reason she started drinking that night was to make her problems go away."

The nonusers or infrequent users tended to assume the "carer" role frequently. In some cases, this decision was very conscious, and a couple of women mentioned that they wanted their friends to be safe. Karen took her role as caretaker very seriously. She had made a conscious decision to be drug free and as a result had the added responsibility for her female friends: "I don't drink or use drugs. Although I don't I'm not uncomfortable around alcohol—drugs (pot) yes. It's not my thing and everyone respects that, just as I respect their decision to use. I do tend to look out for people and have been made the designated driver more than once. This I don't mind at all, and I want my friends to be safe. I have a good time without drugs/alcohol and everyone appreciates that." Most of the regular caretakers, as Karen did, wanted to keep their friends safe.

The designated driver. The role of the designated driver was taken very seriously by every one of the women who mentioned it. Women who broke the rule, and drove drunk, or got into a car with someone who was drunk were sometimes reprimanded by their friends, and some repented in their journals. Women with cars appointed a designated driver if they wanted to drink, but mostly they reported that they were the ones who rarely were "out of control" because they had to drive. Cathy wrote: "We drank in our dorm room and then down to [local bar]. The most sober person drove. At the bar everyone drank extra for the big celebration. Then we found a sober friend to drive my car home."

Mara said that she didn't drink much when she went out because as she said in her interview: "I have a car here so I'm usually the one driving so that's like a big problem for me too, like if we're not walking back, I'm driving. . . if I'm going to drink there I can't drive back. . . so that's another reason why I pretty much stay in control."

Staying sober to drive was also frequently reported as an excuse to "stay in control" if one did not want to drink very much. Dell wrote about this after a long week of drinking during pledging, she did not "feel like" drinking so "I drove to the bars because I was not in the mood to drink, and the easiest way to 'get out' of drinking is to drive."

Women who were submerged in cultures where they were expected to drink frequently and excessively sometimes seemed to search for excuses to avoid drinking as if they could not "just say no" because they needed a reason— driving was one.

The caretaker role as "shifting." Regular users sometimes played the role of caretaker if they happened to be "in control" when a friend was "out of control," or at least in more control than a friend who needed help. In these instances, they seemed to "sober up" quickly. Laren, who was a fairly regular user, described an incident when she was forced to play the caretaker: "On Saturday night my roomie, who has a heart condition of some kind smoked too much and started freaking out to me that her heart was freaking out and she wanted to go to the hospital, so I spent like an hour trying to find a ride to get her to the hospital and she was so stoned. She is so dumb every time she smokes she says her heart freaks out so why doesn't she just stop. I hate taking care of people unless they're drunk so this just sucked."

Heavier users tended to become more annoyed with people who did not know their limits and could not control themselves, especially if this placed them in a position where their fun was ruined because they were forced to take care of somebody who had gone beyond their limits.

Paula had been in both the caretaker role and the cared-for role at different times. I have quoted her at length here because she wrote in her journal a vivid description of what the caretaking role could entail, and how this sometimes affected these women's lives beyond the caretaking relationship (in this case her academics):

Looking at Janet, I realized that her puking was inevitable and I was the only person around who could help her. I shoved the garbage bucket in Janet's vicinity and next thing I knew her head was in it and out poured her dinner. I left the room as the vile sloshing sound of her barf hitting the bucket got louder. Luckily, a few of her friends came down to check on her. They pulled her up once she was done yakking her guts out (which were all over the carpet as well). It took three of us to get her onto the bed. She was limp with absolutely no muscle control. We placed her on the bed we laid her on her side with a bucket next to her. . . .

Once again, I took my watch station beside Janet. Five minutes into my shift she started throwing up—in her sleep! I pulled her up by her bra straps and stuck her head in the blue bucket. Vomit continued to fall out of her mouth in clumps. Finally she finished and climbed into her bed.

An hour or so later I went to sleep as well, with the door open because I didn't want the room to smell in the morning and because it was too cold to open a window. By this time it was five in the morning. My first class was at 10:40.

Caretaking was often a challenging endeavor and sometimes resulted in personal sacrifices on the part of the carer. In Paula's case with Janet the sacrifice was sleep. Paula, however, was cared-for on a few occasions as well. She described one time when she did not know who had cared for her: "When I awoke the next morning I had no recollection of how I got back into my friend Debbie's room, why I was asleep in her roommate's loft or how I got into my pajamas. My last memory was wandering around the halls. I remember seeing other drunk people. I think I even talked to them."

Carrie also recalled her time caretaking for two other women, the week after she had needed to be cared-for: "I was funny drunk, but there were two other girls there that weren't having much fun. One girl was throwing up in the bathroom (kinda like me last week), so I was helping her out and giving her glasses of water. Then another girl got really drunk and was fighting with her date. Well, she threw a glass at him and then she was crying in the bathroom. So I was helping her out all night too."

There was a general sense among many of the women in this project of social reciprocity in these caretaking situations. That is, a sense that "if I take care of this person who needs my help tonight, if I'm ever in need from drinking too much or using too much of another drug, somebody will take care of me." Some women would become annoyed, however, if the same people required care on a regular basis, as Laren describing her friend with a "heart condition" mentioned earlier.

Blackouts and being cared-for. Blackouts were quite common, and during a blackout women often took care of the one who was the most drunk or "out of control." In many of these cases, female friends help piece together what one did the night before: "I only remember drinking my 5th beer and then I can't remember—at all—the rest of the night. The next thing I remember is waking up in my bed. My friends told me the horror stories and all the gory details which I don't feel like going into right now. In a way I'm glad I don't remember because right now I'd have to classify it as one of my worst nights ever."

Her following journal entry began with, "Well, I've decided never to drink again. After last weekend I'm just scared." And she didn't drink again, at least in the remaining four weeks of the journal entries. These blackouts usually provided a scare that resulted in a temporary reduction in alcohol use. It usually led to some reflection on what one's limits were, but rarely to a reflection on the responsibilities taken on by caretaking female friends.

Sandy mentioned that she probably would not have survived this one night if her friends had not helped her during her blackout: "After a few, maybe 15 jello shots—it finally hit me. I blacked out. I was walking around, talking went to the dining hall. Don't remember a thing. It's pretty scary to think your *[sic]* functioning and not knowing what happened the next morning. I could have done anything, said anything. I was very lucky to have my friends with me."

There seemed to be an implicit understanding among women that someone would be responsible enough to take care of a person who was ill or in a blackout. And some women went out in groups when they were drinking. The implied notion was that these women felt that they needed to protect themselves in some environments, like fraternity parties and public bars, more than others. Nina, who did not drink but would occasionally attend fraternity parties, commented on this in her journal: "I am always curious what it is that makes people want to drink in *[sic]* such access *[sic]* and especially in such a seemingly threatening scene such as a fraternity party. The party is full of strange people who don't generally get to know each other. It's not like drinking wine with dinner, or getting drunk and acting silly with a bunch of close friends."

Many women made subtle comments similar to Nina's suggesting that they travel in groups to protect themselves from drunken men, although none of them explicitly stated that. It seemed that many were concerned about passing out or blacking out in a "threatening" environment where they could be assaulted. Thus, caretaking became more than just the obvious care of helping someone back to his or her room, or holding a person's head while they vomited, but protecting them from men who might take advantage of them in a sexual way while they were passed out or blacked out drunk.

In most cases, caretaking was expected. It was often not reflected on with gratitude. In fact, it was rarely reflected on at all, as in the case of Paula, who described in detail holding her roommate's head while she vomited repeatedly, or in examples of other women who accompanied friends to the hospital with alcohol poisoning, or called the ambulance for neighbors who had passed out in their rooms from alcohol poisoning. Nancy wrote:

A few friends of mine had been at a party with their team. They had drinking contests and partied pretty hard because generally they couldn't drink during crew season. About two hours earlier I had seen them be practically carried back to their rooms and placed in their beds. We hadn't heard a peep from the room since.

We decided to check on them. We pounded on the door, called them, screamed their names but to no avail. Finally, we gathered the senior staff and went in. They were both passed out, covered in puke. It was a sickening and horrible sight. The ambulance came and took them to the hospital. A few agonizing hours went by while they were examined and pumped out. Finally, we heard that they would be OK. I was relieved, but at the same time, disturbed. What if we hadn't broken into their room? They would have been found dead the next morning. It was a very scary experience. Since then, I have taken a passionate stand against drinking.

Many of the women wrote detailed accounts of caretaking for people who had near-death experiences from drinking where they were the responsible caretakers, but it was a thankless (and scary) job. Caretaking of this type often served to reinforce light-using or abstaining women's negative views on different substances, and sometimes these experiences led regular drinkers or illicit drug users to reduce their use (at least temporarily).

Sometimes those who relied on the caretakers seemed aware when they were being taken care of, as in the case of Rachel: "I remember putting myself to bed, my friend placing the trash can next to my bed—just in case. And in the middle of the night, I took advantage of the trash can and thanked my friend in the morning."

Within this particular college environment, women found that a significant part of keeping female friends was to party with them, and this sometimes meant taking care of them when they had exceeded their limits. Many of these women (more often the infrequent users) were learning the roles of taking care of people who had overindulged in drug use, or people who had demonstrated some problems with their use. The way the caretaking role was constructed seemed to assume that men were the providers of substances, both women and men used the substances, some women and some men abused some of the substances (alcohol most of all), and the women most "in control" were expected to take care of the person (or people) who needed it the most.

The caretaking role was expected and was one that very few of these women challenged. Given these expectations that women would play the caretaking role in excessive drug-using situations, I have begun to challenge the discourses surrounding the topic of codependency. The topic of codependency will be covered in Part II because women's excessive focus on taking care of others tended to be more problematic in their romantic relationships with men than in their friendships with women. Despite all the time devoted to taking care of other women, most of the women devoted much of their discussions and journal entries to trying to take care of the men in their lives who had drug-related problems.

Chapter 3
Drug Use and Separating
from Friends

Sometimes women changed their thoughts about drugs or their own personal drug use. Differences in drug use or attitudes about drug use often resulted in a separation from friends. This separation was difficult, and often began with harsh criticism and judgments of a friend's drug use or her behavior when she used drugs.

CRITICIZING, PREACHING, AND JUDGING FEMALE PEERS

Many of the women judged how their female friends acted in particular drug-using or drinking situations. When a woman was sober in instances when her female friends were drinking, she tended to become particularly judgmental and critical of her drinking friends, particularly when she described how her drinking female friends interacted with men. If a woman was "out of control," she was sometimes judged very harshly by women who were in control at the time, as well as by women who were usually in control (i.e., infrequent or nonusers) using morality-laden discourses loaded with dichotomies such as good or bad, right or wrong. Some of the women were critical even when they knew that occasionally they might act exactly like the other women they were condemning. Sometimes, if situations where a woman was highly critical of a friend happened frequently, the woman would choose to separate from this female friend.

Light users or nonusers were often the most severe moral judges of "out-of-control" drug use among their female friends, perhaps because they claimed always to be "in control." This criticism may have been made in part because they resented being placed in the caretaking role so often. Gilly was a self-reported nonuser, and her feelings of pride were evident throughout her journal entries and her moral judgments of other women's use. For her, as well as for many of the other light users or nonusers, loss of control seemed to be what separated problem users from infrequent users and nonusers. She wrote: "I think it's pretty scary to do something that makes you loose *[sic]* control of your body and mind. . . . I am a college student, and I have had my share of liquor and pot, but it's not something I do often, and I am proud that I know what my limits are."

Perhaps as a result of being forced into the caretaking role so often, many of the light users or self-proclaimed abstainers used the phrase "I know what my limits are" with pride. Many of the infrequent or nonusing women, like Gilly, set themselves apart from the women who did not know their limits. They considered those who did not know their limits and failed to stay "in control" to be "wrong" or "stupid" or "bad."

When women lost sight of what their limits were, they opened themselves up to criticism from the light or nonusers. Perhaps because the decision not to use drugs ran so counter to what they perceived the majority of their peers were doing within this culture, the language of the infrequent users or abstainers sometimes seemed defensive and morally based. They intimated that knew they were "right" for making the decisions to abstain, even though it seemed to them that nobody else made these decisions. Many White women who made these difficult decisions to remain drug-free (except some who did use alcohol occasionally or drank coffee or soda with caffeine), felt "naive," "out of place," or deviant. Bev wrote this simply in her journal: "Drinking seems to be the main thing that people do in college, more than studying. Sometimes I feel like I am out of place because I really don't like getting drunk and can't stand the taste of alcohol."

This feeling of being outside the perceived norm might also explain many of these women's needs to criticize those women who used drugs more excessively than they personally did (who were viewed as obeying the perceived norm). The decision not to use drugs (or to use legal drugs infrequently) took strength and personal conviction in a culture where the perception often was that abuse was the norm. This often sounded like preaching and judging in the narratives, but this tone or the words used might have been partially due to the limiting nature of the discourses available to nonusers (or light users) around drugs. Gilly seemed to "preach" the most in her journal: "I feel people should have their fun, but know their limitations, that's the key. Don't drink to get drunk, that's not a purpose or goal to go out and have a good time, you can have an awesome time without alcohol, or with alcohol using your judgment. I had to learn it the hard way, but I did learn." Perhaps her role as resident advisor required her to preach to her peers because Candy who was also a resident advisor tended to preach as well. Eden and others who were self-proclaimed nonusers (or tightly controlled users of licit substances) seemed to use "preaching" discourses that were morality-laden throughout their journals.

Preaching or judging seemed to be the beginning of the end of a friendship. Sometimes when women began to think that a friend was becoming annoying as an out-of-control drinker or illicit drug user, they would begin to separate from her. Jude described this when one of her female friends was out of control and dealing large quantities of illegal drugs: "So basically she was taking all of it [the marijuana she was selling] and giving me like $20/30 less than I had given her, and after twice of that I was like, I'm not dealing with that anymore, and she just didn't understand why I was mad at her for it. I said, 'friends just don't do that to friends it's just not right.' She's not a true friend she's like, I don't know, I can't stand that girl, she left and I'm happy, I'm so happy she's gone."

Because she and Donna (the woman in this passage) had been friends and had the same group of friends, socializing was difficult for Jude until after Donna left the university to be with her boyfriend in another state. This made separating a lot easier for Jude because she did not need to take the initiative.

Richy mentioned fighting with one of her friends, and stated that she and her friend Megan discussed how socializing with their same group of friends would be difficult if they were no longer friends: "We [Richy and Megan] constantly get into fights. If we are drunk or even if we're not drunk, and it is so weird because we hang out with the same people that we say if we ever ruin our friendship it is going to make everyone feel uncomfortable. But basically we hang out with the same people."

Richy also reported that during her first semester of college when she would bring men home after drinking, her relationship with her roommate suffered because Richy would make her find someplace else to sleep. Richy described:

The first semester, we hated each other's guts. I mean we were like best friends in high school and then like this semester, when we came back from Spring Break, we became very close friends, but she was getting tired of the many guys that I bring home. We have a split double [a double room with a wall dividing part of it], so usually I would tell her like, "Sally (if she doesn't have exams or anything else like that), Sally could you like sleep somewheres else?" And she will do it. Because she told me "Richy if you ever whatever, if you ever have guys, tell me to leave." But now she kind of regrets that she ever said that.

Richy's relationship with her roommate had its ups and downs. As much as they wanted to separate, they waited until the end of the academic year to find different roommates.

CHANGING DRUG USE AND SEPARATING
FROM FEMALE FRIENDS

When drug use was consistently "out of control" (by a woman's own definition which varied dramatically among the women in this project), this "problem" use sometimes led people to change in ways that caused the breakup of a friendship (or at least a separation). For example, if her roommate started to use more than a woman was comfortable with, this often caused problems in the relationship. This was the case with Jude who was trying to get out of her circle of friends once their use exceeded her personal comfort level. She wrote: "Pot continues to be everywhere and I'm liking what it's doing to people less and less each day. No one is the same anymore. I only have about 5–6 close friends at school right now and those are the people who have cut down too."

Laren experienced this as well. After a period of "drinking into oblivion" and smoking marijuana daily, eventually she decided to move out of her room so she could be "good" (i.e., not smoke marijuana and drink as much any more) because her roommate was a regular user and a "bad influence" on her: "I did get out of my room though which is awesome because that will eliminate a lot of my drug hassles [sic]. I can be good now."

Carol described her experience as an infrequent drinker and nonillicit drug user living with her first roommate, and how they went their separate ways at the end of the semester:

I would like to tell you about my roommate from last year because I observed her taking drugs and I watched the changes she went through during her first semester that year. First of all, she began to smoke marijuana every night, and then she would eat afterwards, so she gained some weight. She also became very moody, and she would snap at her friends when she wasn't high, or wanted to get high and couldn't at that time. She also told me once that she wanted to "shroom," but she was scared. A few days later, she told me that she did it, and it was fun, but weird, yet she did it again and again. By the end of the semester she was so moody, and didn't care about anyone but herself and her "smoking buddies." She asked me many times if she could smoke in our room, and I said no, because I do not smoke. These arguments caused her to move out at the end of the semester, where she got in trouble numerous times with the authorities.

Some women would wait until the end of the school year to separate from a roommate relationship, but some would try to get out immediately. For some, separation was not always as simple as moving out of a residence hall room. Sometimes a woman wanted to separate from a female friend whose drug use was a problem, but the woman who exhibited problem use was still friends within the same social circle. For Jude, her fallout with Donna (described earlier) meant staying away from several of her close friends. She described this separation in the interview. She said that she started to "separate" from some of her other female friends:

Last year, 'cause they don't have any personalities. They all, there's three girls who worship the ground Donna walks on. Actually the apartment is Donna's, Janet's and Annie's. Annie is the only one with her own personality and Janet is totally schizophrenic. I've never seen anything like it in my life, oh and Lana moved in kind of. But her life and Janet's life revolve around Donna, every phrase Donna uses, they use, every thought Donna has. . . it's disgusting and I can't stand watching it. It's been going on. . . it started last year and I started separating myself from it last year. I basically can't stand them anymore, 'cause they make me sick, even to look at them, and their apartment looks so sketchy anyway, because so many people are coming in and out all day long. . . last semester [Donna] was smoking more than anyone I think. I'm not even kidding, if you wanted to get high all you'd have to do is walk into her room.

After Donna left, Jude began to "hang out" more with her group of friends, still separating (at least temporarily) when she needed to complete her school work.

Because separating from female friends was difficult, many women often waited for uncomfortable situations with female friends to resolve themselves. Often the end of the semester came, and women could leave uncomfortable roommate situations, but often in the case of closely knit drug subcultures, this separation seemed more difficult.

CONCLUDING THOUGHTS ON RELATIONSHIPS WITH FEMALE COLLEGE FRIENDS

Friendships, particularly those with other women, were very complicated for many of the women in my project, and drug use often further complicated these relationships. In Part I, I focused on how these women described the role of drugs in finding other female friends, keeping female friends, and losing or separating from female friends. Finding friends was influenced by race because, as many women observed, the campus was racially segregated, and drug use among racially segregated groups seemed fundamentally different. Athletics, sororities, and residence hall placement also played a significant role in finding female friends. Keeping female friends frequently involved caretaking and using drugs at similar levels. Within their relationships with other women, many of these women played a caretaking role for others who used excessively or went beyond their personal limits. Some reported being "cared for." Losing friends was difficult and complicated for the few women who described this loss as occurring because of differences in drug use. Many of the women made critical judgments of other women whose drug use was greater than their own. Sometimes these judgments informed their decisions about the women with whom they would associate and from whom they would separate. Separating from female friends whose drug-use patterns became dramatically different than one's own was difficult.

Not only were relationships with other women affected by drug-use decisions (and vice versa), but so were relationships with men. These women's relationships with men, particularly their romantic relationships, seemed to be more important to them than their relationships with other women. Drug use played a complex role in these relationships as I will describe in Part II.

PART II

DRUG USE AND ROMANTIC RELATIONSHIPS

Chapter 4
Drug Use and Finding Boyfriends

The overwhelming majority of the women in my project emphasized their heterosexual, romantic, sometimes sexual relationships. Drugs, mostly alcohol, played complex roles in this culture where finding and keeping a heterosexual romantic relationship was a significant focus. Many of the women used alcohol to facilitate the "hooking up" process. Rarely after the drunken hookup did women feel they had made good choices. Most women felt they made poor romance choices after the drunken hookup, and some were victims of sexual violence or assault in these settings. Fear of male violence was often cited as a reason for controlling one's use of alcohol and drugs in particular settings, particularly, as one women wrote, in the "threatening environment of the fraternity party." Some of these women experienced physical violence at the hands of their boyfriends, usually when their boyfriends had overindulged in the use of a particular drug.

The relationship between drugs and sex is very complicated. Some people use drugs to enhance sexual pleasure, others to reduce inhibitions to become more comfortable with their sexuality, and still others as a replacement for sex. Some individuals become more sexually aggressive when using drugs. Drugs have varied effects on sexual functioning. The themes of romance, sexuality, and sexual violence emerged as significant for many of the women in my project when they described how drugs intersected with their lives. A great deal of literature has also examined the drug–sex connection.

SEX AND ROMANCE: A LOOK AT THE LITERATURE

The advent of the oral contraceptive during the 1960s sent powerful messages about chemicals relative to female sexuality (Ray & Ksir, 1993). One influential message was that women could use chemicals for more control of their sexuality and their choices about reproduction, allowing people to realize that drugs could be used by "healthy people" to alter their state of consciousness. As

Ray and Ksir (1993) stated: "For the first time, powerful chemicals clearly labeled as drugs were being used not to prevent or treat disease, but by healthy people in order to gain control over their bodies. This may have helped pave the way for attempts to control emotions and thoughts through chemistry in the 1960s" (p. 7).

Sex and romance were important to the women in my project as they were to the women in Holland and Eisenhart's (1990) qualitative study, *Educated in Romance: Women, Achievement and College Culture.* Holland and Eisenhart analyzed women's experiences navigating the college experience in the late 1980s (in both a historically Black college and a predominantly White institution), addressed issues surrounding sexuality for the women in their study, but made no mention of alcohol or other psychoactive drugs. They described the differences in perception between men and women's sexuality, and the notion of the "sexual auction block." The sexual auction block Holland and Eisenhart described was a metaphor for the way college men would bid on women whom they were interested in sexually, but they did not examine the role of alcohol and other drugs in the bidding process. They wrote: "male and female sexuality is differently interpreted, and the outcome is that female sexuality is more constrained. Female sexuality is interpreted in the framework of how the man treats the woman in return for her 'sexual favors'; male sexuality is subjected to no such interpretation" (p. 106). Holland and Eisenhart did not address the compromising sexual positions that women all too often find themselves in— situations that are often accompanied by excessive use of alcohol and other psychoactive substances.

Ethnographers such as Moffatt (1989) in his book *Coming of Age in New Jersey* acknowledged that he did not have enough information to analyze effectively the role of drugs (including alcohol). Nevertheless, he did describe many other important aspects of the nature of sexual relationships within the college culture. However, during his lengthy analysis of the sexual culture of college, he devoted only a parenthetical description of the role of drugs in sexual relationships. He wrote: "seven or eight students mentioned using drugs, or 'illegal substances,' to enhance sexual pleasure; two specified crack" (p. 250). Moffatt, like many researchers, separated alcohol from other psychoactive drugs. However, his description of the role of alcohol in the sexual relationships in the college culture was also limited. He analyzed college women's description of sex and their loss of virginity, but failed to problematize alcohol and other drug use. He used quotes from young women describing their sexual experiences (many of which could easily be construed as "rape"), which all made some allusion to alcohol, but he did not factor this into his analysis. For example, one young woman describing her first sexual experience with her boyfriend who was coercing her to have sex said: "my boyfriend was too drunk to remember the night, so I had made the wrong decision to let him do whatever he wanted" (p. 192). Alcohol was relevant to the discussion of this incident and other similar ones that Moffatt referred to as "loss of virginity." However, Moffatt, like several other scholars, failed to make the cognitive leap to associate drugs such as alcohol with sexual expression and sexual violence.

Many women spent a great deal of time discussing and writing about relationships with the men in their lives. Some of the women stayed in relationships with men who abused substances and tried to help them, and some found better alternatives. Felmee, Sprecher, and Bassin (1990, p. 15), in their study of nearly six hundred surveyed undergraduates in intimate heterosexual relationships, found that "the comparison level for alternatives, amount of time spent together, racial dissimilarity, support from partner's social network, and duration of the relationship are significant predictors of relationship termination." Some of the women's words among those in my project might support some of these findings reported by Felmee et al. Nevertheless, I was more interested in how these women made sense of drugs in their daily lives. Yet I realized that for most of these women, drug use in their daily lives centered around their boyfriends' or love interests' drug use within the culture where heterosexual romance was the focus.

THE SEXUAL AUCTION BLOCK AND THE CULTURE OF ROMANCE

Holland and Eisenhart (1990) described the priority women placed on romantic relationships in college, often at the expense of their own personal and professional growth. Alcohol played a major role in facilitating the process of romance for women in my project, which often began with "hooking up." Hooking up generally involved drinking alcohol, sometimes getting drunk, and becoming intimately and sexually involved with a man, not always for intercourse, but at least for foreplay (kissing and touching). Some of these women reported that men would pressure them for sex in these foreplay situations. Part of the process of hooking up was similar to what Holland and Eisenhart described as the "sexual auction block," which was a metaphor they used for college men judging and selecting college women. Drinking alcohol, often to the point of drunkenness, gave women the "courage" to put themselves on the "block" and men the courage to "bid" on them. Much of the auctioning happened at parties or bars where heavy alcohol use occurred.

Drunkenness served as a woman's excuse if a man bid on her and she later regretted "hooking up" with him, and a man's excuse if he bid on a woman he later regretted. It seemed acceptable for a man to blame a poor "sexual auction block" choice on being too drunk and not knowing what he was doing. Women did not seem to forgive each other or themselves as easily. They were often judgmental and critical of themselves and each another and their drunken hookup choices. Occasionally, if a woman made a good choice, she was commended, particularly if a hookup evolved into a romantic relationship. However, most of the time, women themselves or their friends derided them for their choices in the drunken hookup.

Romance was facilitated by drinking. When a woman did not already have a boyfriend at the university, romance was frequently the sought-after goal of going out drinking. Some of the women in this project acknowledged that the goals of drinking seemed to be different for men and women, and some of the women seemed to understand this. For example, Maria wrote: "I feel that there are so many people that get together after the bars. The way that I hear my male athlete friends talk about these girls is repulsive. They have no respect for any of the girls. They only want one thing from them and that is sex."

When some women talked or wrote about the men in their lives, they thought most men's goal from the "drunken hookup" was to have sexual intercourse, but most women seemed not to have this as their goal. Most of the women without boyfriends, and some who had boyfriends "back home" had kissing, and maybe touching and fondling, as the desired outcome of a hookup.

Richy was the only woman who mentioned purposefully trying to pick up men to have sex with them. Some of Richy's female friends criticized her for having sex with so many guys and for playing the initiator role. Richy described her female friends, and how she was different from them because she wanted sex and admitted to becoming aroused from drinking:

I am the only one [of her friends who has sex frequently and with various partners], so basically I have enough sex for all my friends actually. I really do. . . . There is [sic] so many times that I tell my friends, "get all dressed up, you know, or just get dressed up and pick up guys and just like tease them sometimes," but they never ever really got so totally so bad that they will try to pick up guys. . . they [her female friends] are too shy to even if they were drunk. . . . My friends, when it comes to like, getting drunk, they totally do not get sexually aroused. None of them. I mean two of my best friends, my guy friends, they do. But they can go somewhere else for the night. Like none of my guy friends, no matter how drunk I get, I will never go with any of my guy friends, no way. They are like brothers.

Richy observed that she was different from the women she knew because she did become aroused, acknowledged her arousal, and acted like her "guy friends" and sought a man to "fulfill [her] needs," as she said later.

Men were expected to get sexually aroused when drinking, but women were not. Some women mentioned in their journals that other women they knew who had several sexual partners were "embarrassing" to have as a friend. Women who actively tried to pick up men were also "embarrassing," and drunkenness was not always a good enough excuse for this behavior. Sober women frequently would become annoyed if they observed their female friends engaging in such behavior. Debbie described one of her female friends within the drunken hookup context as follows:

This past weekend, unlike all my friends, I chose to have a completely sober weekend. On Saturday night I still went to [a bar] with everyone. In the beginning, I was having a great time, dancing and drinking my soda. As the night went on my best friend Amy started to get on my nerves, she was hanging all over the guys and it started to get embarrassing. Everyone that I was with kept getting louder and more obnoxious. I finally had to leave because I felt like I was going to kill one of them. I never really noticed how annoying drunk people can get. This is probably because I'm usually as drunk as them (if not more).

Debbie was annoyed at her female friend because she was "hanging on the guys." This was often unacceptable because the men were supposed to do the "bidding" and "hang on the girls," but not vice versa. Women seemed to expect men to engage in the "hanging" or auctioning process and rarely criticized men for doing this, but on the rare occasions when women wrote about or spoke about their female friends taking the initiative, they frequently condemned that behavior as Debbie did in the above example.

Women expected initiating behavior from men, and many women described taking precautions against drunken men by taking care of one another when drinking. This suggested that men were expected to take advantage of drunken women. The expectation that men would take advantage of women was subtly expressed by some of the women, and more explicitly stated by others: "I feel that the whole fraternity idea is to get a girl drunk and see who can score. I realize this is a stereotype, but yet it does happen."

Not all relationships began from drinking experiences, but alcohol frequently facilitated taking an existing nonsexual relationship to the next level of intimacy. Maggie described this when she discussed Andy, the man with whom she had recently become romantically involved. Maggie had been interested in Andy for a year. She thought she was "crazy" to introduce herself to him in the student center (a nondrinking site). The relationship did not become intimate until a year later when they were at a party drinking together, after which their relationship progressed very quickly. She said, "I introduced myself to him last year in [the student center]. When I was crazy, and I could do that, and so then I saw him again at this party. And hung out together all night. . . then we hung out for like the last week. He's wonderful."

Romantic choices were very important to many of these women, and many of these choices originated under the influence of some drug, usually alcohol, frequently supplied by men, as was the case with Maggie and her new boyfriend at the party she described.

Men Controlling the Supply

Men were often responsible for giving women the substances that led to their needing to be cared for by others, as described in Part I. Fraternities were the homes of Jell-O shots with vodka and highly flavored mixed drinks that were very high in alcohol content. Suzy described this as a nondrinker:

Last night I had the opportunity to attend a fraternity party; something I sometimes participate in and always find interesting. The only drug visible was alcohol. Since I am friends with one of the brothers, we got together before the party and he provided my friend with some wine coolers. Once we went downstairs to the party there was [sic] numerous people standing around talking, drinking cups of either beer or a mysterious purple punch concoction that I commonly see at parties; sometimes the punch is red though. I've tasted the punch and to me it tastes like cough syrup, but I think it's a mixture of Kool-aid and some type of hard liquor. I am always curious what it is that makes people want to drink to such access [sic] and especially in such a seemingly threatening scene such as a fraternity party. . . most people go to the party with the sole intention of getting drunk and meeting people and the taste and quantity is unimportant. I was struck by the conversations I had that night. A guy who *[sic]* I had never met before approached me and started conversation. Shortly into the conversation he asked me why I wasn't drinking and I explained that I didn't. This in the past has been the starting point for a conversation on the topic. He was not only surprised, but almost in awe of a person who didn't consume alcohol in their second year of college. I think this is a good indicator of the extent of alcohol consumption on campus. He told me he "would never be able to do that" because drinking is what gave him confidence and ease to socialize at parties. I could relate because I am a quiet person and going to parties isn't always the easiest way for me to meet people.

Suzy's passage described the role of alcohol in facilitating the sexual auction, as well as how she resisted this culture that placed a great deal of emphasis on using alcohol to facilitate romantic relationships by abstaining from alcohol use.

The heavy alcohol content of the "purple concoction" at these parties made the onset of drunkenness happen quickly. Several women mentioned experiencing blackouts after having been to these parties, but stated that they were with friends who took care of them. In many cases, however, women were alert and functioning during a blackout. As Kelly wrote in her journal: "This past Saturday we were invited to a frat and we were excited to change the scenery. Each room had a different specialty and you could find jello shots around the house. Anyhow, the night ended not as I had expected. *Supposedly*, we went to [the food court] and then back to our room. The thing that bothers me is that I have no idea what happened from leaving the frat until the next morning. I know it wasn't very wise of me to drink to an extreme but I didn't realize how many jello shots I was consuming." Men were expected in many instances to provide alcohol. Fraternities had parties with alcohol, but sororities did not. The man's role in the provision of substances was not limited to alcohol. Of the several drug dealers mentioned, only one was female. Also, men were often the ones who made the transactions with the dealers (i.e., bought the bag of marijuana or the "doses" of LSD).

Men controlled the supply and sometimes expected something in return (attention, affection, sex). Caren described how her boyfriend wanted her attention exclusively in a drinking situation, and was angry and jealous when she did not provide it: "I noticed that the more beers my boyfriend had, the more jealous he became. He thought everyone in the whole place was looking at me or hitting on me and he didn't like that very much. On Saturday night, my boyfriend supplied the stuff. I really haven't smoked that much, but enough so that it now effects *[sic]* me."

In Caren's case, her boyfriend supplied the marijuana and the alcohol and expected that she should not be paying attention to other men. When she did he was jealous and possessive, perhaps because he felt as though he had rights to her and other men did not. Women with boyfriends did not go out to sites where drunken hookups happened as often as unattached women. Perhaps their boyfriend's jealousy was one reason why.

Men supplied their girlfriends not only with marijuana, but with other illicit substances as well. Maggie described how her new boyfriend, Andy, supplied her with Ecstasy for the first time: "He's a lot, he's a lot more experienced with drugs than I am, he's been through a lot. He's done a lot more drugs than I have, and he's the one who first got me thinking about Ecstasy. At first he was really hesitant, he was like, I don't want to be the one to give you this at all. And I was like I'm going to do it anyway, whether you give it to me or someone else gives it to me, I'm going to try it."

Andy ultimately gave Maggie the Ecstasy, and she did it a couple times within three days because it was "so wonderful." Generally, male friends and boyfriends were "a lot more experienced with drugs" than the women were.

Christine's boyfriend supplied her with cocaine, and he, also, like Maggie's boyfriend, initially expressed his concern about "getting [her] into it," but ultimately did anyway: "The funny thing was that I was like, he'd be like, 'I don't want to get you into this, I want you to do this for yourself.' So I was like okay, this is what I want. So I tried it and I wanted it for a while, and then I realized that I didn't want it anymore."

Part of why Christine wanted to use cocaine was because she wanted her boyfriend to like her more. When this did not happen, she began to realize that she did not want to use cocaine anymore.

Men and the Caretaking Role

Men were typically not expected to fulfill the caretaking role in drunken episodes even if they were the providers of the substances. In the couple of instances where men were mentioned as trying to play the caretaking role, they usually ended up doing more harm than good, and a female friend or friends usually ended up picking up the pieces. Becca told the story of her friend: "At around 2:00 Kelly came stumbling in, waking everyone in the hall up (she got dropped off by two other guys—we didn't know them). Kelly fell in the middle of the hall (she could not get up) and began vomiting. A half an hour later she began vomiting blood."

These men dropped Kelly off and left her alone vomiting repeatedly as if they were not expected to take care of her. Some men did attempt to take the caretaker role, sometimes with good intentions, but usually when it was at the end of the night and all the fun had been had. It seemed that whenever a more fun alternative arose, the men would take it and neglect their good-intentioned caretaking. For example, Maggie described an example of her male friend's acknowledgment of her need for help, but his failure to help her at all until the end of the night:

I ran to the bathroom and looked in the mirror. I was pale White. I threw up and then stumbled out and laid on the ground. Not more than 2 minutes passed when I had to throw up again. I felt like death. Well, I threw up four more times (or I mean 4 total) and then walked over to my friend Mick. I only looked at him, and I guess I didn't look too good because he dropped his cards and said we were leaving. "You really look pale" was all I remember him saying. I walked outside in the snow with just a T-shirt on and ran to my car. I got in the back and laid down but then tons more people came and I was squished into the middle. My friend Matt decided that it was a good night to go offroad-ing through the graveyard. I think that if I could have spoken I would have disagreed. But we went and I was being thrown all over the car and my stomach decided to voice it's [sic] opinion and I threw up out of the car window. After we finished offroading and dropped everyone off, Matt drove me home. I remember trying to talk to him. I could formulate words in my head, but nothing would come out when I tried to speak. He car-ried me into the house and put me in bed.

Matt helped Maggie, but not until after he had his own fun with his friends, even though this fun made Maggie's suffering worse. In the very few mentions of men attempting to take the caretaker role, it seemed clear that it was not a priority and that they resented it taking time away from their fun. In a couple of cases, men helped women carry their friends when they were passed out and put them in bed, but in these cases, a female friend was overseeing the caretaking project.

Cathy said in her interview that when her "guy friends" tried to take over her typical responsibility for her "out-of-control" best friend they failed miserably and that she knew all along that she would have done better: "I've seen my friends do dumb things like one of my friends becomes totally out of control when she drinks. Like one night we were taking care of her and my guy friend was tak-ing care of her, and I'm like, she's my best friend, and I'm like, I know how to walk her, I know how to take care of her, better than you guys do, and they're like no, no, no get her out of here. . . they're like, no we'll take care of her, we'll take care of her. She wakes up at 6 in the morning in her underwear and T-shirt in our lounge."

Men were expected to provide substances and be the initiators of a sexual encounter, or "bidders" in the "sexual auction," but they were not expected to be the primary caretakers. Men controlled many aspects of the auction that sometimes resulted in a caretaking situation and sometimes in the "drunken hookup."

Views on the Drunken Hookup: Good Choices and Bad Choices

It seemed as though the heterosexual romantic relationships that emerged when couples were drinking heavily were open to public scrutiny and often resulted in women being extremely critical of each other in such situations, but rarely critical of men. These events were often referred to as "random drunken hookups." It seemed that in most examples of random, drunken hookups between men and women, female friends of the woman thought she was either "stupid"   or "embarrassing" except in the very few cases where female friends approved of a woman's choice. Drunken hookups sometimes resulted in the woman (and sometimes her friends) thinking she made a good choice and sometimes a bad choice; sometimes a series of bad choices resulted in a woman being in a position where she was assaulted or dominated by a man.

Good choices. Occasionally during a drunken hookup, women thought they had made a good choice. Richy, who really enjoyed smoking cigarettes (and spent a great deal of time describing it in her journal), described a "typical" Friday night out at the bar she frequented where on one particular night she smoked nearly a pack of cigarettes and drank a couple of drinks. In her journal, she offered a detailed narrative of the experiences prior to the drunken hookup. She was the only woman who reported initiating a hookup:

I found out that alcohol and cigarettes sexually arouses *[sic]* me. . . . I've noticed that when it comes to picking up guys, I definitely feel more at ease and confident of *[sic]* myself. I'm more easy going than I usually am. I seem to be wittier and plain outgoing. I might say, I was pretty smooth. It all began when my friend TJ and I started playing pool with him and his friend. While waiting for our turn, I found myself standing next to him and just started talking to him. A few minutes later, I just asked him what he was doing afterwards and he said that he was going to his fraternity party and I then smoothly said that I was hoping that he would come back with me and he agreed. That was around 11pm. From then on, he left his frat brothers and sat with me and my friends. He was so cute. When we finally left to go to his frat house, because he didn't bring his car, we ended up walking hand-in-hand, which I thought was really cute. Well, anyway, my friends and I ended up leaving the party early and before I left I told Stan and he said that he was going to meet me later at my hall. Which I did not believe I would ever see him. But to my surprise, he got to my hall before my friends and I ever got there.

Richy concluded this journal entry with her friends' judgment of her hookup. In this particular instance her female friends approved of her romantic choice (perhaps because her friends benefited from free alcohol): "All of my friends were talking about him the next day. All of my friends were also complementing *[sic]* me, for my good choice because Stan ended up inviting us all back to his fraternity party, which by the way served alcohol. When he woke up, I got kind of nervous. At first he really didn't seem like he knew where he was, but a minute later, he gave me a kiss and called my name out. Wow!!! What a relief. That would have been totally embarrassing. Before he left, he promised he'd call back. We shall see."

Richy was not embarrassed about picking up guys and having sex with them, but she wrote that she would have been embarrassed had she had sex with a man who could not remember her name. Richy was the only woman who openly admitted to "picking up" guys to have sex with them. Even in Richy's case, the final decision to "hook up" was left to the man—to her "surprise" he came back to her residence hall. In later passages in her journal, she waited for him to call her and became very depressed when he failed to, but was thrilled when he did. She would not call him. So even though Richy was perhaps the most sexually assertive woman and admitted taking far more control over her own sexuality than any of the other women in the project, she still waited for men to make the ultimate decisions in her romantic endeavors—particularly in day-to-day interactions when she had not been drinking: "To my surprise, when I got home, I find a note that said that Stan called, which absolutely made me the happiest person in the world."

Richy's happiness seemed to be controlled by her romantic partners or interests. If he remembered to call her or stop by her room, she was thrilled. If he failed to call, she was depressed and would go out drinking to forget about him and find someone else.

Most of the other women who described the "drunken hookup" described it as something that happened *to* them, and not something that they took an active role in. If a woman did take personal responsibility for a drunken hookup, she often blamed her behavior on being drunk. In Cathy's case, she described how she wanted to hookup with her "guy friends" but would not take the initiative: "I got home to the dorm and hung out with my friends, the funny thing about being drunk with your guy friends is there is always one that you want to kiss. At least it always happens to me that way. However, I controlled my hormones and kept my lips to myself."

Perhaps part of what kept Cathy from acting on her "hormones" was fear of being embarrassed, either by her female friend's reactions to hooking up with her "guy friends" or her "guy friend's" reaction to her attempt to kiss him—breaking the norm and making the first move. Embarrassment or looking bad in front of others was to be avoided at all costs. Women were often their own harshest critics of their romantic choices. Perhaps Cathy did not act on her "hormones" because the norm to let the man make the move to bid on the sexual auction block was so pervasive that she felt she would violate the norm by initiating a sexual encounter.

Good choices were those where a woman ended up with a "cute" guy and the hookup evolved into a relationship. Good choices also seemed to be those that resulted in friends benefiting—meeting other men, free alcohol, or a ride home.

Bad choices. Most of the time when women reflected on "drunken hook ups," they did so with regret and remorse. Women were very hard on themselves when they "hooked up" with men after a night of heavy drinking and made bad choices. As Laren wrote: "After this weekend I wish I could say that I'd never drink again but I know I will. Drinking makes people so horny and that sucks. I really didn't like this guy but I definitely did more with him than I would have if I was sober. It is so dumb because I went into the night promising myself that I wouldn't be bad."

"Being bad" seemed to include, for some, doing more sexually than one would have done sober. Laren, like many other women, had a boyfriend "back home," but this did not take her off the sexual auction block. It seemed that women with boyfriends at college with them were off-limits to other bidders, but those with hometown sweethearts were not, except on the weekends when their boyfriends were visiting. Laren, like many of the other women, blamed poor romantic choices, and being "horny" on being drunk. These women consistently denied their responsibility when they were drunk for their sexual choices with men because as Laren wrote "drinking makes people so horny," suggesting that the desire to have a sexual experience with someone else was caused by the alcohol and was not about one's own desires. The excuse that "the alcohol made me do it" was one that was not always good enough for their female friends, however. Many of the women who were lighter users or abstainers, who tended to be more critical of their female peers than the regular users, did not accept this excuse. Maria, an athlete who drank only rarely and never to drunkenness, wrote: "I do not care how drunk you are, you always know what you are doing. You may not care about your action but you know your actions. If everyone could drink and handle their alcohol. Then it would be fine. But when people start to act crazy it really gets on my nerves. Alcohol in college is a way to mask problems/feeling with my friends."

Paula described her negative experience with a "drunken hookup" and her friends' and her own disapproval of her choice:

Drinking definitely distorts your judgment, and the championship game was a prime example of that. After downing my two forties [40 ounces of beer] I bumped into a male friend of mine who I never in a million years would ever dream of hooking up with. He's only five foot two and always smells like weed. But since I had eighty ounces of malt liquor zipping through my veins I thought nothing of it when this guy started kissing me. The next morning though, I felt like a donkey when all my friends started heckling me about hooking up with him. I definitely need to be more careful when I'm drinking.

"Bad" choices during drinking situations often led women to be "more careful." None of the women mentioned two "bad" hookups within the seven-week period.

Zoie, Alana, and Mara reported in their interviews that among the relatively small, tightly knit group of mostly Black and Latino/Latina students, there tended not to be many "random drunken hook ups" because everyone knew each other, and drunkenness tended to be infrequent. At the time of their interviews, both Zoie and Alana had boyfriends at the university. Their relationships with their boyfriends evolved from intimate friendships during their time of difficulty breaking up with their boyfriends from home. None of the other Black and Latina women mentioned drunken hookups in their journals, nor did Zoie or Alana mention the concept of the drunken hookup in their interviews. In Mara's case, her friends knew she had a boyfriend at home because they had met him on numerous occasions when he came to visit her. Mara said that among her Black and Latina friends random, drunken hookups were uncommon, but among her White friends these were common:

I've never been drunk and like randomly hooked up with someone, it's like thank god I've never done that. But I just know other people that have done that and it just seems like it's very common. . . . I don't think people realize at the time what they can get themselves involved in. . . . It happens a lot. . . in general I'm a very paranoid person. Like I would worry about like "oh what does this person have, who have they been with," you know. . . . But you know, my one friend who had random hook ups and two weeks later we were in the health center you know getting pregnancy tests, and she wanted an AIDS test, you know just things like that, and it's not worth it.

Perhaps among the groups of Black and Latino/Latina students, fears about AIDS had arisen through personal experiences. Jana's father and Tara's aunt had recently died of AIDS. None of the White women reported having personally experienced the loss of a family member or loved one to AIDS.

A couple of other women mentioned fears of AIDS in their journals, as Mara did in her interview—accompanying friends to clinics to be tested, or being concerned that they might have contracted the virus from unprotected sex. One of the White women mentioned her concerns about her boyfriend (with whom she did not use condoms because she assumed she was safe and her boyfriend was monogamous). Sammi mentioned her concerns about her boyfriend:

I was talking to a close friend of mine Caley, one night on the telephone. She had just broken up with her boyfriend after finding out that he had cheated on her. He was the first guy she had ever had sex with—the only. She became very worried and upset over the fact that he had been messing around with another girl. She asked him that he go and get tested for HIV with her also. In talking with her this made me think about my life. I had been together with Mike over the end of the school year and into the summer. Our relationship was not very strong at all. The situation was horrible and manipulative. He went away for two weeks this summer and slept with a couple of girls—honestly I am not sure how many one or four. I do not know. I found this out from him; he had a moment of guilt and he started to tell me the stories. I never had even considered that I might have gotten HIV from him.

None of the White women mentioned knowing anyone personally who had AIDS or HIV or had died from the disease. The majority of women did not mention AIDS or fears of contracting HIV when discussing random drunken hookups, nor did they mention issues of protection against the disease. Perhaps not using protection was what women meant when they wrote or said that they were "stupid." A couple of narratives involved accompanying female friends to clinics to have AIDS tests, suggesting a failure to use condoms during drunken hookups. None of the women directly mentioned whether or not they had unprotected sex during hookups.

When I asked Richy if she used protection when she had intercourse with men, she mentioned that she "always" used a condom and never let herself get too drunk that she would not think to use one (she had them in her room). Richy said in her interview when I asked her if she used condoms:

Yes of course always. [I asked "who usually supplies that?"] I usually do. I always have something to cover me. I was like so nervous, like this year, I have had so many guys, right, that I even got tested and I always have something, I always use something. Especially if I don't know him, no way. Even if I know the guy really, really well, I mean . . . I am just like, I just get sexually aroused. But I am not in a state where okay just do whatever you want with me. I just like I want someone to fulfill my needs and usually, but I am still, I am not totally out of it.

Richy was the only woman who used discourses of desire when describing relationships with men. For most women, sexual encounters were described as "bad."

Bad choices: Drugs and sexual violence. Inaba and Cohen (1996) wrote that sexual violence happens to "one out of every three women in this country" (p. 289) and that many of these instances occur on college campuses. A recent study involving college men and women revealed that 75% of rapists and more than half of those who were raped were using psychoactive drugs (including alcohol). In this same study, every one of the reported gang rapists were under the influence of alcohol (Inaba & Cohen, 1996). Mohanty (1991) wrote: "male violence must be theorized and interpreted within specific societies, in order both to understand it better and to effectively organize to change it" (p. 10). To date, the culture in which sexual violence occurs on college campus has not been described from the point of view of college women.

Some studies have attempted to examine qualitatively the role of alcohol and other psychoactive substances in violence against women, but often focus more on the statistics than on the stories of the women and men involved. For example, a recent study interviewed forty-two males who had a history of abuse with their partners and fifty men without such a history. They reported that "stepwise logistic regression indicated that higher perceived quality of the intimate relationship, black race, and greater depression were significant predictors of male violence toward female intimates" (Julian & McHenry, 1993, p. 39).

What is it about the characteristics of alcohol and other drugs that increases the likelihood of violence against college women? Alcohol, which lowers inhibitions, may increase the likelihood that students will be in risky or dangerous situations where they are less able to defend themselves, or acting on impulses and desires that may not be reciprocated. Other "downers" such as marijuana and Quaaludes or Valium also tend to lead to lowered inhibitions, which may have the same results as alcohol. Cocaine and other stimulants often lead to increased confidence, increased sex drive (in smaller doses), and aggression. In the past two decades, the literature has begun to acknowledge that alcohol and other psychoactive compounds play a significant role in campus violence against women, however, this validation is still accomplished through a predominantly statistical, quantitative discourse.

Other sociological factors, such as stereotypes about women who abuse alcohol and other psychoactive substances, contribute to a culture of violence against women. Nechas and Foley (1994) stated that "by far the most damaging stigma that women who drink or use drugs must contend with is that of sexual promiscuity. The prevailing attitude is that women who drink excessively become far more sexually aggressive. Yet research does not support this notion, no matter how popular it remains" (p. 158). The stereotype of the sexually promiscuous female heavy drinker or drug user still remains popular among the general population (Nechas & Foley, 1994). Because it is so widespread, it often results in women alcoholics becoming victims of sexual assault, and the reaction of others (including police, judges, and jurors) is that *she wanted it*. One comparison study between alcoholic and nonalcoholic women reported that 16% of the alcoholic population had been raped, but no one within the comparison group of nonalcoholic reported having been raped (Nechas & Foley, 1994). The stereotype has also been reinforced in past literature by studies reporting that half of college women surveyed had sexual intercourse with the males who supplied their alcohol or drugs (Bowker, 1977).

In addition, research has demonstrated that college male attitudes contribute to campus rape. For example, Fisher and Sloan (1995, p. 166) summarized the literature on campus rape and found consistently that about "one-third of college males have reported that they would rape women under some circumstances, if they knew that they would not get caught. . . . Gang rapes are such an institutionalized activity in some fraternities that they are given names like 'trains' and 'spectrums' by fraternity brothers." Studies have suggested that the Greek system on campuses is at least somewhat to blame for creating a microenvironment in which sexual violence against women is tolerated—by both men and women. For example, Kalof's (1993) study comparing the "rape-supportive" attitudes of sorority and nonsorority women indicated that significantly more sorority members were likely to accept rape-myths and accept sexual violence against women. These women were also more likely to have been victims of sexual violence. This study also helped establish the important link between the substance abuse culture and the rape culture by indicating that sorority women who were victims of sexual violence were more likely to have been under the influence of alcohol at the time (Kalof, 1993).

Past studies such as Bowker's (1977) showed that as many as two-thirds of fraternity men surveyed used alcohol and other drugs to make a date more responsive sexually. More recently, Frintner and Rubinson (1993) supported this notion by providing statistics from a survey of a representative sample from a large midwestern university, which showed that sexual assault against women happens at an "alarming rate" and that alcohol use and fraternity membership were significantly correlated with acquaintance rape. Martin and Hummer (1989) argued that the "fraternities' general social construction of men and masculinity" is what fosters sexual assault against women in this culture. They analyzed open-ended interviewed with students around one specific gang-rape case and found that some common themes emerged around the culture of the college fraternity: alcohol is used as a "weapon," women are viewed as "bait," "servers," and "sexual prey," and violence and physical force and competition are encouraged (Martin & Hummer, 1989).

The danger in the shifting focus of the literature seems to be reinforcing the belief that sexual violence against women is *just* a fraternity problem. It is important to emphasize that this violence seems pervasive in all settings where alcohol abuse and abuse of other psychoactive substances are promoted and where there is a removal of personal responsibility in drinking and drug-use situations. LeJeune and Follette (1994) suggest that college males were more likely to use alcohol or other drugs as an excuse for violence against women. It is very important to analyze the drug culture of abuse in order to begin unraveling the competing forces that result in perpetuating the rape culture on college campuses.

Some of the women in my project would describe how they had made poor romantic choices because of excessive drinking, but some women did not have any choices at all. They experienced physical domination and violence within the drunken hookup context. Women who described such domination and violence often viewed these experiences as innocuous.

Many of the women played a passive role in their romantic relationships with men. Sometimes, within the initial hookup phase when drinking, women would take some initiative, but only up to a point—usually flirting or, to use Richy's word, "teasing." It was almost as if many of these women did not want to take personal responsibility for a romantic relationship in case it did not work out (i.e., develop into a relationship). It seemed easier to blame poor decisions on drunkenness or on the man who pushed her to go further than she wanted. Because many women wrote about and spoke about the regrets they had in their drunken hookups, it was difficult to determine whether anyone other than Richy had pleasurable experiences. I began to wonder if drinking was a site where women could take some sexual initiative because their inhibitions were reduced, and they had an excuse if they were disappointed with the results of the hookup. However, later they often felt obligated to speak and write about their experiences with remorse because the larger cultural norm (at least in this college environment) was that men were supposed to take the initiative and men were supposed to want sex, whereas women were not supposed to do either of these two. Perhaps in their sober moments, the women felt uncomfortable that they had broken societal norms. It was difficult to determine, but the guilt and remorse throughout women's narratives describing drunken hookups was widespread.

In drinking and other drug-using situations, some women in my project found themselves in positions where they were dominated or assaulted by men—emotionally or physically—but often did not describe these events as domination or assault. This dominance began with something as seemingly harmless as a man controlling the supply of alcohol or other drugs, but the domination did not always end there. For example, Eden gave a detailed narrative of this process where she was the only woman with several of her "guy friends" playing the drinking game "Asshole," which she described as if it was fun and funny:

They also knew that I hate beer, so they were kind enough to buy me a bottle of Boone's [Boone's Farm is an inexpensive sweet wine, similar to a wine cooler]. When I got there we had a change of plans. No one owned Pictionary, so we played "Asshole" instead. Asshole is a card game (most often played when drinking) in which the winner is the President, the next person is the Vice-President, and so on and so forth until the last two people are the Vice-Asshole, and the Asshole. Basically, the president can make up any rules they want to, and they boss everyone else around, especially the asshole. Of the six of us, I was the only girl (which is how it always was last year too), and they thought it was really funny to make me the designated asshole. They would do things like, call a "pee break" and when I was the last person back (since the girls bathroom was much farther away than the boys bathroom), they would demote me to the "asshole" position. . . . I was careful to take little sips when I was drinking (much to my friends dismay) but I most definitely was not sober when I got home. I was in control, and I didn't do anything to be embarrassed about. I just had a good time.

While this experience may seem harmless enough, it contributed to a culture in which men were expected to dominate women in subtle ways within drinking situations and women were supposed to protect themselves. In Eden's case, this meant taking "little sips." Several of the women reported "hanging out mostly with guys" as friends, and some of these women experienced what might be construed by most as "violence," but the behavior was not considered violent or troubling by these women.

Violence as initiation to acceptance as "one of the guys." Fine (1994, p. 40), in her chapter entitled "Over Dinner: Feminism and Adolescent Female Bodies," wrote about her conversations with four teenage women. She found that these young women "rejected femininity in favor of a benign version of masculinity that enabled them to function as one of the guys." In my project, some of the more regular users also rejected femininity to be accepted as one of the guys. For example, Jude, like Eden, had male friends. She rationalized their domination of her because she was just being treated like "one of the guys." Jude experienced physical violence at the hands of these male friends. She excused these "rough" situations and defended her male friends' actions to other friends and authority figures. Jude explained some of the consequences of being treated like one of the guys (although she laughed as she said this, in a somewhat boastful way):

I've always been viewed by the guys on my floor as just one of the guys. They talk to me like one of the guys. They beat me up, literally. I was getting dragged into the office by the head master so many times [in high school] saying "I saw this happen. . . I heard this happened, do you want to press sexual harassment charges. . . I've already got them filed . . . do you want to press them?" And I would have to try to convince them that these guys are just treating me like a guy and not looking at me like a girl and treating me like you'd want them to treat me. I'd come home with bruises. My prom pictures I had bruises all down my legs 'cause my two guy friends had a contest to see who could give me the biggest hit.

The women who "hung out" more with "guys" like Sally, Maggie, Lee, Eden, and Jude each seemed to condemn femininity. Jude did this rather harshly in this passage during her interview: "I'm moving out after second semester. . . I can't hang out with girls. Normally I hang out with guys. . . guys have always been my friends and they don't care what I look like, they don't care about hair and makeup and all the stupid petty little things." "Hanging out" and drinking with "guys" seemed preferable to being with female friends for the women who were more regular users. These associations with men with no other women around to take care of them sometimes had a price—violence in excessive drinking or drug-using situations.

Violence at the hands of romantic partners in drug-using situations. Much of the data suggested that some of the women in my project were demeaned physically or emotionally by men in drinking and other drug-using situations in not-so-subtle ways. A very clear example of this was Maggie's: "He basically started holding on to me and not letting me go even when I persisted. I was humiliated sitting there with Ken holding me down and kissing me. He was so drunk that he couldn't even sit up. I finally broke away from him and ran out of the room."

Ken was Maggie's boyfriend at the time. However, these situations did not only happen with boyfriends. Some women experienced this aggression as part of the drunken hookup. Paula described a night when she was "really drunk," and how the "hookup" progressed into a situation that was very frightening for her: "I bumped into him, and then I was at the keg talking to him and the next thing I knew we were in my room. He was on one side of the room and I was like sitting in a chair, he was sitting on my bed. . . the bed looked really big because I pushed two together. . . and then just passed out on it. It was like three in the morning, so I just wrapped myself up in a blanket and he just jumped on me. It was the scariest thing in the world, and then he left. And right before he leaves he was like, 'where does this put us emotionally?' I said, 'get out!'"

Paula described the "tug of war" that frequently happened during a drunken hookup where the men typically pushed to get as much as they could sexually from a woman, and the woman's role was to resist:

But he shows up in my room, okay fine. So I am in there talking to him and he weighs 350 pounds and I am like 10 beers deep, he was having his way with me, and I was just like. . . not into it sexually, but he would not leave for like two hours I am fighting him off. It was terrible. I was like go away. Stop it I am tired, I am drunk, I want to pass out for two hours. . . somehow I just fell asleep. So it was tug a war kind of thing. All the time he is like, "but you are so pretty and blah, blah, blah," and I was like "yeh some other time." So I fall asleep and I wake up like at 9:00 the next morning and he is still in my bed. And I was like, "why haven't you left?" Finally he jumped ship.

Paula was too drunk and too tired to resist the aggression. Cathy described (as did Paula and Sally) what a "typical" drunken "hookup" was like for them when they had experienced times when they just did not care to fight against the man's advances (often aggression), so they just "let him do what he wanted." They were either too drunk to care or just did not have the energy. Cathy said: "You're not thinking straight or you just don't. . . it's like you're caught up in the heat of the moment, you just don't care or like sometimes it's like he's physically aggressive and you don't like. . . . I'm a passive aggressive person, like I hate confrontation. I hate it. I would rather be silent about something than talk about it or whatever. . . confrontation wise. And I think it's like private. . . it's like. . . part of you doesn't want it and part of you doesn't care and stuff and I mean."

Paula and Cathy each admitted that sometimes it was easier to "give in" in instances when a guy kept pushing because they were tired (or about to pass out from drunkenness or exhaustion), and they just did not feel like "fighting him off." These episodes were often not viewed as violent or oppressive but as annoying. Cathy described what she considered to be violence when she was hit by a "guy friend" whom she had "hooked up with" on a previous night. She said that they were in a bar, and they were both "drunk" when he swung and hit her after she brushed him accidentally with her hand: "They [the friends she was with] thought he was swinging across to hit a guy that's how hard he went. He went like this across [makes a swinging punching motion]. He was so drunk that he missed my face, thank god. Because the pain from my arm. . . I couldn't even imagine what he would have done with my face."

Cathy also mentioned that she had been hit before by a boyfriend when he was drunk. She described it during her interview:

And both times, one time. . . we would kid around and stuff like that, like we would wrestle and I would come home with these bruises on me and my friends would be worried, and I'd be like, "oh yeah Jay and I were kidding around." And they were like "don't you think that he's a little bit rougher than he should be?" And I'm like, "well no, he's an aggressive kid, he's a brother, his father is a very aggressive person, his father's an alcoholic," I'm like, "obviously his father has a temper, and Jay has a temper." I'm like, "no, no, no, no, he's kidding around, like we just kid around." And then one night, after the first time he ever hit, he was drunk.

Cathy described the process of making excuses for this behavior when she was questioned about it. None of these women called these instances "rape" or assault. To most of them, it was more that they "didn't care" at the time when they were drunk, but afterward, when they were sober, both Paula and Cathy said, "oh my God!" suggesting that each did regret having "let" the man "have sex" with her. Often, it seemed that the violent behavior of male friends or romantic partners was excused or downplayed as insignificant or as being due to excessive drinking or drug use.

In one case, Janie wrote in her journal about how various drugs would affect her high school boyfriend and the impact this had on her decisions:

Many people don't believe that I have never used drugs, but it is true I have seen bad things because of them. My ex-boyfriend when we were juniors used to be very violent and put that anger towards me. He was only like this when he smoked up though. He would hit or push me until I gave in. I lost my virginity to him after a lacrosse game because he was high and pinned me down, he was a lot bigger and stronger than me [sic]. It was only a month later that I was able to escape that relationship because of a mutual friend, who also smoked up, but never grew violent. He helped me one night when he saw me getting pushed around.

Janie never called her boyfriend's action "rape" or "sexual assault." She wrote that she "lost her virginity" to him. As a result of her experiences, she wrote about a more recent experience (in college) with her new boyfriend: "I do not like to be around guys I don't know when they are smoking up. My boyfriend recently became violent when he was drunk and he scared me. His friends had to take care of me. I was in tears and scared out of my mind. I know his friends would never let him hurt me because some of them were mine too. I can only hope that he does not do this again, although I don't think he will because he is not an aggressive person at all."

A couple of the women mentioned in their interviews that they knew women who had been sexually assaulted when drinking, but it was still not labeled "rape" or "assault." Cathy described her friend: "They had been drinking and she went into her room, she didn't feel good, and he kissed her and then he like pinned her down and like she couldn't, and she was yelling and screaming and no one came to her rescue. She's a girl emotionally messed anyways, her father had died right before we came to college, and she's had a lot to deal with and then that happened." These stories were frequently about women who were, as Cathy put it, "emotionally messed anyways," as if they were somehow deserving of their fate.

The narratives of these women suggested a culture in which the men were expected to be the aggressor in every situation, from the provision of substances to the initial "pickup" through the "hookup." Then a man was expected to make the next move if he wanted to continue to "see her" (i.e., become boyfriend—girlfriend). Men's violent behavior in many instances of sexual assault when using drugs or when drunk was excused or forgiven. In friendship relationships with men, violence was sometimes viewed as part of being considered "one of the guys"—a status that some of the women sought.

Women, like Maggie, Janie, Cathy, Sally, and Jude who had been with men who had treated them violently and who had stayed with these men, either as friends or romantic partners, have been labeled various terms in treatment circles and the literature (e.g., codependent, lacking self-esteem, etc.). Behaviors that often are associated with the "codependency" label were common to many of these women. This will be described in the next chapter.

Chapter 5
Drug Use and Keeping Boyfriends

Keeping boyfriends was important to many of the women in the project. Women who already had boyfriends, and reported that their boyfriends used drugs excessively, often learned to tolerate their boyfriend's decisions quietly. Sometimes a woman would increase her own levels of drug use, often beyond the level where she felt comfortable, to approximate the level of her boyfriend. Some of these women adopted what often is described as "codependent" behavior where they had an "excessive focus on" their boyfriend's drug use or abuse or "addiction," and spent a great deal of time trying to help their boyfriends who often had academic difficulty from their excessive use.

In the 1990s, feminists have begun to critique the way in which those involved in the study of drugs (mostly psychologists) have organized and labeled some of the key problems associated with excessive, problematic use—particularly codependency and addiction. Babcock and McKay (1995, p. 3) wrote of codependency: "This author's repeated impression has been that the term is most frequently used, by addictions workers and the public, to mean a disordered syndrome (often called a 'disease') of excessive focus on the other, which typifies most addicts' significant others (especially female), is chronic and is invested in the continuation of the addiction (as indicated by the prefix co)."

Van Den Bergh (1991, p. 6) focused her feminist critique on the addictions which she defined as "characterized by a mental obsession as well as compulsive behavior related to ingesting a substance (food, alcohol, drugs) or engaging in a process (gambling, sex, work). Schaef (1987) suggested that "societal structures can predispose persons to develop addictions; this purview is complementary to a feminist perspective." Schaef's study seemed to suggest the importance of examining the societal structures, which for the purpose of my project were specific to the college culture in which drug-using behavior that could be classified as "addictive" as well as behaviors that could be construed as "codependent" seem to be happening. Women in my project took up these discourses in complex ways.

Many women told vivid narratives about the way the men in their lives (friends, fathers, uncles, and boyfriends) used, abused, or had abused drugs in the past. Many of the women seemed far more sympathetic or concerned about men's problems with drugs than they were with women's (sometimes including their own).

Initially, I was reluctant to deal with the theme of codependency because the term has become so engendered (i.e., it is mostly used to describe female partners of alcoholics or drug addicts). It has often been used to blame the partners for enabling the addict to continue his or her behavior. Also, the term failed to address adequately the nature of the issue for the women in this study. It was not simply that some of these women were in codependent relationships with addicts, but more that many of these college women (particularly abstainers and infrequent drinkers) devoted a great deal of time and effort to worrying about, and trying to solve the drug problems of friends, boyfriends, and family members. Using Babcock and McKay's (1995, p. 3) definition of codependency, several of these women had an "excessive focus on" men's drug problems.

I became increasingly aware of the many women in my class who approached me after class to ask me what they should do to help their boyfriends or ex-boyfriends or male friends who were using more drugs than the woman felt comfortable with their using. I found myself reexamining the issues of codependency—how it has been written and spoken about and the implications of the way the discourse has been shaped. Women came to me wanting answers, wanting advice, wanting to "fix" the drug problems their friends or boyfriends were experiencing. The label of codependency was insufficient to explain the behavior or the amount of time many of these women spent being concerned about (and wanting to alter) other people's use, particularly that of boyfriends whom they wanted to keep. Women cared for their boyfriends and wanted to "help" them. This "help" took on various forms as Annie, Sally, Jude, and others described.

After devoting nearly seven weeks of journal entries to describing her involvement in trying to get her boyfriend to stop smoking so much marijuana and start going to classes, Sally finally described her frustration in her last entry: "He still doesn't really go to class. He's only taking 9 credits this semester anyways. He thinks of it now as 'well, I know what I have to do next year. I'll stop then and get my act together.' He says I make such a big deal out of things. I tell him—if I knew something was responsible for creating all this trouble in my life—I wouldn't do it. He knows I say all this stuff to him because I care about him."

Annie wrote almost her entire journal about her concern over her ex-boyfriend's use of marijuana. She was a first-year student, and her boyfriend was still in high school. She was from a local high school, so she had frequent contact with him. She approached me after class to ask me what she should do.

In her journal, she wrote extensively about his drug use and her relationship with him:

My ex-boyfriend, Brian, has been telling me he has started using marijuana a lot. Every week-end and during the week now. I am really worried about him. I do not know what to say to him. He wants to listen to me but at the same time he doesn't. I just don't want to get in a huge fight with him over this, because we do not get along very well anymore anyways, and we just started talking again. I am really worried and do not know what to say to him or if I should go to his mom. But the thing about it is his parents know he uses marijuana, so I don't know if I should even bother.

Annie was clearly concerned and wanted to help Brian, but she was unsure of what to do or say. Many of the women in these situations voiced frustration over being unable to help or change these men they cared about. Jude acknowledged feeling that she was acting like her boyfriend's mother but that she "didn't want to." He had "failed out" of the university, and she was trying to help him get back in to school. She described this in her interview: "He's just lazy and it is completely pot. . . . It bothers me how nice he is and like what a good person he is and how much potential he has, and I want to show him that, and make him live up to that, then I feel like I'm a mother, so it's a boyfriend and girlfriend relationship, but its also more of a mothering relationship. I don't know, I've never been in that type of relationship before."

Women wanted to help the men in their lives find a balance between their drug use and their responsibilities, and they spent quite a bit of time trying to figure out how to do that. They often expressed frustration because they felt unable to talk to people (particularly boyfriends) that they cared for about their troublesome level of drug use. The discourses around drug abuse were so limiting and limited that women frequently said nothing, instead of risking offending their boyfriends by calling them "drug addicts." This was the case for Annie, Jude, and Sally who were currently involved (or had recently been involved) with a "boyfriend" who used drugs in ways that seemed to lead to problems in their lives.

PUTTING UP, SHUTTING UP, OR PREACHING

Some women with boyfriends described wanting their boyfriends to reduce their drug use or alter their behaviors while they were using drugs. According to Maggie, Ken was her "boyfriend," at least at the time that she wrote her narratives. She continued with a classic example of what I have termed the *codependency narrative* because she remained in this relationship for at least a brief time after the incident described below, and dealt with his drinking problem and his occasional violence against her by keeping this information to herself. While she acknowledged that she was afraid of being raped, she still confronted him the next day:

The next day, I went to tell Ken exactly how angry I had been, only to find out that he didn't really remember any of the night. It's kind of hard to yell at someone when you have to tell them what they did wrong first. . . . I didn't yell at him instead I just told him that I never would trust him around me when he was drunk. . . . I really began to believe that Ken could possibly be an alcoholic and as I read through the questions [in the textbook for the course] which defined an addict, Ken fit right into the category. I never did anything about it—never telling anyone, but I didn't need to because I knew myself.

Many women who were light or nonillicit drug users reported discomfort when trying to "preach" to their boyfriends or other male friends. Perhaps this discomfort was a result of not having a more appropriate discourse available to approach those whose drug use caused a woman concern. For example, Eden wrote of her frustration when confronting drug-using behaviors in the case of a male peer but hid her true disappointment from her boyfriend: "He [her boyfriend at the time] told me that he was going camping with his father this weekend, and that it would be fun, but he was upset because the whole frat house was planning on going tripping on 'shrooms, and pot. I think he could see the disappointment in my face, because he asked why I was upset. What could I say? It is his life, it just makes me sad that it is starting to revolve around drug use. I let it go because I don't feel like I am close enough to give him a lecture without his resenting me in the long run."

Eden, like many other women, elected to keep her concern about her boyfriend's drug use to herself. Keeping quiet was often easier and would not result in an open conflict about drug use. Women did not want to be perceived as "mothering" or "nagging" their boyfriends, so this often led them to shut up within relationships with heavier drug-using men. The excuse was usually like Eden's, "it is his life. . . I let it go."

Sometimes women who were worried about their boyfriend's drug use would keep quiet like Eden did in the above passage and just let her facial expression of disappointment speak for itself. Some women would occasionally preach, as Sally and Annie both tried to do a couple of times. These women often emphasized the importance of "being in control" or "knowing one's limits" because failure to do so was viewed as a problem. The women who preached to their boyfriends had already, in their minds, learned their limits and wanted to help others (particularly their boyfriends if they had problems) learn their limits, and seemed frustrated when they did not.

CONCERN OVER LOOKING GOOD FOR BOYFRIENDS

An important part of the culture of romance was being attractive to a possible mate. Most women wanted to "look good" for their boyfriends or potential boyfriends in terms of the choices about the drugs they used and how much they used. This meant different things depending on what their boyfriends, or the men they were trying to attract, used. For example, for Mara this meant not drinking too much: "Because when you're there with your boyfriend. . . for me like I don't think your boyfriend likes to see you get really drunk. You know what I mean, I think like if you're out of control like it's just very unattractive to the person."

For some of the women, being an attractive partner meant remaining in control when drinking or using other drugs, as Mara described. However, women with boyfriends who were more regular users thought that using drugs at similar levels as their boyfriends would make them more attractive. Many of the women also reported that their boyfriends used illicit drugs at or above their own levels. In many cases, the boyfriend's use exceeded the woman's and there was a not-so-subtle pressure to join him. However, in no instance did a woman feel that her drug use (or abstinence from drug use) affected her boyfriend's use. Some of the women reported using other illicit drugs than they felt comfortable using, believing they would become more attractive partners. For example, Christine described this with cocaine: "My boyfriend and his three friends were high and they brought some [cocaine] with them. This was a very hard situation for me. I do not think I was pressured in a direct way, but sort of indirectly. Maybe it was me, but it was too hard to say no. Maybe it was because I liked him a lot, I really do not know."

Christine spent nearly her entire journal and much of her interview talking about her boyfriend, who was her ex-boyfriend by the end of her journal and at the time of her interview. She told me about "getting into the Rave scene": "Like I did everything I think for him more or less. 'Cause like all my friends weren't into that. And they were like, 'you're not going, you're not going to go' [to Rave parties]. [She described that she would use] every kind of drug, cocaine, meth, speed, acid. . . dancing all night until like three in the morning. And then go home, and sleep all day Sunday, and then I wouldn't go to class on Monday." She said these parties weren't "that much fun," but that she went because her boyfriend wanted to go. She wanted to be with him and share these experiences thinking he would grow to like her more. She wanted him to stop using drugs and thought he might someday. When he did not cut down, and his drug use escalated and he began to sell drugs, she eventually stopped seeing him.

Body Image and Drug Use

Some of the women in my project mentioned the connection between drug use and their body image, but past research has not analyzed such a connection. Volumes have been written about college women and eating disorders. Slade (1994) pointed out in his essay entitled "What Is Body Image?" that the concept of "body image" which is often associated with eating disorders has been difficult to define. Within literature on eating disorders, distorted body image has been cited as one of the major symptoms. Slade offered a typical example, that anorexia nervosa is defined as having body image distortion in the form of an "overestimation of body size, and is linked to a sociocultural norm in developed societies" (p. 497). Myers and Biocca (1992) asserted that women's body image was "elastic" and that one's body image was strongly influenced by the media. Their study involved seventy-six female college students who watched videotapes and television commercials emphasizing the "thin ideal body image." They demonstrated that women's ideas about their own body size were significantly influenced by this viewing. They suggested that "watching even 30 minutes' worth of TV programming and advertising can alter a woman's perception of the shape of her body" (p. 108).

Few studies have examined a woman's body image and how it influences decisions about drug use. Barker and Musick (1994) in their study of adolescent mothers from Latin America, Asia, Africa, and the United States found that these women tended to have poor body image and demonstrated self-abusive behaviors including but not limited to drug abuse. This study suggested a link between poor self-image including poor body image and teenage pregnancy and drug abuse (and other labeled "self-abusive" behaviors).

Part of looking good for boyfriends meant paying attention to one's body image. This meant being thin, at least to several of the women in my project. Staying thin within the culture of romance was important. Women's emphasis on staying thin intersected with their decisions about drug use in complex ways.

Some of the women in this study mentioned issues related to their perceptions of their bodies and how their decisions about drugs were influenced by their images or ideas about their bodies. First, drugs were sometimes viewed as harmful for one's body (and drug use was sometimes limited based on this perception). This will be described in Part III. Second, drugs were used to control body size through diet pills. Third, drugs such as alcohol and marijuana were seen as leading to increasing body size (a problem that quite a few women were concerned with). Alcohol and marijuana use was sometimes limited as a result of this perception, or in a couple of cases, behaviors such as vomiting would be used to counteract the potential weight gain from overdrinking. One of the women mentioned using food as a drug—that is, to reward herself, and how this resulted in a poor body image. The women who were more heavily involved with a variety of drugs (e.g., Maggie, Lee, Jude, Darla, Jackie) failed to mention their bodies or the negative influence of various drugs on their bodies.

Only one woman, Missy, acknowledged that she had used diet pills to control her weight: "I've had experience with past uses of diet pills. I was able to purchase these at a local drug store—with no problem at all—over-the-counter. When taking these pills, I usually became easily irritated and moody. I sometimes felt really energized and hyper but at other times I would feel dizzy, at times faint, sleepy, withdrawn and very tired (these usually occurred when I ate very, very little while on the pills). Initially I lost weight, but once off the pills I gained the weight back right away."

Andrea, who was an infrequent drinker and did not use illegal drugs, wrote about her struggle with her weight. She did not use drugs to relieve stress or to reward herself, but she did use food. She wrote:

Eating becomes my reward system for having taken a really hard exam or done a lot of work. I eat to relax and not think about my work, but all I get is fatter! I am not an overweight person, but I do have extra pounds that a person my age does not need. No one ever does need it, but I know that controlling my weight will only get harder as I get older and less active. So I say, well maybe next week I'll find time to work out, but next week comes and goes with no changes. The change has to start somewhere, but I'm not sure where that will be. The other thing that makes it hard is that I am not an insecure person, so I feel no desire to be ultra thin like a lot of the girls on this campus. My roommate is constantly battling her desire to eat and always loses. She is much heavier than me, so I always feel safe when I compare myself to her.

Attractiveness (including weight) was frequently measured in relation to others. Women talked about other women's battles with their weight. For example, Alex described a woman who lived near her who used cigarettes to control her weight:

One of the girls who lives nearby smokes constantly. The hallway in our apartment constantly stinks like smoke, despite the fact that she lives three floors above. She seems to need cigarettes for their calming influence in her life, but I think also to keep from eating. She has absolutely zero body fat, but she keeps saying she wants to go for the waif look. She doesn't ever let herself eat anything at our apartment except on very rare occasions. Then when she has eaten, she suddenly has to go upstairs for something. This Saturday night we all went out for dinner. She left the table three times during the course of the meal to go to the bathroom! I don't believe it was because of an upset stomach, I think she may be bulimic.

Cigarettes were a popular way of controlling hunger—perhaps this is the main reason why cigarette smoking has been so popular among young women. Other drugs such as marijuana and alcohol were described as having the opposite effect, and concerns about weight gain from these drugs were described in some of the women's narratives. For example, in her interview Cathy described how she was gaining weight from her drinking her first year. She said that she used to vomit regularly when she would drink and that would help prevent weight gain.

Smoking pot also adds a few pounds because you eat so much at such a late time of night. Through my freshman year at college this is what I have learned through experience. Not only can dining hall food put on the pounds but so can alcohol. I swore I would not gain weight but drinking caught up with me. Now I must spend the summer working it off. I used to throw up every time I drank more than 3 beers or anything else. Now I wish I would so the calories would not pack on. Unfortunately as I adapted to college lifestyle so did my system.

Cathy took extreme measures (vomiting) to avoid weight gain. She said that she was not "bulimic." Carrie also mentioned that she threw up, while writing defensively to me that she was not "bulimic": "Well let's just say that marijuana and alcohol don't mix well with me because I was throwing up in the bathroom all night. I guess I should've known better because it's happened to me before. The only good part about it was that my stomach was really flat the next morning. But don't worry, I'm not bulimic or anything."

Women who described vomiting in relation to drug use (usually drinking) denied any bulimic tendencies. Many women were concerned about this weight gain, and for some, this fear was enough to cause women to limit their use. For example, Eden mentioned in her journal that part of her desire not to drink was because of the link with weight gain: "I really hate beer, and feel no need to 'acquire a taste for it,' because, as I tell my friends, why should I acquire a taste for something that will make me fat?"

Some of the women noticed when their girlfriends or roommates gained weight from drugs. The weight gain from the marijuana "munchies" was frequently mentioned in class and in the journals. Jenny wrote about watching her roommate's drug use lead to her weight gain: "I would like to tell you about my roommate from last year because I observed her taking drugs and I watched the changes she went through during her first semester that year. First of all, she began to smoke marijuana every night, and then she would eat afterwards, so she gained some weight."

Cathy mentioned in her interview with me her perceptions of gender differences in drinking and weight gain: "For girls it's harder because you gain weight. Like I gain weight easily anyways. I gained like 15, I gained the freshman 15 and it was partly from food, but when I cut down the food it was still partially because of drinking. I cut down drinking too and I don't have a tolerance that's the thing is I don't need to drink a lot to get drunk. But you, I mean you do it anyways."

By "it" Cathy meant drinking more and drinking until she would throw up, because this would keep her from gaining weight. As she described, she did this intentionally, until she stopped after her first couple of months at college: "I stopped throwing up I'd say in like November. And that's when I started gaining weight was in November and I had lost weight when I went home for Thanksgiving. But Christmas time the weather didn't help and Christmas cookies, you know holidays. . . and at home I don't drink as much, my friends work a lot."

Women raised the issue of drug use and its intersection with their bodies and body image in different ways. Attractiveness and being in control were critical pieces of courtship and in keeping a boyfriend. Caretaking and "partying" together were also important elements of a boyfriend—girlfriend relationship. Most of the women with boyfriends were concerned about being "good girlfriends" and wanted to be attractive, "in control" or "know their limits," take care of their boyfriends without being a "nag" or too much like their "mother," and wanted to "party" with their boyfriends. This was sometimes a difficult juggling act.

Similar to their friendships with women, part of keeping boyfriends meant partying with them (which often meant using drugs with them at least for many of the White women). This did not seem to be the case as often with the women of color. Within drug-using settings, women were expected to be the caregivers. In addition, women were expected to take care of or help their boyfriends who had problems that their girlfriends attributed to drug use. An "excessive" amount of time spent worrying about or taking care of a person with a drug-related problem or "addiction" has often been labeled in the literature on drug abuse as "codependent behavior." The behavior that many of the women described in my project would likely have received this label.

Chapter 6
Losing or Separating from Male Friends and Boyfriends

In some cases, when a woman could no longer tolerate her boyfriend's troublesome drug use, she would break up with him and seek another boyfriend whose drug-use levels were more compatible with her own. Sometimes women were forced to separate from their male friends and romantic partners because the men were academically dismissed as a result of their chronic drug use.

"BREAKING UP IS HARD TO DO"

Many of the women in my project were first-year students, and several were in the process of ending their relationships with their "boyfriends from home." Some of the women described breaking up with their boyfriends "from home" or college because of drug use—often because of differences in drug use. In their interviews, Alana and Zoie both talked about their boyfriends from home who were drug dealers and from whom they had recently separated. They had each made a conscious decision not to use illicit drugs and were not swayed by their boyfriends who used and sold drugs. They both said that their boyfriend's drug dealing was kept secret during much of their relationship, suggesting that they weren't directly exposed to it. Alana said when she first met her boyfriend from home: "Yeah. He's like 28, he has his own business. He has a store by my house. A store, and I met him there. But I didn't know that's [selling drugs] what he did. I just thought he was business owner."

The excessive drug use and drug dealing of their boyfriends from home was part of why Alana and Zoie broke up with them. In their interviews, they both recognized that their close associations with their drug-dealing boyfriends needed to stop before they became teachers. Alana asked the question when she was trying to decide if she should break up with her boyfriend: "I can't be a teacher and have my husband sell drugs. . . even though he does not like you know what I mean sell the worst drugs. . . like crack." This statement described how women ranked drugs hierarchically and traditionally, as if her boyfriend's drug dealing would be "worse" if he was selling "crack." More about this will be described in the next chapter.

Alana described the "trauma" of the breakup briefly in her narratives: "This weekend I went to stay with my boyfriend for Easter Break. It was traumatic because I wanted to break up with him but I didn't want to tell him, so I kept pushing it off. When I came home, I told him on the phone and he told me he is going to start drinking to forget me. He's not a drinker, he's fucked up off 4 drinks, but he's doing this to forget his problems." This experience was "traumatic" for her partly because she was worried about his drinking to "forget his problems." Many of the women constructed drinking to forget problems as the sign of a "problem." Alana told me in the interview that this same boyfriend from home stalked her for a while after their breakup. He came to see her at school and threatened her, and threw her television out the window. These experiences made breaking up especially difficult for Alana.

Alana had another boyfriend at school at the time of her interview. She had positive things to say about this relationship, but she was concerned about being taken for granted or controlled. When I asked her about her new relationship, she compared her new boyfriend to the boyfriend from whom she had recently split:

I don't know like guys when you say I'm going to be with you like once they know that they love you and they think you're the woman for them they don't want to let go. And they don't understand. And I see the same pattern with Jose. That he wants to be with me like forever. . . . Forever like you're the one I want to marry. You know cause he's that kind of person. And it kind of scares me because I mean even though I have this feeling for him, I don't want him to think that way always, because if things change then it's hard to handle. It sounds kind of mean, but. . .

These concerns about a major commitment partially stemmed from her "horrible" breakup with her boyfriend from home who behaved violently toward her when she broke up with him, even though in her words he "was not a violent man" and he "apologized."

Several women did not want to discuss the future or long-term commitments such as marriage during the interviews. When I would ask women during the interviews about how they saw their futures with their boyfriends, each said they "didn't know" and would not say anything else. Perhaps because most of the women were in their first and second year of college, and future commitments such as marriage seemed in the distant future, these women could not talk about or would not speculate about this. Alana was the only one who mentioned her boyfriend discussing marriage, and this discussion made her nervous. Her new boyfriend was a senior at the time of the interview, so perhaps he was more future-oriented than she was.

Zoie described her high school boyfriend who was also a drug dealer and user: "I found out he did cocaine, he did heroin, he smoked cigarettes, he drank, he dealt."

When Zoie found out about her boyfriend's drug use from her cousin who was one of his friends, she tried to break up with him. He came up to see her at school and in her words "stalked her." After nearly a semester of this (which adversely affected her academic performance), she said she was going to file a restraining order. She told this story in her interview with me:

Yeah, on Christmas Day his whole family called me and insulted me. And said it was all my fault because he was trying to kill himself or something like that. And I said, "well if he's going to kill himself tell him to come over to my house and I will give him a gun, and I will take care of it myself and we'll go to the Empire State Building so we can leap. And I'll be there to make sure he does it." And they went "oh, oh," In January, I received a letter and it was like the last thing I was going to take from him, and I called his mom and said, "look if he writes me or he calls me once more I'll have him arrested. I don't want to hear from him ever in my life again." And that eventually stopped him. And I think it was because he was smoking a lot . . . of marijuana.

Zoie was angry about her ex-boyfriend's harassment. Alana and Zoie had the difficulty of dealing with being stalked and harassed after breaking up with their drug-dealing boyfriends as well as the struggle of finding new ways to finance their educational expenses. As Alana said: "I didn't have to work up here [when her boyfriend was supporting her financially] just because he always gave me money. I had work-study, but I only used like $200 of it." The added fear of not having enough money for college made breaking up particularly difficult for these women.

Zoie had a new boyfriend at school within a month of her breakup with her boyfriend from home. She told me how they ended up together: "That's probably why we got together, because my boyfriend, he became like my best friend. . . we have so much in common, it's unbelievable. And everything that was happening I would always cry on his shoulder or whatever, but we were just friends, and eventually I guess it developed into something else. Maybe I saw how good he was, how much different he was from my boyfriend, I don't know but then like a month after I broke up with my boyfriend, I became involved with him . . . now it's perfect."

Many of the women stayed in less than perfect relationships with their boyfriends where they would tolerate drug abuse and being neglected by them until a better option arose, usually a more suitable boyfriend who shared similar attitudes about drugs and many other things. Sometimes these new boyfriends evolved from friendships with men who were supportive during a difficult breakup with a boyfriend "from home," as was the case with Zoie. Better romance options were a good excuse to get out of a romantic relationship with a partner who was abusing drugs.

Alana was the only one among the Black and Latina women who briefly mentioned her boyfriend in her journal. However, most of the White women mentioned either boyfriends, hookups, or both. Each of the Asian-American women mentioned their boyfriends or hookups in some way in their journals.

For example, Richy spent a great deal of time in her journal and in the interview discussing her ex-boyfriend. She said that the reason she came to this university was to be with him, and he broke up with her shortly after she started school. She described their relationship after they broke up:

On Thursday night I saw the love of my life and made an absolute fool of myself!!! I got so drunk and so high from cigarettes that I ended up making a pass at him. My ex-boyfriend is a junior here and he is an absolute doll. I absolutely love him to death, but in a now friendly manner, rather than sexual thing. I admire him so much! He's like an older brother that I've never had and to make a pass at him, totally insulted him. We've known each other for almost 5 years now and to think that I almost lost everything we had. Though, he was also drunk he still has a great deep respect for me and would never in any way take for granted of me [sic].

Rachel, who was also Asian-American, mentioned her ex-boyfriend and how the ending of their relationship led her to drink excessively: "It was after the breakup with my two-year boyfriend when I started to explore with alcohol every weekend. I never became an alcoholic, but I knew that I needed to feel good when the weekends came. I knew alcohol was the only way to alter my state of consciousness. To forget him, the whole breakup. Throwing up every time I drank was worth it."

Several women mentioned their ex-boyfriends and the role of drugs in the breakup—often as either the reason for or the remedy to forget the breakup. In some cases where her boyfriend used drugs more than a woman felt comfortable, this could result in a breakup. In other cases, like Annie's, she was worried because her boyfriend began to smoke marijuana more heavily after they broke up. Alana's boyfriend used his drinking as a means to evoke her concern and to try to get her back into his life. In Rachel's case, she used alcohol or other drugs to get over a painful breakup.

LOSS OF HETEROSEXUAL FRIENDSHIPS

Women who used more illicit drugs more frequently, such as Lee, Jude, Maggie, and Hetty, tended to "hang out" more often with male friends and boyfriends than female friends. However, unlike their male friends who would disengage from their academics to engage in regular drug use, most women usually found a balance between drug use and their academics.

Jude, Maggie, Lee, and Hetty spoke about their separation from male friends because they had been "kicked out of school" on account of poor academic performance from excessive drug use. Lee said: "they're all nice guys, like a lot of them had gotten kicked out for academics like recently. So a lot of them aren't here anymore, which is kind of hard, it's weird." However, neither journals nor interviews mentioned female peers, or even acquaintances, being dismissed for academic reasons.

These women's friendships with men who used drugs excessively were not ended by choice but because of academic dismissal. These "breakups" were sometimes painful, as Lee described. Jude, Maggie, and Hetty each described this loss of their male friends to academic dismissal as difficult. Loss of male friends, like separating or breaking up with boyfriends, was difficult but several women experienced it.

CONCLUSIONS ABOUT DRUGS AND ROMANCE

The theme that emerged for nearly all of the women was the important role of drugs in these women's relationships with men. For White and Asian women, alcohol and cigarettes were often an integral part of romantic pursuits, but rarely was any other drug mentioned in relation to romance (with the exception of Ecstasy described in the next chapter). The Black and Latina women did not mention boyfriends or their seeking of boyfriends as often in their journals as the White or Asian women did. Nevertheless, in their interviews, Zoie and Alana spent a considerable amount of time describing their ex-boyfriends and current boyfriends and the role of drugs in these relationships. None of the Black and Latina women described any drugs as playing a facilitating role in their romantic endeavors, but many of the White and Asian women did.

Romantic relationships were very important to these women, and drug use sometimes made these relationships easier and more fun, but more often difficult and painful. Drugs played an important role during many of these women's efforts to find romance and permanent boyfriends—that is, during the "hooking up" process. Second, various drugs made negotiating the boyfriend—girlfriend relationship difficult as boyfriends often encouraged their girlfriends to use drugs at the same levels as they did. The emphasis placed on finding and keeping boyfriends had serious implications for some of these women in terms of body image, sexual violence, and codependency because women often placed themselves in situations that were physically and emotionally dangerous. Finally, breaking up was difficult to do, but in some cases when drug use was "out of control" or women became increasingly uncomfortable with their boyfriends' drug use, they broke up with them.

PART III

THE SOCIAL CONSTRUCTION AND RANKING OF DRUGS WITHIN RELATIONSHIPS

Chapter 7
The Social Construction of Drugs

Women described a variety of drugs that they encountered in college: caffeine, nicotine, alcohol, marijuana ("pot" or "weed"), nitrous oxide ("nitrous"), prescription medication (Ritilin, Codeine, Clonopin), LSD ("acid"), Psilocybin mushrooms ("shrooms"), MDMA ("Ecstasy," "E," or "Ex"), Ketamine ("Special K"), cocaine/crack, and heroin. Women constructed each drug they encountered differently and attempted to determine their personal use limits for each drug they used based on their prior personal and vicarious experiences with these drugs within their important relationships. Experiences with and constructions of the various drugs were often different within the racially segregated groups on campus. Drugs such as caffeine, nicotine, and alcohol were often not considered "drugs." Some women labeled many of the illicit drugs as "bad" and "hard-core," using antidrug rhetoric. Women who were regular drug users constructed most drugs as "good," using a discourse of pleasure.

A BRIEF INTRODUCTION TO HOW EACH OF THE DRUGS WAS CONSTRUCTED

Women constructed each drug differently as they struggled to learn their limits for the drugs they deemed acceptable to use. In this section, I describe each drug individually: how these women tended to make meaning of each one; if appropriate, how women set their personal use limits for the drug; and the differences in the constructions of some of the drugs within racially segregated groups on campus.

Caffeine

Caffeine was considered a safe drug for each of the women to report. The first reason is obvious—it is legal and accepted. It is not even socially constructed as a drug at all. In fact, there were no questions about caffeine use on the U.S. Department of Education's Core survey that was administered to students at this university (see Appendix A). The second reason is that caffeine is often associated with doing *good student* things such as allowing them to stay up late to study or stay alert for early morning classes. Paula expressed this use very well: "When I first discovered Vivarin [and over-the-counter caffeine pill] first semester, I loved it because if I took one at eight at night when I started doing my homework, I would be up until three in the morning. This really came in handy the week I had a statistics test because I would have enough energy to relearn an entire chapter."

Most of these women wrote or said that caffeine should not be classified as a drug. The reasons for their belief helped uncover some of the concerns and fears some of the women had about other drugs and the stigma attached to the word "drug." For example, Melissa wrote: "I don't even think of caffeine as a 'drug' per se because it is not negatively looked upon by society."

The negative association that a drug must have before it is constructed as a "drug" affected the way many of these women perceived drugs and how willing they might have been to describe accurately their own involvement with what they labeled as "drugs." For many, drug was a dirty, four-letter word and one they learned to fear or hide. The way the word "drug" was used seemed to mimic the larger society, which does not use the word to describe the legal drugs caffeine, nicotine, and alcohol. It seems now to be used in the same way that the word "narcotic" was used in the early propaganda films. It is associated with all things evil about drugs, and it is distinctly separate from legal drugs or medicines.

Women often learned their limits for caffeine use from their own personal experiences or observations of others. Some women set their own caffeine limit after taking too much or from watching a friend who was "bouncing off the walls" from too much coffee or too many caffeine pills.

Nicotine

Nicotine, despite its recent slip in status in our culture, is still not constructed as a drug because people who do not "do drugs" still smoke cigarettes. For example, people in recovery programs leading "drug-free" lives can still drink coffee and smoke cigarettes within the Alcoholics Anonymous model.

The *majority* of women reported smoking at least occasionally. They often felt that most of their peers smoked as well. In many cases, this addiction started quite early. However, many reported smoking socially because it seemed as though everyone else was. Those who did not smoke reported its widespread nature. The U.S. Department of Education Core Survey conducted at the University showed that in the Spring of 1996, 41.3% of the students smoked cigarettes.

Much of the social smoking was done in conjunction with drinking at bars or parties or public places. As mentioned earlier, Black and Latina women did not go to these places, and none of these women smoked cigarettes. The smoking in this particular college culture, at least among the White students, seemed to illustrate the power of the local cultural norms despite powerful negative publicity in the larger culture. Cherry illustrated this point: "Very few of my friends smoke regularly. I, myself, stick to smoking only at the social scenes and every once in a while during the day. I tend to smoke more around smokers and less around nonsmokers." Cherry, similar to other smokers, only smoked with her friends who were smokers.

The self-identified smokers focused a great deal on wanting to quit, trying to quit, or at least repenting for this habit that they realized had a negative reputation outside the college culture. Several said or wrote that they would quit after college. In addition, three of the women admitted being chronic smokers and having asthma that was exacerbated by their smoking. For example, Emma wrote: "Smoking is a big problem for me. I have been smoking for three years. I have asthma—which is often irritated by it. I have tried to quit over and over."

Limits were difficult for smokers to determine even if they had health problems due to smoking. They knew the larger societal sentiment was not to smoke at all, but if one wanted to smoke this was acceptable in bars or at parties. Many of the regular smokers claimed that they tried to quit, while some tried to quit during the seven-week course (most unsuccessfully). However, some of the women who tried to quit smoking cigarettes continued to smoke marijuana and failed to make the connection that marijuana smoking can be even more harmful. Some studies demonstrated that smoking one marijuana joint is as damaging to the lungs as smoking seventeen to twenty cigarettes (Inaba & Cohen, 1996). Richy, as a pack-a-day cigarette smoker, but nonmarijuana smoker, discussed this common hypocrisy: "One day, Matt and I were talking about my smoking habit. You should have seen how much he criticized me for it!!! Then he admits to me that he and his roommate smoke weed together. What a hypocrit [sic]!!!!"

The general consensus, however, particularly among women who smoked cigarettes and marijuana, was that cigarette smoking was more harmful than smoking marijuana. Most cigarette smokers claimed that they wanted to quit smoking cigarettes, while none of the marijuana smokers claimed that they wanted to quit smoking marijuana.

Alcohol

The widespread nature of alcohol abuse on college campuses has been well-documented quantitatively in the literature on college students. The U.S. Department of Education's Core Survey administered at this university in the Spring of 1996 reported that 86% of students drank and that 43% of women and 64% of men engaged in binge drinking (i.e., more than five drinks at a sitting). Nearly 55% of bingers binged one to two times in the previous two weeks. A new question was added to the survey about whether or not one preferred to have alcohol available to them at college, and 26% said they preferred not to have alcohol available (see Appendix A).

Little has been written about how alcohol abuse on campus is experienced, thought about, or written about. Nothing has been written from the perspectives of college women. Women did not consider alcohol a drug—and like most people in our culture, they frequently used phrases such as "drugs and alcohol."

Each of the women's narratives noted that they were affected by alcohol abuse in some way—regardless of their own drinking patterns. Many also recalled their early alcohol experiences, including their initiation into the adolescent culture promoting abuse. In some cases, a profoundly negative experience with alcohol early in adolescence was used as a reason why a woman did not drink heavily in college. Early negative experiences seemed to force a woman to learn her limits before arriving in college, although this was certainly not the case for all of the women. Regardless of a woman's current level of drinking, there was almost always a narrative of a woman's own alcohol abuse or that of a close friend or boyfriend marked by vomiting, passing out, or blackouts. Some of the narratives of alcohol use did involve responsible use, and a period of responsible drinking frequently followed an episode where a woman had gone well "beyond her limits." For example, one of the women (a division I athlete) wrote about a heavy night of drinking where she "passed out" on her boyfriend. She wrote: "I have never passed out in public before. I decided to take a break from drinking for a while."

From this point on, she did not mention any drinking at all in her journals, so to keep from sounding too "boring" she wrote down past experiences in high school and college when she had experimented with other drugs (all legal).

Perhaps most of the women did not describe incidences of moderate or responsible use because they feared sounding too "boring." Almost every mention of alcohol was of drunkenness, not unlike this example from Dani which was simply put: "The other night we all stayed in and got drunk." Or Jude's: "I don't remember much of Thursday or Friday nights except I was so drunk I almost puked."

Blackouts and becoming ill from excessive drinking helped women determine their personal limits and what they wanted to avoid. There were no cases in which a woman reported more than one such blackout or vomiting episode in the seven-week period. In fact, the women who mentioned any such event cut down their drinking quite dramatically after it.

Alana, Mara, and Zoie mentioned that some students of color might drink a little alcohol or smoke a little marijuana before a dance or party to, in Alana's words, "get nice"; drunkenness or being "stoned" was not the goal. Although drinking did help one loosen up to dance, the amount was less than that which they thought the White students drank or smoked. Alana said: "They'll [some of her friends] drink but it's usually at a party and they're drinking, you know what I mean, like it's music and dancing and drinking. It's not like just go to a bar. . . . I mean there's some people that do that but I would say for the majority of us it's more dancing, partying, whatever, and drinking. Not let's go to a bar and just sit down and drink and play drinking games. . . . We drink to get nice."

Alana, Zoie, and Mara's perceptions were that the White students' drinking centered around getting drunk and playing drinking games to facilitate getting drunk and using other drugs to excess. For her friends (mostly Black and Latino/Latina students), dancing and listening to music was the focus, and drinking was only sometimes a small and unnecessary part of it.

Marijuana: Individual Morality and Difficulty Learning Limits

The Core Survey reported that 41.3% of students reported smoking marijuana (see Appendix A). The widespread nature of marijuana use was reflected in the journals and the interviews as well. Smoking marijuana marked the beginning of the drugs in the acceptability ranking composite (see Appendix C and Chapter 8) that women described as "doing drugs."

These women's words supported the commonly held belief in the literature of marijuana as a "gateway drug" (i.e., it was the illicit drug that these women began with before progressing to other illicit drugs, often referred to as "hard-core drugs" by many of these women). However, what has been unknown is how women construct meaning about marijuana and their decision to use or abstain from using this illegal drug. For most, these constructions and decisions were based on experiences within relationships.

Marijuana was viewed as part of almost every woman's everyday reality within their relationships, regardless of whether or not she elected to smoke it. Nonsmokers would comment on a neighbor's smoking, and on smelling it at parties and through their heating vents in their rooms. To many, marijuana was viewed as completely harmless. Some argued that it is less problematic than alcohol.

Women did not voice any concerns about marijuana causing physical harm, but many mentioned people they knew who were smoking too much, who no longer went to classes, and who were "failing out of school." This reduction in motivation and this apathetic attitude were typically not seen as a result of drug use but as a character flaw in them. Paula demonstrated this attitude in her observations about her friend who was on academic probation after his first semester. She intimated that he could make a conscious choice to stop using the marijuana and become more academically motivated. She did not mention that the marijuana use could be responsible for his reduction in motivation: "Jon's situation could totally be changed if he would just drop the bong and put his nose in a book."

Sally's discussion of her boyfriend who was "failing out of school" suggested that she too felt his choices to abuse marijuana were a result of a lack of self-control, and not a result of the chronic effects of marijuana smoking: "I think that is where my boyfriend is lacking. He has no self control. He'll be high, and just keep smoking and smoking—even if he's totally blasted. I kinda wish he could realize what he's doing to himself—can you say: YOU'RE FAILING OUT OF SCHOOL?!?"

Many women felt that marijuana is a physically harmless drug, but if one does not have control of it, or one stops going to classes or is no longer involved in any social activities, then one lacks self-control. Women rarely mentioned that these behaviors might be a result of the effects frequently associated with chronic marijuana use.

The norm to use marijuana was so powerful in most places on campus for many of these women that those who decided not to smoke marijuana felt they were missing out on the fun. One young woman athlete expressed her anger at the unfairness of being drug-tested and how this made her feel because she couldn't smoke marijuana with her friends. Another young woman athlete, who had experimented with marijuana and found out a few days later that she was going to be drug-tested, described her search for products she could take that would give her a "clean" test. After this she reflected: "You know, I thought to myself is this really worth it for me? To go through all of this trouble. I want to be an athlete at [school]. It means a lot to me to be a part of the [sport] team. But, do I feel a bit left out, having not had a true experience with pot? Yes. I am feeling sad saying that, though. I want more though, to be a part of the team."

Some women and their friends or boyfriends had difficulty learning limits of responsible marijuana use because excessive use was not marked by frightening or traumatic events such as blacking out or vomiting. Women who had "bad" marijuana experiences used the excuse that the "weed was laced" with some other drug. Excessive use affected some women academically and in their relationships, but most were unwilling to attribute problems to their regular marijuana smoking.

Some women commented on the marijuana smoking of their male peers (friends and boyfriends) who, in the women's opinions were smoking to the detriment of their health and happiness, and had not learned their limits. Some of the women questioned their personal choices about their level of marijuana smoking as they were figuring out their limits. In a couple of cases, efforts were made to cut down. Erin, for example, really began to question her marijuana smoking while she was pledging a sorority: "This past week I had been smoking marijuana more often than usual. I found it was becoming a daily habit therefore I am going to begin to cut back. I have watched too many people let that rule their lives and I would never let that happen to me. I know my limits and I also know what I want to do and there is nobody in this world that can force me to do something that I do not want to do."

Some women, like Erin, seemed to learn their personal limits with marijuana smoking by watching other people and by monitoring and reflecting on their own use. There did seem to be some speculation among peers about who was smoking too much and who might fail out of school because their smoking had gotten out of control.

The way marijuana was smoked was different within racially separated social groups. Students of color tended to smoke blunts (i.e., cigars cleaned out and replaced with marijuana), and Whites tended to smoke from bols (i.e., which are carved out, often unfiltered, small and "pipe-like") and bongs (i.e., water filtered through a fairly long tube). Regular use of marijuana was viewed as problematic for many of the women of color as Alana described her feelings about a friend Hector and his group of friends who were the only students of color whom she knew smoked marijuana regularly:

I went to M street, one day this week with my girlfriend Simone and we ran into this guy named Hector. He told us that he was on his way to get high—smoke marijuana. He asked us if we smoke and we don't. He could not believe it. He insisted that I did, he figured I did, I have no idea why. Well anyway, Simone, and him are from Brooklyn. It's so funny how that became a topic of conversation. Well, not really because Hector is always talking about how he's going to get high and get fucked up. All his friends do that so, I'm not surprised. He told me before the end of our 4 years we are going to get high together. I told him that's not my scene. He's annoying, why do you have to be constantly high 7 days a week—there's a problem???

Some Black and Latino/Latina students smoked a lot of marijuana and drank alcohol frequently, as was Hector's case. None of the women of color in the study smoked marijuana, drank heavily, or used other illicit drugs in college, although Tara and Zoie admitted to having tried smoking marijuana once prior to college and not particularly liking it. Some of them were annoyed, as Alana illustrated above by the excessive use of one of her acquaintances, because excessive use was not acceptable within her social group.

Of the women who used illicit drugs, in addition to marijuana, all started their illicit drug use smoking marijuana, except for Kelly. This exception provided a good example of peers reacting if one "skips" a step on their friends' acceptability ranking (described in the next chapter). Kelly had never tried marijuana because she wanted to "prove she had will power," but she had experimented with nitrous oxide (which can be legally purchased at restaurant supply stores for whipped cream makers in some states if one is over 18) which was often considered worse than marijuana: "when I told my friends, especially my boyfriend, he couldn't believe I did nitrous and won't do pot."

Although nitrous oxide is legal in some circumstances, I suspected that some considered it worse than marijuana in part because fewer people used nitrous. Because it was used less often, some of the women discussed concerns about its effects, and most women were unaware of its legal status. Legality, morality, and safety were all factored into decisions about each drug, and nitrous oxide, even though it was somewhat "scary" and unknown, was legal. Marijuana, even though it was illegal, was considered safe and accepted. Marijuana and nitrous oxide use illustrates how the weight given to each of the factors (legality, morality, and safety) shifted in complex ways for some of the women.

Nitrous Oxide Becoming a Second Gate

Nitrous oxide (known as nitrous to most of the women in this study) deserves special mention because it seemed to be growing closer in status to marijuana, at least for many of these women. Nitrous oxide is legal to buy. It is sold at restaurant supply stores, although some states are beginning to regulate the sale of nitrous cartridges to individuals over 21. Quite a few women had tried nitrous oxide, and it too, seemed to be another gateway to illicit substances that women passed through, usually on their way to the hallucinogenic drugs. According to the Core Survey data, only 5.5% reported using inhalants (including glue, gas, and solvents). It is possible that most people do not realize that nitrous oxide is an inhalant, because when the topic of inhalants was presented in class, most students were surprised that nitrous oxide was included. Therefore, the usage figure may be significantly higher than 5.5%.

Nitrous oxide was mentioned frequently in the narratives but not as much in the interviews. The stories usually began with the woman watching others in a group of people, and getting over her fear and trying it. Sandy wrote a very detailed story of her first time with nitrous:

We got two balloons for the 6 of us. My friend had told us to inhale and exhale in and out into the balloon a couple of times to get the best "hit." So I did about 4. . . . When the balloon came around again I took 6 hits maybe. And then I remembered being in a wet dark tunnel with a light at one end it was misty and I was naked holding my orange balloon. Then I was in a chair back in the parking lot. My friends said I was fishing— convulsing. My one friend got scared and was ready to do CPR. Two guys picked me up and put me in the chair. It turned out that I fell straight back, body tight my beer flew and I started shaking. I was told not to do it anymore. I went out and did a lot more. I've done it again. It cracks and pops your brain cells. But the rush is awesome, indescribable even if it only lasts 1–2 minutes.

Limits were difficult for nitrous oxide, at least partly because the "rush" was "awesome" and short-lived. In addition, use of nitrous oxide seemed to be mostly limited to concerts that White students attended. None of the women of color saw or used nitrous oxide.

Several of the White women drew the line after marijuana or nitrous oxide, and for these women, all other illicit drugs were considered "hard-core" drugs. As one woman put it: "I knew the day would come where I would try marijuana but I was sure I would never go near any of the more intense drugs." Most women did not use any illicit drugs other than marijuana, but some did. In most cases, the women who had ventured past the safety line of marijuana were curious about all the other drugs and experimented with most all of them, generally constructing drugs using discourses of pleasure. Women who did not use illicit drugs constructed these drugs using antidrug rhetoric, often labeling them "hard-core."

The Other Illicit Drugs: Prescription Drugs, Hallucinogens, and Other "Hard-Core" Drugs

Misusing prescription medications: Ritilin and Codeine. Several women mentioned using prescription psychoactive painkillers (e.g., Tylenol with Codeine) that were prescribed for athletic injuries, menstrual cramps, and postsurgical pain. A couple of women mentioned having been prescribed tranquilizers and other antianxiety agents for stress (e.g., Clonopin). These were often not considered "drugs" because they were prescribed by a physician. To use these drugs, women typically did not consider legality, morality, or health concerns because they felt they had a stamp of approval that covered each of these areas—the physician's prescription.

Jackie and Marianne were on a maintenance dose of a prescribed Benzodi-azepine for anxiety. These drugs interfered with these women's ability to use the more mainstream drugs like alcohol and marijuana, but they still tried to use these drugs occasionally. As Jackie stated: "I had taken my Klonopin [*sic*] [a Valium-like Benzodiazepine] and so I did not want to drink too much. I took one shot of tequila but it made me sick so I just drank one beer."

Prescription medications taken without a prescription or in ways that they were not designed to be taken were viewed as problematic for most of these women. The two major prescription drugs that women saw used in this way were Ritilin and Codeine.

Quite a few women mentioned people who had snorted others' prescription Ritilin to abuse for the stimulant-like effects. Women described friends, typically male, who would find someone who had been diagnosed with Attention Deficit Disorder (ADD) and had a prescription for Ritilin, so they could buy Ritilin from them to snort. Ritilin, when used in this way, was spoken of or written about by the women in this study as "wrong." Paula described how her friend with ADD snorted Ritilin and "hid" it from his friends and that she thought this was a prob-lem. Maggie tried snorting Ritilin and described it in detail:

I was at my friend Mick's house one night after a party. We were all sitting around just smoking bols and talking. Then Mick decided it was time to break out the Ritilin. I had never done Ritilin before and never seen anyone do it either. He poured out some pills onto a CD cover and crushed them with the end of a lighter. He crushed them until they were basically powder. Then he took a dollar and rolled it really tight. He cut lines out of the pile with his id card. He then asked someone to hold the CD case while he shoved the dollar end up his nose and snorted a line. The CD case got passed around and everyone did a line. It came to me and I said that I would try it but I didn't know how to cut a line. When I snorted the Ritilin it burned. I only did two lines after that. I didn't really feel anything except a little more awake and buzzed.

Maggie did not use Ritilin too often after this because she did not think it was anything "special." Jackie, too, had snorted Ritilin, and she wrote in her journal that she felt it was "overrated": "It [Ritilin] makes me shaky and it definitely doesn't help me to concentrate. . . . People here love Ritilin. I mean they constantly crave it. Whenever my friends have work they are always searching for Ritilin to get them through the night."

Ritilin, like caffeine, was used for its stimulant properties that allowed students to get their work done. Codeine was also misused. One woman described a young man on her floor asking if he could buy Codeine from her which a doctor had pre-scribed for her menstrual cramps. Tara described the Codeine use on her floor that she observed:

The majority of my floor is addicted to codeine. They will do anything to get it. Codeine puts you to sleep. I had to take codeine after I had an operation. It knocked me out in a matter of minutes. I would only stay up like 4 hours a day. I felt like I was getting addicted, then they ran out. It seemed like I had to have it. The girl across the hall takes a pill every night before she goes to sleep. I went to ask her for a book and she was going crazy because she couldn't find the pills. I said to myself, I don't need it, I'll get tired sooner or later. . . she's a mad woman.

Tara, like other women on prescribed medications such as Codeine, antianxiety agents, and other psychoactive prescription medication, thought about her limits and was concerned about exceeding her limits and becoming addicted. Tara's fears were likely grounded in her having grown up with a mother who was a "crack addict." She watched at first hand the horrors of drug dependence and feared it for herself. Eden, like Tara, drank rarely and reported that she did not use any illicit drugs, but she had painkillers prescribed for a chronic pain from an injury she received in high school. In her journal she mentioned her fears of drug dependence. She used the painkillers only when she could no longer bear the pain: "I have taken the painkiller and the muscle relaxer twice since I've been here. . . . It knocked me out for three days. I was unconscious most of the time and the rest of the time I was too out of it to know what was going on. . . . I have no other medication to take that works, I have little choice when I'm in that much pain."

Eden was concerned about exceeding her limits and becoming "addicted." Jackie too was concerned about becoming dependent on her antianxiety drug Clonopin. She wrote: "I'm getting a little nervous because my Klonopin *[sic]* is running out. This is not a good thing because I don't know if I'll be able to get a refill. I'm really scared that I'm getting too dependent on this stuff. I need to go see my psychiatrist when I get home."

Women who were given prescription medication often did not perceive that they had any decision in the matter. Nevertheless, they still worried about finding their personal limits, fearing that going beyond their limits would result in "dependence" or "addiction."

Hallucinogens: LSD, Psilocybin mushrooms, and MDMA. Even if they did not use hallucinogens, nearly all of the women had intersected with at least one hallucinogenic drug at some point during the seven weeks of the course. In the Core drug survey administered in the Spring of 1996, 8.8 % of students reported having used hallucinogens which included LSD, Psilocybin mushrooms, and PCP. The survey separated out "designer drugs" such as MDMA (Ecstasy), which 6.1% of students reported having used. Only a few of the women in the narratives and interviews admitted to any experimentation with the hallucinogens (i.e., LSD, Psilocybin mushrooms, and Ecstasy), and in nearly every case, these experiences were constructed positively, using discourses of pleasure. Some had used LSD and mushrooms several times in the past. Ecstasy was still viewed as a novelty, but a drug that most women who tried it described as Maggie did: "Wonderful! Incredible!" Maggie had just tried it for the first time the week before the interview. She took it with her new boyfriend and enjoyed it so much that she went out the next night and spent another $25 for a pill to do it again.

Typically, Ecstasy (also known as "E") was mostly still associated with Rave parties—all-night dance parties that tend to have psychedelic lighting or strobes and techno-music, often held in abandoned warehouses. These parties are known for drug use, particularly the hallucinogenic drugs such as Ecstasy, "Special K," and LSD as well as cocaine and heroin. Young people find out about Raves through flyers, the Internet, or word of mouth. Some "fake Raves," as one student called them, are organized dance parties with techno-music and dancing to strobe lights, but they are held at fairgrounds or bars with security present. Even in these settings, however, people easily concealed hallucinogens by taking them before going.

Tara, like the other women of color, had never used any hallucinogenic drug and did not write or talk about their friends who had either. Tara described the Rave from what she heard about and observed from one of her floormates. As a nonillicit drug user, she tended to use antidrug rhetoric when describing illicit drugs, describing only the negative aspects of the drug experiences she heard about or observed. She described how she intersected with hallucinogens:

Last weekend one of the girls on my floor went to a rave at the fair grounds. It lasted from 10 to 8. For the whole semester she wanted to try ecstacy *[sic]* so bad. No one wanted to go with her, so she got in a cab and went by herself. Each pill costed *[sic]* twenty-five dollars. She bought two. While she was there she met this guy and had sex with him. When she finally got home (the next afternoon) she don't *[sic]* remember nothing *[sic]* from the night before. When she came back she was so uppety *[sic]*, but then she got real sick. She became dizzy with migraine headaches.

Tara described nothing pleasurable in this passage, which was typical among the nonusers. She also described another somewhat common phenomenon—sex with strangers at Raves. Ecstasy (popular at Raves) has become known as the "love drug," which as Maggie said "makes you love everybody, and feel like everybody loves you." Within these settings, the sex is likely unprotected. None of the women admitted to having first- or second-hand experiences with stranger-sex at Raves, but some did hear about it.

Caren described in her journal what a Rave party was and what she thought of hallucinogenic drugs from her perspective as a nonhallucinogenic drug user but a fairly regular drinker and marijuana smoker. She did not use antidrug rhetoric, but rather, she used discourses of pleasure:

While I was at the formal my best friends were at a Rave. This is a type of dance party which are very popular. Now you can go and not use any psychoactive substance but most people use mood altering drugs. My friends mostly drop acid. I'm glad to know that it does not make you legally insane because then my best friends would be really crazy. Their description of a rave is a happy and safe place. People dance, hang out play with toys and eat like crazy. I have never heard of any violence at one or people "bugging out" on drugs. It seems like a safe environment to enjoy your "trip." Not everyone does LSD, some people nitrous oxide, ecstasy and even smoke marijuana, some do nothing. My friends are always exhausted because they party all night long and so sleep the whole next day. This time one friend dropped [LSD] for the first time and imagined rolling around in popcorn. He loved it. If I was going to try LSD I would do it in this environment. I see nothing wrong with it in this setting. I don't see LSD as bad unless abused. Also the effects could make me skeptical to use it but then again alcohol has risks and I drink. It especially has risks for me because of my family history and I still drink.

Caren described two conflicting thoughts about drugs that some of the women who grew up in alcoholic homes expressed. She feared addiction because of what she had witnessed in her family environment, but she wanted to try a drug that her friends constructed as "fun." Most women who described profoundly negative experiences in their alcoholic homes abstained from drug use entirely, tended to disregard any positive information they received about drugs, and generally used antidrug rhetoric throughout their journals. However, Caren did not construct her experiences with her alcoholic father as negative. Perhaps this is why she drank alcohol, smoked marijuana, and was receptive to the idea of trying LSD.

Lee had been to a Rave and described her experience with Ecstasy, which she thought was "absolutely the greatest thing." Her first of several Raves was "at the civic center or something so there was like a lot of security. They wouldn't let you bring anything in, and they were checking for everything—markers, stickers . . . and then when we got in there were all these decorations just set up like they knew people were tripping. . . you walk in and just everyone is like kind of dressed like kind of freaky and not like normal style. And it's just crazy, 'cause it was obvious that everyone is doing drugs."

During the course of my project, Ecstasy started to become more mainstream and was likely to be seen in settings other than at Raves. Jackie, who was in one of the classes in the final semester of the project, described a scene in her friend's apartment that involved an unusual way of ingesting Ecstasy: "People were taking bong hits [smoking marijuana] and doing lines of coke. Okay, now was the weird part of the night. There was a group of people in the corner snorting extasy [sic]. It looked really painful. This one guys nose started bleeding. It was really gross. I've never seen anyone snort Ex before, it just seemed so stupid. I was pretty interested and so was everyone else. They were doing line after line like it was coke. I had to get out of there. It was just too weird."

The hallucinogens were frightening to women who did not use illicit drugs, and sometimes particular hallucinogens were "scary" to those who did use other illicit drugs. Each woman who had tried some of the hallucinogens had formed her own opinion about which ones were "safer" or "better." Jude, for example, described why she drew her personal use line after Psilocybin mushrooms but before LSD: "I personally will never do any chemical stuff. What I mean by that is acid, cocaine, etc. If I could get really pure—100% pure ecstasy then maybe that but for right now I am sticking to shrooms and weed. My sisters [sic] only 17 and last year at one point she was taking acid 4–5 times a week for a month and a half. All kinds too—from blotters to Dead family liquid driven in from SanFran. It all just scares me too much to do." Several of the more regular users constructed some drugs as "natural" and some drugs as "chemical." The natural drugs were somehow viewed as safer and less scary.

A word about "Special K." A drug that deserves special mention is "Special K." Only Jana had heard of this drug when I mentioned it in class in the Fall of 1995, but by the next Fall several of the students knew about it. The chemical name is Ketamine, and it is a "close relative of PCP. . . . It is still used as a surgical anesthetic to control severe pain from burns and is not as closely watched as other restricted drugs" (Inaba & Cohen, 1996, p. 169). The few women who did know about it had seen it on campus but mostly at Raves. Jana described in class her use of Special K or "K" with her friends. In class the following year (Fall 1996), when I asked if anyone had heard of it, Dara said that "it makes you retarded—just like really slow and stupid." In a later interview, Lee admitted to having used it. In her journal she wrote: "I stopped by Mike's to say hi to Ray and Jerry who were over there doing special k with him. I stayed and took some bong hits, but I turned down the k when they offered."

This passage suggests that Lee, like many of the women who were involved in subcultures where various illicit drugs were present, did not feel pressured to use different drugs. However, it seemed easier to "turn down" a drug that a woman might not be ready to try as long as she could opt for a drug she considered "safer" (in this case marijuana).

Dara tended to use a discourse of pleasure when describing all drugs (except for LSD). She really enjoyed her experience with Special K, but she had also been using other drugs, as she described in her journal: "I went to a Rave. I drank two Captain [Captain Morgan's Rum] and Cokes. I snorted 5 (20mgs) of Ritilin before I went. When I got to the Rave I snorted some Special K and when I got inside I bought a pill of E [Ecstasy]. I felt incredible. I can't even describe how it felt. I was so content with everything. I had clear visuals. I went home and crashed."

Mentions of Special K were rare, but in the few occasions when it was described, it seemed to be often associated with a Rave. Raves seem to be the place where drugs are introduced before they become more mainstream.

Cocaine and Heroin: The two most fear-inducing drugs. The descriptor of "hard-core" when attached to the word "drug" was particularly intriguing to me because most women assumed they could use this descriptor and everyone would know what they meant. I think for most of the women in my project, "hard-core" meant hallucinogens, cocaine, and heroin. However, women who had used hallucinogens, but not cocaine or heroin, would not have considered hallucinogens as hardcore as cocaine or heroin. Currie (1993), in his book *Reckoning: Drugs, the Cities, and the American Future,* even made a distinction between "hard-core" and "soft" drugs in his appendix where he defined the "hard drugs" only: "I do not include 'soft' drugs like marijuana and LSD, but do include inhalants—which, while they are legal substances, are widely abused, often with usually troubling consequences" (p. 333). He included cocaine, heroin, methamphetamine, phencyclidine (PCP), and inhalants in his definition of hard-core drugs. While I have often heard allusions to this dichotomy, I have never seen it written as definitively as Currie did. Many of the women in the journals and interviews had developed their own definition of hard-core drugs. Although some likely differed on the specifics, most of the women would probably argue that heroin and cocaine were "hard-core drugs."

Jill described what most of these women's sentiments were about cocaine, particularly "crack cocaine" (and similarly about heroin) relative to the hallucinogens and chronic marijuana use: "I know my friends have even done 'shrooms' before too, and that really scares me. . . . I am really concerned about one of my friends who smokes up [smokes marijuana] a lot. She has been smoking for a while and now she is experimenting with other substances. Nothing like Crack Cocaine because she would never do anything like that, but she's thinking about dropping acid, and I don't know what to tell her."

This passage also reflects the concern many women had for their friends. There was a tendency to want to "save" or "help" someone, or keep them from making a mistake and getting hurt, particularly if a friend was starting to use a drug that a woman considered "hard-core." For example, Christine told me about her friends trying to get her to stop using cocaine:

They [her roommate and other college friends] walked in, and they were really upset. They said they were going to call my parents and tell them what I was doing [leaving school for days at a time and using cocaine and other illegal drugs with her boyfriend], and they were like really upset and worried about me 'cause I wasn't going to classes. They were like crying because I was going to go to see my boyfriend. So that night I didn't go back to my boyfriend's. And she [her roommate] said, "I've got to tell you something, it's them [her boyfriend and his drug-abusing friends] or me." And I said, "I can't pick."

Most of the women in this project described cocaine and heroin using strong antidrug rhetoric, and emphasized that friends who used these drugs needed to be saved. Christine was the only woman who had actually used cocaine and used antidrug rhetoric, but at the time of the interview she had been "saved" by her nonillegal drug-using friends and had quit using all illegal drugs. Within Christine's group of friends at college, and most of the women in my project, cocaine was constructed as a "bad" drug and morally reprehensible to use.

Almost every mention of heroin was about someone else, told as a frightening, but true tale, and as a reason to stay away from this particular drug. Women who did not use illicit drugs tended to use antidrug rhetoric and provide illustrations about why they thought certain drugs were "bad." For example, Sherry wrote: "I just heard a few weeks ago one of my friends had been at work and was found passed out on the bathroom floor from the night before. The night before was a night for him to try heroin. He was still effected [sic] the next day at work and immediately fired."

Many myths seemed to surround the drugs that many women labeled as "hard-core drugs" such as LSD, heroin, and cocaine. These narratives almost always ended with death or a near-death (or a hopelessly addicted) experience.

Discussions of crack and heroin often included words such as "losers," "addicts," and "bad neighborhoods." For example, Candace wrote about how her middle-class, suburban neighborhood viewed cocaine and the neighborhood's shock over the murder of one of their "All-American" boys in a cocaine deal gone awry in a "bad neighborhood."

One experience I had regarding cocaine this year dealt with a friend's brother. He was the "all-American" boy from a middle-class suburb. He was found shot in his car and later died at the hospital. His car was found in a neighborhood that was notorious for drug dealing. No one realized that he would be there to buy drugs. What no one knew was that he was shot because he was trying to buy cocaine and sell it back in his neighborhood. He got into a fight with the person selling it to him and the other man fatally shot him. This shocked our neighborhood because he was seen as the perfect boy who did good in school and was loved by his family.

In class, White women tended to share Candace's sentiments about crack and heroin as ghetto drugs used by the poor people from "bad neighborhoods." Women in my project who grew up in these so-called bad neighborhoods (most of the Black and Latina women) saw these drugs at first hand and constructed these drugs negatively based on their experiences observing others in their families and neighborhoods. Tara described her mother who was a crack-addict. Jana described her father who died from AIDS and had been a heroin addict. Zoie had loved ones who were in prison or had been killed from dealing these drugs. These women said or wrote that they did not use any illicit drugs because of these experiences, and so they constructed these drugs as "bad," using strong antidrug rhetoric. In contrast to crack which was socially constructed as a poor, urban, ghetto drug, snortable cocaine was often considered an upper-class drug because it was so expensive to obtain. These kinds of traditional discourses around crack and heroin often focused on race and class.

Most of the more regular users who constructed most drugs and drug experiences positively surrounded themselves with peers who also constructed drugs positively. These women who used discourses of pleasure described how they constructed meaning about cocaine and opiates (i.e., opium, heroin, and prescription codeine which was mentioned earlier). Maggie, Jude, and Lee each said that they had smoked opium (from which heroin is derived) and found it "fun." Maggie had made an unsuccessful attempt to obtain cocaine, and Lee, Jackie, Dara, and Marianne had used cocaine and enjoyed it. Lee enjoyed cocaine so much it "scared" her because she thought she would become addicted.

Marianne, who had stopped using all illicit drugs after hitting her own "rock bottom" illustrated this discourse of pleasure: "If I wanted to party with my boyfriend, we would do some lines of coke and heroin and have a romantic evening." These drugs were not only pleasurable for her but were also linked to romance.

For some, the pleasure was overridden by their fears associated with becoming addicted, or hurt, or "busted." In her interview, Lee described her experience using cocaine at a Rave party that had been "busted" by the "cops": "Like I tried it and like after I did it, like a few days later, like I kept thinking about it and I didn't like that at all. It kind of made me nervous. Like if I had more access to it I might like really get into it and I don't want to do that."

Lee did not use cocaine again after this episode because she feared that she would be unable to determine her limits and would become addicted. The fear of being unable to determine one's limits for cocaine use was frightening for women who had tried cocaine or women who were thinking about trying it. Each of the more experienced drug-using women except for Dara had some fear associated with both cocaine and heroin. Dara, who seemed to "love" almost all drugs, was unafraid of cocaine and heroin, but she was somewhat afraid to try LSD: "One night we went to the Asian Mafia House. We smoked blunts [marijuana] laced with coke (crack). I got so speedy, I loved it. I have not tried that again since. . . . I love drugs of any kind. I think I've been pretty selective. In general, I want to try at least every drug once, then stick to the things I like the best. I'm not a drug feign [sic]. I just like drugs! Most all my friends use drugs. The only thing I will never try is LSD. (I don't know why it's just something I've held back from doing for so long.)"

Dara was the only one who placed LSD at the bottom of her personal acceptability ranking instead of heroin or cocaine (which is what most of the other women considered the most "hardcore" and will be described in detail in the next chapter; also see Appendix E). Interestingly, Dara loved other hallucinogens like Ecstasy. She, like many of the regular drug users, discussed drugs using positive terms and tended to emphasize positive drug experiences more often than the infrequent users or abstainers, who tended to focus on their negative experiences. It seemed that even the most experienced users had at least one drug or category of drugs that they feared or wanted to stay away from. Perhaps having a line or limit is a way to convince oneself and others that one's drug use has limits, and therefore, is not problematic. Nevertheless, women socially constructed each of the drugs differently. These social constructions were affected by their friends and romantic partners, and women used these constructions to make personal decisions about drugs, which will be described in the next chapter.

Chapter 8
The Individualized Drug Acceptability Ranking

Drawing on experiences within their relationships, particularly friendships and romantic partnerships, women in this project constructed drugs in traditional ways using discourses of morality, legality, and health/safety. Women organized their constructions in a way that I labeled an "individualized drug acceptability ranking." This ranking, which seemed to be fairly consistent for many of the women in this study, typically began with what a woman considered the most morally acceptable, physically safe, and legal drugs and progressed downward to what she considered morally "bad," "hard-core," "dangerous," "addictive," and illegal drugs. (See Appendix C for the drug acceptability ranking composite.) For most women, these rankings were complex and shifting. A woman's personal drug acceptability ranking seemed to guide her decisions about what drugs were acceptable to use. Because no research on drugs has ever examined such an idea, I examined the literature for historical messages about drugs and their link to legality, morality, and health.

Public anxiety about drug use and abuse has waxed and waned throughout America's history. This anxiety has often resulted in attempts to create antidrug education and media campaigns preaching against drug use by constructing drug use as unhealthy, immoral, and un-American (and worthy of legal sanction)—messages that have been frequently intermingled. However, various drugs have been socially constructed in different ways at different periods in history. Below I will elaborate on a few examples: the Women's Temperance movement and the social construction of alcohol as immoral; some major historical events around nicotine products (smoking, chewing, and snuff) focusing on the health risks; and drug legislation of the early twentieth century surrounding the now illicit drugs using moral, health, and racist beliefs to demonstrate that certain drugs were worthy of harsh legal sanction.

WOMEN, ALCOHOL, MORALITY, AND THE
TEMPERANCE MOVEMENT

Alcohol use became linked to morality in the United States perhaps around 1785 when Dr. Benjamin Rush began to warn against excessive use of alcohol and the need to use alcohol within one's *limits* for good health. In 1785 Rush published the "Moral Thermometer," which indicated that "temperance" or light drinking could lead one to "cheerfulness, strength, nourishment, when taken only at meals and in moderate quantities." If used more than that (i.e., liquor in the form of a toddy or a grog), the result could be jail, the whipping post, madness, murder, anarchy, palsy, apoplexy, and even death (to name only a few) (reprinted in Inaba & Cohen, 1996).

The Women's Christian Temperance Union started as a relatively small group of women in the late eighteenth century (around Rush's era) and did not begin to pick up steam until the 1830s in response to the highest per capita alcohol consumption in our nation's history (7.1 gallons per person per year average in 1830 versus 1.8 gallons today) (Inaba & Cohen, 1996).

Women played a major role in the Temperance movement that began to increase its numbers in the 1870s. Bordin (1981) described women's role in the Temperance movement and the impact of this mass involvement of women on politics in the decades to follow: "Temperance became a cause that large numbers of women actively embraced, and women in turn became the most important force behind the temperance movement. Also, by the 1880s temperance had become the issue that drew tens of thousands of women to rally behind general women's and reformist causes and demand a more equal share in the political process. Through temperance, which women saw as protection of the home, women from many social and economic strata were caught up in feminist goals" (p. 3).

Leaders of the Temperance movement used discourses of morality in an attempt to construct alcohol use as immoral. This perhaps marked the beginning of drugs, politics, and moral arguments combining to fight a common battle—to criminalize a psychoactive substance.

The Temperance movement which sought to criminalize alcohol use was closely connected to politics and religion. The Temperance movement, under the leadership of Frances Willard (the president of the Women's Christian Temperance Union) and her colleague Annie Wittenmyer, believed that using religious and moral appeals would be the best strategy for eliminating alcohol and its societal problems (Bordin, 1981). They thought that "the Union's program should emphasize personal reform of the drunkard and of the whole liquor industry by moral suasion. This was the route the Crusade had taken—religious conversion, Christian commitment, acknowledgment of sin, and willingness to abandon evil ways" (Bordin, p. 46). Wittenmyer focused more on a moral than a political crusade. She wanted to avoid any political action that would lead women to fight for the right to vote, believing that this "campaign for the vote would 'strike a fatal blow at the home'" (Wittenmyer in Bordin, 1981, p. 46). Perhaps ironically, the Temperance movement created a site for women to rally around important issues including, eventually, the right to vote.

As today, where many women suffer from domestic abuse at the hands of their drunken spouses, in the late nineteenth century part of what drew the women involved in the Temperance movement together was the violence they suffered at the hands of their drunken husbands. As Bordin (1981, p. 7) wrote, "the nineteenth-century's drunkard's reputation as a wife beater, child abuser, and sodden, irresponsible nonprovider was not undeserved." When delivering a speech at the National American Woman Suffrage Association in Chicago in 1875, Susan B. Anthony said that "women were the greatest sufferers from drunkenness, and graphically pictured the virtuous woman in legal subjection to a drunken husband" (Bordin, p. 7).

It is important to mention that women of color were absent from this movement, as were women who were Catholic or Jewish. The majority of the half a million members of the Women's Christian Temperance Union were Methodist, White, middle to upper-middle class women (Bordin, 1981).

Alcohol's More Recent Popular Social Construction

My grandmother, who was born in 1910 is a very devout Methodist, and she still believes strongly that alcohol use is immoral. Perhaps one reason why she has lived a very healthy eighty-six years is because alcohol has never touched her lips. She does recognize, however, that her opinion is not shared by the majority in American culture and that it is considered "old-fashioned." Nevertheless, to her the belief that alcohol is an extremely dangerous and immoral drug is as real as many people's beliefs about heroin and crack.

Alcohol has also had its ups and downs in the American public opinion polls after the Eighteenth Amendment, which made the manufacture or sale of alcohol illegal, was passed in 1919 and repealed thirteen years later. According to Inaba and Cohen (1996, p. 19), the repeal came about not because Americans had changed their feelings about alcohol but because they discovered that "Prohibition created other devastating problems for America. Unfortunately. . . a new coalition of smugglers, strong-arm thieves, Mafia members, corrupt politicians, and crooked police had discovered a lucrative trade in the distribution and sale of illicit alcohol." These "other devastating problems" have historically accompanied any drug after it has been made illegal and been forced underground.

Shortly after the Eighteenth Amendment was repealed, rates of alcoholism rose over the pre-Prohibition level. In response to the rising rates, Alcoholics Anonymous (the twelve-step program designed to help alcoholics stay sober) was created in 1934.

Driving while intoxicated has vied for the leading cause of death of teens since the automobile was invented. More recently, however, during the early 1980s, stricter laws, the raising of the drinking age, as well as increased education, awareness, and student programs such as SADD (Students Against Drunk Driving) have perhaps contributed to the reduction in alcohol-related traffic fatalities since the late 1980s. Nevertheless, alcohol continues to be the most used and abused drug by teenagers. In 1993, Ray and Ksir reported that 88% of high school seniors reported ever using alcohol and 54% had used it within the last thirty days. Inaba and Cohen (1996), using the National Institute of Drug Abuse's Household Survey data, reported that of the 22 million young people aged 12 to 17, 21.1% had used alcohol in the past month. Several reports in journals such as the *Journal of the American Medical Association* during the early 1990s have argued that alcohol-related illnesses are the second leading cause of premature death of Americans (second only to cigarette smoking). Inaba and Cohen (1996) reported that "used separately or in combination with other psychoactive drugs, alcohol kills over 130,000 persons a year in the United States, compared to only 8,000 killed by all other illicit psychoactive drugs combined. There were an estimated 10 to 12 million Americans suffering from alcoholism in 1996." Despite these rather grim statistics, most Americans do not consider alcohol an immoral and hard-core drug. Perhaps my grandmother's fears of the dangers of alcohol, though grounded in morality, may be grounded in reality as well.

Why the link between morality and the social construction of drugs? Duster's (1970) book *The Legislation of Morality* described at least part of why Americans have so readily connected drug abuse with discourses of morality. He wrote: "the answer is simple enough. A 'moral' or 'good' man in Western society is responsible, independent, respectful of the rights of others, and in conventional wisdom, able to face the reality the rest of us have come to know" (p. 154). He argued that the drug abuser (or at least the stereotypical drug abuser) does not meet this description of a moral person. According to Duster, "history and logic reveal that there is nothing intrinsically moral or immoral about injecting an opiate into the human body. Yet, many have come to believe there is" (p. 80). Duster also described some of the problems with making drug abuse and addiction a moral issue, or at least blaming it on character weakness or immorality "if someone believes that drug addiction, alcoholism, and prostitution are caused by devils possessing men, then the solution conceived is calling out the devils. . . if you believe that drug addiction is caused by weakness of moral character and psychological disturbance, then the solution is equally charted by that conception" (p. 115). Traditional social constructions of drugs have often used discourses of morality, and the women in my project often took up these discourses.

To Gilligan, morality was based on relationships with others. Similarly, Noddings (1992) wrote: "women who speak in the different voice refuse to leave themselves, their loved ones, and connections out of their moral reasoning. They speak from and to a situation, and their reasoning is contextual" (p. 21). I believe that context and standpoints are critical in moral decision making and that morality is more complex than simply an essential part of feminine identity. Building on the work of pioneers such as Gilligan, and feminist methodologists such as DeVault and others mentioned in previous chapters, I describe how many of the women in this study spoke and wrote about issues of morality and their decisions about drug use.

NICOTINE: AMERICA'S NUMBER-ONE KILLER

Antismoking campaigns have used discourses of morality and health/safety to convince people not to smoke cigarettes. Since the time when America was "discovered" by Europeans, different drugs have been construed as somehow possessing inherently evil characteristics, and nicotine, despite remaining legal throughout American history, is no exception. One of Columbus's traveling companions returned to Europe after having been initiated to tobacco by the American natives, and introduced smoking tobacco to the Europeans. He was immediately put in jail and believed to be possessed by the devil because he had smoke coming from his nose and mouth (Ray & Ksir, 1993). Pope Urban VIII threatened excommunication for smoking, and King James I of England said of smoking, it is "a costome lothsome to the eye, hateful to the Nose, harmefull to the braine, dangerous to the Lungs, and the Blacke stinking fume thereof, neerest resembling the horrible Stigian smoke of the pit that is bottomless" (King James I, 1604, in Inaba & Cohen, 1996, p. 11). However, according to Inaba and Cohen (1996, p. 17), "by the middle of the [nineteenth] century, both men and women used snuff (snorted tobacco) and smoked pipes. In addition, men smoked cigars, chewed tobacco, and spat tobacco juice when they pleased." In the later nineteenth century, the automatic cigarette rolling machine was developed; public spitting began to be frowned upon, and cigarette smoking increased dramatically (Inaba & Cohen, 1996).

In the twentieth century, R.J. Reynolds developed a "mild" cigarette that was "marketed to women (as a symbol of female emancipation), to young people, and to those on diets" (Inaba & Cohen, 1996, p. 17). However, activists, inspired by what Prohibition achieved (albeit temporarily) through the efforts of the WCTU's Temperance movement, managed to redouble their antismoking efforts. These antismoking activists had some limited success passing state laws regulating tobacco use in the 1920s. However, these laws were repealed by the later part of that decade (Inaba & Cohen, 1996). By the 1930s, the federal government was receiving a great deal of tax revenue from cigarettes, and many tobacco farmers and manufacturers were becoming very wealthy and politically powerful. According to Inaba and Cohen, by the middle of the twentieth century smoking was "entrenched in American society. It was a source of revenue for advertisers, retailers, tobacco farmers, the media, and government. Warnings of health hazards of smoking were issued as early as 1945 by the Mayo Clinic. Warnings continued throughout the early 1950s from the American Cancer society" (p. 18). The first Surgeon General's report that cigarette smoking was hazardous to one's health was not published until 1964.

Since the Surgeon General's reports on the dangers of smoking, antismoking education has become very popular. Most of the antismoking campaigns in the past few decades have centered more around the health risks of smoking than making moral appeals (as had been the case in the earlier part of the century). Despite other reports, such as those by the American Medical Association naming cigarette smoking as the number-one cause of premature deaths in the United States, nicotine has still not been socially constructed as a morally "evil" or "hard-core" drug as drugs such as heroin and cocaine have been. The number of young people smoking has been rising. The National Institute of Drug Abuse Household Survey released in August 1996 showed that 38.1% of 12 to 17 year-olds had used cigarettes (in Inaba & Cohen, 1996). Twenty percent of American high school seniors in 1991 reported smoking cigarettes daily (Ray & Ksir, 1993). The number of premature deaths in 1995 attributed to smoking was as follows: 115,000 heart disease, 106,000 lung cancer, 32,000 other cancers (related to smoking), 57,000 chronic lung disease, 28,000 stroke, and 52,000 other conditions (related to smoking). "One out of every five premature deaths in the world is caused by the use of tobacco, 390,000 in the United States alone. Another 50,000 die from second-hand smoke" (Inaba & Cohen, 1996, p. 124).

As the killer of more Americans than alcohol and illicit drugs combined, it is curious why appeals to health and wellness have not worked to reduce the number of smokers in this country. President Clinton has recently launched an antismoking campaign charging that the tobacco industry will now (for the first time in history) be regulated by the Food and Drug Administration. (Until recently tobacco has been the only drug exempt from FDA standards.) President Clinton has attempted to use the bully pulpit to preach the dangers of smoking and to convince young people to avoid smoking. Despite these efforts, large numbers of young people continue to take up the smoking habit, perhaps because nicotine has not been constructed as an inherently evil or hard-core drug the way that the opiates and cocaine have been.

FEDERAL LEGISLATION OF THE EARLY TWENTIETH CENTURY SURROUNDING THE NOW ILLICIT DRUGS

A number of historical events in American society have led to the social construction of many of the now illicit drugs (particularly cocaine, hallucinogens, and heroin) as hardcore and somehow inherently worse than alcohol, tobacco (nicotine), and caffeine, and worthy of harsh legal sanction. In the late nineteenth century, the hypodermic needle was invented (1860), and refined injectable drugs such as morphine were developed (1890s) (Inaba & Cohen, 1996). Kits with hypodermic syringes and holders for heroin and cocaine were sold at such popular department stores as Macy's in the very early twentieth century. And from the mid-nineteenth century into the first decade of the twentieth century, heroin and cocaine were found in tonics and patent medications.

Despite the laissez-faire attitude of the federal government that drug use was a "victimless crime" and that any attempts to control one's own decisions about one's own body were unconstitutional (Ray & Ksir, 1993), after the turn of the century the United States government began to regulate use of various psychoactive substances. Pressure from various groups and the popular media resulted in significant early attempts at federal drug regulation such as the 1906 Pure Food and Drug Act, the Opium Exclusion Act (1909), and the Harrison Narcotic Act (1914). The 1906 Act was a labeling regulation that required all food and drugs to be properly labeled. It did not prohibit psychoactive substances from being put into tonics and medicines. However, by the 1914 Harrison Act, most psychoactive substances that are currently illegal (e.g., heroin, cocaine) became available only with a physician's prescription.

During the time of the Eighteenth Amendment (1919–1933), almost every psychoactive substance with the exception of nicotine, marijuana, and caffeine was illegal at least without a prescription, and the sale of these substances went underground. During this time, marijuana became the target of antidrug sentiments. By 1937, marijuana became illegal without a prescription with the passage of the Marijuana Tax Act. Most of the antidrug laws in the early twentieth century (with the exception of the Eighteenth Amendment) were tax laws, not punitive laws. These tax laws, such as the Marijuana Tax Act, required that dealers (primarily physicians) had to register every year, pay an annual fee, and use only the special prescription order forms issued by the Bureau of Internal Revenue. Ray and Ksir (1993, p. 42) wrote that during this era "there would have been no support and no constitutional rationale for a federal law prohibiting an individual from possessing or using these drugs. The Congress would not have considered such a law and if it had, the Supreme Court would probably have declared it unconstitutional."

The Marijuana Tax Act placed marijuana in the same category with the drugs controlled during the earlier Harrison Act. The Marijuana Act was partially the result of the labors of Harry Anslinger, who was the first commissioner of the Federal Bureau of Narcotics. He sought to make cocaine, heroin, hallucinogens, and marijuana illegal, and he was successful with passage of the 1956 Narcotic Drug Control Act. He began his efforts to demonize marijuana and other drugs with unsubstantiated rumors such as that of "degenerate Spanish-speaking residents in the Southwest going on criminal rampages while smoking marijuana." He also publicly referred to marijuana as the "assassin of youth," arguing that marijuana was the most dangerous drug and posed the most significant threat to our nation's security. With the 1956 Narcotic Drug Control Act, "any offense, except first-offense possession had to result in a jail term; no suspension, probation, or parole was allowed. Anyone caught selling heroin to a person younger than age 18 could receive the death penalty" (Ray & Ksir, 1993, p. 50). This was the critical turning point in the now illegal drugs and their criminalization and stigmatization.

The Power of Race in Social Construction of Drugs: Linking Various Drugs to the Ghettos

Cocaine and "crack." The media and politicians have almost exclusively linked crack to the inner-city ghetto since crack was first created as a simple way to smoke cocaine in the 1980s. However, crack was not limited to the inner-city ghetto. As Inaba and Cohen (1996, p. 97) wrote: "the words 'crack cocaine' appeared on the streets and in the media in 1985, as if society were trying out a new nickname. By 1986, there seemed to be a 'crack epidemic' that crossed all economic barriers. By the 1990s, it was ingrained in the American psyche as one of the main causes of society's ills: gang violence, AIDS, crime, and addiction." Crack is smokable cocaine, yet when students in my class (men and women) spoke about crack it was as if it was almost as horrible as heroin (but not quite as bad because it wasn't injected). Recently in my class on drugs, a young woman in this project, Marianne, asked with horror: "crack is smoking cocaine—so if I've smoked cocaine, I've essentially done crack?" When I said, "Yes," she gasped and put her head down on her desk as if she was ashamed and embarrassed. The social construction of drugs is very powerful. For example, snorted cocaine which is frequently considered a drug of the wealthy, yuppie, "rich college kids," is acceptable, while the smokable form of the same drug is frequently considered inherently more evil or dangerous because it is used in the inner-city ghettos. Not only is the drug itself socially constructed as better or worse, but the different routes of administering a drug into the body are also constructed in this way.

The difference between snortable cocaine and smoked cocaine (crack) has been argued in the courts. The National Association of Criminal Defense Lawyers argued that the law that penalized crack cocaine (cocaine-based) crimes one-hundred times more severely than powdered cocaine (snortable cocaine) crimes was racially biased because more Blacks were arrested than Whites for crack cocaine offenses (Nando Times, 1996). A study conducted in Los Angeles demonstrated that of fifty-three crack cocaine cases from 1991 to 1993, none of the defendants was White, suggesting that the law was racially biased against African-Americans (Nando Times, 1996). Recently (1997), the case *U.S. v. Booker* (1995) went to the Supreme court. Booker (who was African-American) pleaded guilty to crack cocaine possession and was sentenced to twenty years in prison because he had "cocaine based" or crack instead of "cocaine" or snortable cocaine. Had he been charged with the latter, the maximum sentence he could have received was 125 months. When this law was appealed to the Supreme Court, the Court ruled that the law was race-neutral and constitutional. My argument is that lawmakers and citizens of this society have socially constructed crack as a drug of poor and Black people and therefore as somehow inherently more "dangerous" or "bad" than snortable cocaine used by wealthier Whites. This popular social construction has resulted in much harsher penalties for crack users. The drug is the same, yet the law treats people differently based on their method of administering the drug. The end result of these popular social constructions is that the poor or people of color are penalized more severely than Whites.

The opiates: Codeine, morphine, heroin. Throughout the United States' history, attempts like Anslinger's were made to stigmatize drugs by linking them to immoral and criminal behavior, and often to those groups that have historically been oppressed. Morgan (1981) stated that "the racial imagery that was so common at peaks of concern about drug use is. . . complex. Every such image represented profound conflicts and fears. The Near Easterners who figured in the early concern about cannabis use symbolized passivity and backwardness that seemed diametrically opposed to the developing American nation. Opium use appeared to be a major factor in China's apparent stagnation and inability to become modern. The Black who figured in the sharp debate over cocaine represented violence and irrationality, as did the Mexican in the later debate about marijuana. And the hippie flower child, the most recent analogous stereotype, was supposedly passive, unproductive, and hostile to the basic values of thrift, productivity, rationality, and realism" (p. x). The American values that Morgan referred to were often tied to antidrug campaigns. The efforts begun late in the nineteenth century in order to criminalize various drugs also cited these values. Morgan (1981, p. 32) wrote: "That drug use undermined basic American values fueled the public debate. . . . When the concern about drugs first developed, most Americans lived in small towns and in the countryside, and the various sections of the country were both separated and self-conscious. The myth of agrarian virtues was powerful in the national consciousness. It was difficult to imagine the legendary farmer as a morphine user, however much he imbibed spirits, brews or cider. Yet the early estimates of distribution reported considerable use of habit-forming drugs in rural areas." Nevertheless, attempts to link opiates and cocaine to the cities and its social woes continued, as did attempts to construct the users of these drugs as immoral and un-American.

Courtwright, Joseph, and Des Jarlais (1989, p. 14) wrote: "Blacks were not considered heavy drug users early in the twentieth century. They lived mainly in the rural South, were poor, and had less access to opiates than Whites who could afford doctors and patent medicines. Black workers used cocaine occasionally as a pick-me-up, a few hands smoked marijuana, and some unemployed men drank excessively, but, with these exceptions, Blacks had neither a disproportionate nor a very serious drug problem. On the contrary, the prevailing racial stereotype of the narcotic addict was White or Oriental." At this point, early in the twentieth century, when the prevailing racial stereotype was of a White or Asian user, few attempts were made to outlaw these drugs. The popular views of opiates changed dramatically when people started to believe that drugs like heroin had spread to the cities and were linked to violent crime, the poor, and people of color.

Courtwright, Joseph and Des Jarlais (1989) conducted an oral history of narcotic use in America entitled *Addicts Who Survived: An Oral History of Narcotic Use in America, 1923—1965*. They described the changing social construction of opiates as these drugs (heroin mostly) began to be associated with poor, inner-city, Black men. After the Second World War, the perception of heroin began to change dramatically. Many middle-class Whites believed:

Ghettos were filled with Black men mugging Whites for money to pay for heroin and then injecting this evil drug so that they can spend the rest of the day nodding away into a blissful vacuum. . . . Not only were Black addicts turning up more often in federal treatment centers, they were being booked more frequently by the police, to the point that, by the 1950s, half or more of all narcotic arrests involved Blacks. Something similar was happening in Hispanic communities. In 1936 only about 1 percent of the addicts treated at Lexington were Hispanic; by 1966 over a quarter were—13.9 percent Puerto Rican and 12.2 percent Mexican (p. 14).

The shift in America from White and Asian heroin and other narcotic users to inner-city poor African-American and Hispanic resulted in the popular belief that heroin was an inherently more evil drug than all others. Perhaps as a result of the racism that was so pervasive in this culture, the federal legislation surrounding this drug in the 1960s created penalties that were severe, and people of color often paid these stiffer penalties. Heroin became a Schedule 1 substance (legal under no circumstances), and if one was found guilty of possessing this drug, one paid a much stiffer price (legally in terms of jail-time or fines) than for any other drug.

Women and the Opiates: Prescription Medications as Socially Acceptable

People had varying views about which drugs were considered worse than others, and unlike today when opiates (like heroin) are often considered more "hardcore" than alcohol, in the late nineteenth and early twentieth centuries, the reverse seemed to have been true. The average opiate user was upper middle class, White, middle-aged, and female, and even after the Harrison Act, she was still able to obtain these drugs with a physician's prescription.

Palmer and Horowitz (1982, p. 21), in their book chronicling the writings of women during the late nineteenth and early twentieth centuries entitled *Shaman Woman, Mainline Lady: Women's Writings on the Drug Experience,* wrote: "alcohol, coffee, tobacco were much more socially taboo for women than for men. . . . While a few avant-garde women later dared to smoke and drink in public and visit opium dens, patent medicines were used in mass quantities by their sisters for psychological as well as physiological problems. Women became addicted to the pleasurable effects of the opiates, which were medically over prescribed and cheaply available, just as female 'complaints' today are overtreated with mood-alterants and tranquilizers." Today, prescribed psychoactive medications tend not to be viewed through the same lens as most other psychoactive substances, even though their effects may be similar. The physician's prescription pad has almost always given certain drugs public and private approval, and prescribed psychoactive drugs are often taken without anyone questioning their effects.

However, just prior to and following the Harrison Act of 1914, the opiates that were once used as a "soothing elixir for baby's cough" and to cure women's "monthly distress" began to be constructed as a "seductive and deadly weapon on the Devil's arsenal" (Palmer & Horowitz, 1982, p. 101). Palmer and Horowitz described how "scare stories in the press about American women held in bondage by Chinese opium purveyors and about sex crimes committed by cocaine-crazed southern Blacks made ideal propaganda for the anti-drug forces" (p. 101). These images are somewhat similar to the images conjured up regarding crack today.

White women, like men of color from the ghettos, were used in antidrug campaigns. Portrayed as "more easily led astray by drugs" than men, and more likely to fall victim to violence from drug-crazed men of color (Black, Hispanic, or Asian), images created of women contributed to the powerfully negative images of different drugs.

Women in My Project and the Popular Messages of Their Youth

Different drugs have been socially constructed in different ways throughout history, and some powerful messages and images have continued throughout this century. Heroin and crack continue to be considered the most "hardcore," while nicotine and alcohol are not in this category, despite the fact that these two drugs have been the number one and two ranked (respectively) killers of Americans.

During the 1980s, when most women in this project began receiving influential messages about drugs, the popular approaches to educating young people about drugs were based on the social inoculation theory. Goode (1993) wrote: "Social inoculation is based on the idea that students live in an environment in which drugs and the temptations to use drugs are endemic; to resist them, they must first understand how these pressures and temptations operate." One popular application of this theory in practice was the "Just Say No!" campaign. Programs such as this, designed to make children afraid of drugs and teach them effective refusal skills, have shown questionable success (Goode, 1993). Another proposal under this model, made by William S. Bennett, the secretary of education during the 1980s, was called "Drug Free Schools and Communities" (Ray & Ksir, 1993). The focus was not on a drug education curriculum, except to teach students the laws against drugs, but instead on school policies and punitive measures that schools should take in response to drug use. Ray and Ksir (1993) wrote that "this approach wants to make it clear to the students that the society at large, the community in which they live, and the school in which they study have already made the decision not to condone drug use or underage alcohol use."

To provide a flavor for the political climate in which most of these women received most of their early messages about drugs, I quote President Reagan's speech to the nation given on September 14, 1986: "Drugs are menacing our society. They're threatening our values and undercutting our institutions. They're killing our children. . . . It is an uncontrollable fire. And drug abuse is not a so-called 'victimless crime'. . . there is no moral middle ground. . . . I implore each of you to be unyielding and inflexible in your opposition to drugs" (quoted from the official text in Ben-Yehuda, 1990, p. 168).

The discourses the women in this project used reflected the moralistic and fear-producing climate in which they were educated about drugs. Some drugs have been socially constructed as "hard-core" drugs, while others have been considered acceptable to use and, in some places, abuse.

WOMEN'S RANKINGS: FROM THE LEGAL, MORAL, AND SAFE TO THE ILLEGAL, IMMORAL, AND HARMFUL DRUGS

Most of the women in my project seemed to unknowingly rank-order drugs based on their personal drug experiences as well as on their observations of friends' and boyfriends' drug experiences. Women constructed drugs in hierarchical ways, resulting in what, as noted earlier, I have labeled an "individualized drug acceptability ranking." Women tended to use traditional discourses of morality, legality, and health/safety when constructing their ranking. This acceptability ranking helped women determine which drugs they would use and which they would not. The notion that individuals might create their own individual hierarchy or "drug acceptability ranking" has not previously been identified in the literature. In addition, these women did not acknowledge an awareness that they used such a ranking to simplify the complex decisions they frequently were forced to make about drugs that factored in their experiences within their relationships and their perceptions of the legal, moral, health, and safety issues associated with each drug.

These women seemed to develop an acceptability ranking of the drugs about which they had some awareness. Their ranking served to guide their personal decisions about drug use as well as their decisions about their relationships with others. For example, women would experiment with drugs down their personal acceptability ranking—caffeine, alcohol, cigarette smoking, marijuana smoking, and so on—until they reached the point at which they drew their personal line. Women would not use drugs beyond where they drew the line because they were afraid of physical harm or dependence, legal trouble, or not being accepted by people who were important to them (e.g., friends, boyfriends, family members). Sometimes women would change their minds about where they drew the line and would move the line to the next drug in their acceptability ranking. In addition, women also tried to determine their limits for each drug they used within their ranking. That is, once a woman had set her limit of what drugs she would use, she attempted to determine how much of that drug she could use. Also, how a woman made meaning about or ranked drugs also influenced her decisions about her relationships with others. That is, women tended to select peers who had created similar drug acceptability rankings, were similarly located on their personal acceptability rankings, and had similar ideas about their limits for each drug.

The composite of a drug acceptability ranking I developed (see Appendix C) was based on the comments about various drugs the women in my project made. Many of these women seemed to have created a personal acceptability ranking similar to the drug acceptability ranking composite in Appendix C, and thirty-five of the seventy-two seemed to draw the line after alcohol and did not use any illegal drugs. Twenty-two of the seventy-two women drew their personal line after marijuana. From Maggie's and Darla's comments, I created examples of what their individual drug acceptability rankings might look like and where they might have drawn their personal lines. For a more comprehensive picture, please see Appendices C, D, and E.

The drug acceptability ranking seemed to be a combination or reconciliation of at least three different rankings many of these women conducted: a legal ranking, a moral ranking, and a health or physical harm ranking. These "subrankings" were complex, weighed differently by each woman, and each woman's thoughts about them were constantly shifting. Women also modified their rankings based on their perceptions of their close friends' and boyfriends' rankings.

Because many factors were considered when developing a personal hierarchical acceptability ranking, the task quickly became complicated. For example, Marianne, who had used every drug on the drug acceptability ranking composite (Appendix C), had recently quit using most illegal drugs, although she was on a number of prescription medications and occasionally smoked marijuana. Quitting caused her to rethink her personal acceptability rankings of different drugs. She summed up her confusion in her first journal entry after the first day of class:

Today's class discussion was slightly scary for me, because I knew that admitting to doing some of the drugs I've done would raise a few eyebrows. At least I don't know any of these people. I'm pretty confused about how I feel about drugs as a whole. I don't really have a strong sense of what I think is okay, and what I don't mind using, or being around. Sometimes when I claim that I don't want to be around people using pot, I feel like a hypocrite, since I used to smoke so much. I also know that I still use it every now and again, and I feel guilty every time I do. I find myself becoming more and more opposed to drugs in general, but only certain ones, again hypocritical. Is it insane to think that certain drugs are okay, or is any mind altering substance "bad?" I truly think that this is an issue that each person must think about and decide for themselves. I just haven't figured it out yet.

Marianne was in the process of reformulating her personal acceptability ranking because it had changed so dramatically when she "hit her own rock bottom," and many of her heavy-drug using friends had been to drug rehabilitation for using so many drugs excessively. She also believed, as many of the women did, that these decisions were personal. Marianne was the only woman who had used every drug on the drug acceptability ranking composite, and began to have problems as a result. She wrote: "I know my own story, and what made me quit. To put it simply, I hit rock bottom. My own rock bottom. Life didn't seem like it could get much worse. I was doing terribly in school, my friends were all compulsive drug users, and I was not enjoying much of anything anymore. My every thought was consumed with what drug I would do next. I had it down to a science. I knew what mood I wanted to be in, and which drug, or combination of drugs would get me there. . . . Drugs became my soul and my spirituality."

I attempted to describe the complex ways women made meaning of drugs in their lives rather than provide a simplistic framework. However, it seemed that often some women created simplistic frameworks or acceptability rankings to simplify the complex decisions they were confronted with daily about drugs. Many women constructed meaning about various drugs in their writing and in their interviews in a hierarchical (stepwise) fashion (i.e., cocaine is worse than LSD, LSD is worse than marijuana, marijuana is worse than drinking alcohol, etc.). Marianne in her excerpt above seemed to be attempting to reconfigure her acceptability ranking after a major disruption in her previous acceptability ranking.

Alex described some of her personal questions regarding a drug's legality, morality, and potential for harm and how these affected her decisions about different drugs as she attempted to reconcile her acceptability ranking. She recognized some of her own hypocrisy in judging others' decisions about drinking and driving when she recognized that she was willing to ride with someone if they had been drinking if she had also been drinking.

I scream at my friends all the time about driving when they have been drinking, but at 4:00 in the morning when I'm buzzed outside the bar, who really wants to be so particular about the absolute sobriety of the driver? Despite the fact that I know these things, I continue to do the things I want to. I hope I won't learn my lesson the hard way, but it's really easy to continue in the same old habits. I hope this drugs class will teach me enough about the effects of alcohol or marijuana that I will start making the right decisions. Speaking of which, what are the "right" things to do? I know that driving after drinking is wrong, but I don't know that I feel marijuana is such a bad presence in my life. I'm a lot safer when I smoke than when I drink! For one thing, I am always at home in the presence of people I know when I smoke. When I drink, I lose my judgment in the presence of strangers, most of whom wouldn't think twice about taking advantage of this fact. So which is the lesser evil?

Alex sought answers to the complex questions of legality, morality, and safety as if to rank-order and determine which of the two major drugs she used, alcohol and marijuana, was better. Many of the women factored in these issues when creating their own personal drug acceptability ranking. One's own personal drug ranking seemed to be an attempt to reconcile the complex issues associated with a drug's legal status (or at least the woman's perceptions of the amount of legal trouble she thought she could get in for her drug-related activity); the woman's perception of how a drug was perceived by others morally; and her perception of how potentially harmful a drug could be to her. However, the weight each women placed on legality, morality, and potential for harm varied at least partly based on the ways important friends and boyfriends constructed drugs and her personal and vicarious experiences with friends and loved ones.

Legality and the Drug Acceptability Ranking

The perception of how illegal a drug was, or at least the perception of how much legal trouble one could get in for using a particular drug, was part of what many women considered when creating their personal acceptability ranking that influenced their decisions about personal drug use. Women who were nonillicit drug users and infrequent drinkers, who also tended to associate with nonusing peers, and tended to internalize their parents' messages to avoid drugs, seemed to weigh legality and morality more than fear of physical harm when constructing their drug acceptability rankings.

The drug acceptability ranking composite in Appendix C reflects the importance most women placed on legality. For example, caffeine was always legal for these women from the time that they had their first sip of Pepsi, but nicotine (cigarette smoking) was illegal until they turned 18, and alcohol was illegal for most of the women and would be until they turned 21.

Marijuana was the first illicit drug (illegal for all regardless of age) that most women used, and many felt they would not get in trouble for using it. However, despite this false perception that many women had, marijuana was one of the few drugs on the acceptability ranking, with the exception of all the hallucinogens and heroin, that is a Schedule I drug (as designated by the Controlled Substances Act of 1970). Hanson and Venturelli (1995) described the legal meaning of the Schedules as follows: "Schedule I substances have a high potential for abuse and have no currently accepted medical use in treatment in the United States (currently include heroin, LSD, peyote, MDMA "Ecstasy," marijuana)" (p. 91). (Despite the recent attempts by some states to legalize marijuana for medical purposes, at the time of this writing, this was the federal law that would override any of the state laws.)

Many women consistently considered cocaine (especially if injected or smoked as crack) among the most "hard-core" drugs, yet it is a Schedule II drug. Schedule II drugs are defined as having a "high potential for abuse, with severe psychic dependence potential. They have some currently accepted medical uses in the United States, but their availability is tightly restricted. Currently, amphetamines, raw opium, morphine, methadone, cocaine and pentobarbital are in this category" (Hanson & Venturelli, 1995, p. 91).

Most of the women's individualized acceptability rankings did not mimic these federal drug schedules but were more likely to consider what penalty they thought they would pay if caught. The perception was that one would only get into very minor trouble with marijuana and alcohol but would get into much more legal trouble if found with other illicit drugs. This perception tended to be accurate because women who were caught smoking marijuana once were only given a verbal warning from the university's administration, yet the punishment for other illicit drugs was far more severe. Women with male friends who had been "busted" for dealing other illegal drugs knew this. Maggie said that after her friend Eric had been "busted" for having large quantities of marijuana, LSD, Ecstasy, and Psilocybin mushrooms: "It scared a lot of people. We got called a lot, and it was horrid. And then I realized, I don't want to be a part of this, it's just, it's horrible. It's horrible. Like he got caught with so much stuff, like when I was over there the night before, and I wake up the next morning and there were fire trucks, and they were in the police cars all day long."

Maggie's friend Eric was "kicked out of school," but his parents hired "good lawyers" to keep him out of prison. Missy, like some of the other women in their journals and interviews, made some observations about the problems she saw with some of the drug laws—particularly around alcohol and marijuana: "All the pot smokers I know think it should be legal and not alcohol. I knew this one kid who was the sweetest stoned and this out of control @#%&7 when he was drunk. I really wonder how life would be different."

Many women in class, in journals, and during interviews viewed the federal scheduling of marijuana as a Schedule I drug as ridiculous. Perhaps this was why their discourses on marijuana so rarely used the language of the law, except when disagreeing with existing legislation.

The overwhelming perception was that with or without laws, certain drugs would be used more often than others—particularly cigarettes, alcohol, and marijuana. Lisa who did not drink alcohol or use illicit drugs felt that the laws were ineffective and that some people would figure out how to get these drugs and use them: "When people are using drugs, I don't think that they understand nor care about the consequences. Drug abuse is so prevalent in this country that it is somewhat overlooked. Cigarettes, alcohol, and even marijuana are everywhere on college campuses. They are in the dorms, on the Quad, down the street and some "drugs" are in the bookstore. Drugs are always going to be present, legal or illegal. There seems to always be a way of getting marijuana, alcohol and other types of drugs."

Several of the women of color from large urban communities (Alana, Zoie, and Richy) mentioned the illegal nature of drugs. Zoie mentioned her cousin who was a drug dealer and his run-ins with the law as well as other people she had known who had gone to jail for selling drugs. Richy admitted that the main reason she did not smoke marijuana was because it was illegal. She was not concerned about the health consequences or the morality of these drugs as much as she was afraid of getting caught with something illegal. Richy said of the one and only time she tried smoking marijuana: "I only took like a couple of puffs, but it just kind of totally scared me. Like it is bad you know. I mean cigarettes are also really really bad for you but sometimes. . . I mean the really scary part like is it is illegal."

Richy did not break the laws with any drugs before or after this time of taking a few puffs. She was 21, so alcohol and cigarettes (the only drugs she used, albeit frequently) were legal for her. Many of the women wrote and spoke about the alcohol laws, particularly the legal drinking age. Most women were not of legal drinking age, and were frustrated about having to jump through many hoops to obtain alcohol or to go to popular bars where, as Dell wrote, "everybody who was social" was. Alex was one of the few women who was 21, and she discussed the differences between her illegal alcohol use (before she was 21) and her now legal alcohol use:

What is the difference between our alcohol use now and back then? Now we are considered legal and then we weren't. I'll tell you honestly, it was often more fun back then when we weren't supposed to be doing it! Sometimes we got into bars, other times we were "negged" and turned away, but the desire to be there in the middle of all the action was always there. During my freshman year of college, one of the two bars that allows

18 year olds entrance was closed for serving under-age patrons. Illegal? Yes, but that bar was still the greatest meeting place on this campus. Now everyone just has to be a little more secretive about their age by asking older siblings for IDs, or faking their own. There is a highly lucrative market for fake IDs on this campus! I know I found one in the bathroom of a party when a drunk girl left it on the sink as I came in.

Laws were meant to be broken and worked around for many of the women who were under 21 and drank alcohol, smoked marijuana, and used other illicit substances. These laws and campus rules created hassles, and these women devised elaborate strategies for obtaining drugs of choice: using fake identification and changing driver's licenses to get into bars if under 21; blowing smoke through a dryer sheet around the end of a toilet paper roll to mask the scent of marijuana from the resident advisor; hiding drug use from parents and other authority figures; befriending drug dealers; and moving off-campus or to the less closely monitored campus housing.

Maggie, Lee, Jude, and Hetty feared that their male friends or boyfriends who were drug dealers would get in legal trouble. Maggie wrote about Andy, her drug-dealing boyfriend: "He's really paranoid about getting caught. Like that's why I'm hesitant about talking to you. That's the biggest scare. And the fact that you shouldn't get caught because it's so stupid, like he's smart about it, and he's not into mass quantities of it like other people are that should be caught before him, but like he still has this huge fear." Maggie was worried about him being "caught." Interestingly, as a drug user, Maggie and the other regular users did not fear that their own illegal behavior would result in their being "caught" or "busted," but rather, they feared more for their male friends and boyfriends who were drug dealers.

The popular perception of the laws (including campus rules) and the perceived likelihood of getting in trouble for using a certain drug typically increased as one went down the acceptability ranking, even though this may not have been based on the reality of the federal laws. Most of the women who did use marijuana or alcohol illegally thought there was only a minimal chance of getting caught, except for most of the women of color who thought they would be caught and treated more harshly for the same offense. For some, the legal status of a drug factored into their decisions when they first decided to try a drug, but once a woman had been using alcohol, marijuana, or other illicit drug regularly, the drug's legal status, or illegal activities associated with obtaining the drug, rarely factored into her decisions or daily reality.

Morality and the Drug Acceptability Ranking

I examined how discourses of morality were taken up by the women in my project. For many of the women, particularly for those who did not use many of these drugs, decisions about illicit drug use, alcohol use, and cigarette smoking were at least partly moral decisions that considered the perception of loved ones and context. Part of what many women in this study seemed to take into consideration when creating their own personal acceptability ranking of drugs was what drugs were viewed (by others and by oneself) as morally "okay" for personal use and what one would tolerate one's peers using. The acceptability ranking progressed downward to what one considered "hard-core" or morally unacceptable drugs, the use of which would not be tolerated (by oneself or one's peers) and would likely result in avoiding those who used or abused these drugs. Kathy, like many women, thought that the drugs she felt were "hard-core" drugs (in her case all illicit drugs) were "wrong" to use, but that alcohol was acceptable, and that breaking the laws regarding alcohol use was acceptable because the laws were too strict and wrong: "Yes, I think it is wrong for those people that do heavy drugs to do them, especially daily and I don't think that it should ever be legal. However, I do not feel that drinking is a choice that should be made by authorities until you are twenty-one. Society tells us that we are adults when we hit age eighteen. We can do almost everything and I think we should have the choice whether to drink or not."

Many of the women thought that there was nothing "wrong" with drugs up to and often including marijuana (i.e., caffeine, nicotine, and alcohol) because they were so prevalent and accepted. What was considered wrong or right seemed to be based on what was popular, and therefore acceptable, for some of these women, but for other women the legal status of a drug was tightly linked to morality (i.e., using illicit drugs was morally wrong). However, the "everybody's doing it" logic seemed to influence women's decisions about each drug's morality more than a drug's legal status. This distinction is identified somewhat subtly in Heather's passage: "There were cigarettes, drinks, marijuana all around. It's really hard to notice these things nowadays because I have become so used to it, it doesn't seem like anything is wrong with them."

The issue of what drugs were considered morally okay to use was sometimes connected to what drugs were legally accepted. Some of the women who made decisions not to use illegal substances mentioned fears of getting caught because a drug was illegal as guiding their decisions, but many women used words that indicated that use of some substances, or some behaviors around drug use, just were not "right." Even Jude, for instance, who used many illicit substances, thought that selling drugs to a youngster (in this case a freshman when she was a sophomore) was "wrong." She also captured here part of the moral code that existed for many of the women who were regular drug users—the notion of individual morality: "The weed and alcohol continue to flow around here. I even brought some freshmen I know down from the dorms because they wanted some. That was wrong, I know, but I do it so who am I to tell someone not to?" Regular users tended to live by a moral code that was based on personal choice as Jude described here.

Regular users and the "live and let live" moral code. Women who used illicit substances somewhat regularly, made the decision to use various substances according to their social context. These women tended to surround themselves with like-using peers, creating a typical social context where regular use was validated and discourses of pleasure were used when constructing various drugs.

The morality for more regular illicit drug users was more of a "live and let live" notion that people can decide for themselves what drugs they want to use, and that they did not want others imposing their morality on them—including the government or the school.

Fine's (1988) work in the area of sexuality, desire, and the discourses around sexuality struck me as analogous to some of the themes I noticed in my project with women's writings and discussions about their drug use. Her article, "Sexuality, Schooling, and Adolescent Females: The Missing Discourse of Desire," was quite useful in helping me frame some of these themes around morality. She wrote about sexuality as individual morality and about how this individual morality gives agency to young women to explore their own ideas about sex, but still often in this paradigm, abstinence is the preferred option (until one is married). This is similar to the larger societal ideal that abstinence from drugs is the preferred option (and abstaining from alcohol until one is 21— like abstaining from sex until married). Many of the women in my project wrote about choices not to use different drugs, or to use different drugs as one's own to make. Those who chose abstinence described feeling out of place, but they did so with conviction and pride. Many women who used drugs argued that it was their personal choice and did not feel they should pass judgment on others' levels of use.

Morality and context. Drug use was partly a moral issue for many of these women, and one they contemplated and made conscious decisions about, although in some cases these decisions were often changed. It was clear that most of the women were aware, at least on some level, of a larger societal (outside college) preference for abstinence from all illegal substances. However, within the college environment, the use of marijuana, although it is an illegal drug, was widely accepted and rarely severely punished. It was seen as morally okay to use in college by most of the women, despite the larger societal disapproval (although even perceptions of societal disapproval seemed to be changing with the current attempts to legalize marijuana for medical purposes).

Context and relationships were important in determining morality around drugs. Discourses of morality were used when some of the women discussed their contextually defined limits, as Nancy illustrated in her journal: "On the weekends I would have wine with my family if they were entertaining. Although college has changed that scene a lot. I still have good morals, and know my limits. To this day I have never had the joy of hugging a toilet due to excessive drinking."

In Nancy's case and others, college had a different standard of morality than home. As a result, many of the women's decisions about drugs were contextual and affected by their relationships. Because most of the women associated with others who used drugs at the same levels, their drug use was frequently considered morally okay within their peer groups. Often, women who did not use illicit drugs tended to impose their morality on others and to be judgmental of others who did use illicit drugs.

Drawing the line of and what was morally acceptable from peers. Women who were not regular users or did not use illicit substances tended to consider individuals who used drugs further down their individualized acceptability ranking "hardcore users" and felt that these individuals should be avoided or reprimanded. Not only would women avoid or disassociate from peers whose personal limits were further down their acceptability ranking, but also peers whose limits were higher than those of the women for a particular drug (e.g., if a peer drank more or smoked more marijuana than the woman did or where she had set her limit) were labeled as "out of control" or an "alcoholic" or as having a "problem." Abstainers frequently used these phrases. For example, Nikky, who did not drink and chose to live a "drug-free" life, set her personal limit at caffeine and labeled any cigarette smoking or alcohol use that her friends did as problematic or "alcoholic." For example, she wrote of her friends: "Scott's friends normally have beer in their rooms at all times. They drink when they watch sports, before going to parties, or if they're bored. I swear they're all a bunch of alcoholics."

Being around these friends made Nikky uncomfortable, so she rarely "hung out" with them. Women tended to remain with others who had similar moral views about drugs and separate from those who did not.

Morality and religion. A few women mentioned religious beliefs in their journals or their interviews. In the few cases where religion was mentioned, it was within the discourses of morality that condemned different drug use. Eden demonstrated this:

I got in an argument with his [her boyfriend's] roommate in the car. His roommate is Jewish, and he keeps kosher strictly. He won't eat any meat, and won't eat anything that doesn't have the kosher symbol on it. Ironically, he loves to 'shroom and smoke pot. He kept trying to tell me that I'd enjoy life much more if I would let go, and get high just once. I asked him, "TJ (his nickname), why is it that you won't eat cows, you won't eat cheese, but you'll eat the fungus that grows on their shit?" I was trying to be blunt to drive home the hypocrisy of his actions. All he kept saying was that it was different. I don't understand how, they both go in your mouth the same way, but who am I to judge?

Although Eden was not exactly clear about the difference between keeping Kosher strictly and vegetarianism, she was clear that she had two conflicting thoughts about her friend's and boyfriend's drug use. First, she believed that drug use was morally wrong and inconsistent with her understanding of religious practices. Second, as wrong as she found certain forms of drug use, she thought that the prevailing norm of individual morality (particularly for marijuana use) dictated that one was not supposed to judge the drug decisions of others. For Eden in this particular situation, her desire to speak her mind, using discourses of preaching, was more powerful than her desire to follow the norm of individual morality.

Religious reasons seemed like a sufficient excuse if one did not drink or use drugs. However, Jenny did not use "religious reasons" as her reason for abstaining from drinking "as most people might think." Her passage suggested that when an individual chose not to drink or use drugs, the assumption was that this choice was due to a religious conviction.

Alcohol is something that most people don't see as being a big problem if you drink it. It has become such a part of everyone's lives that I don't think they realize that it is possible to lead a good life without it. I have never been a drinker and never plan to be. Not for religious reasons as some may think, but just because I never have had the desire to go out and get drunk. Too often I have seen the people on my floor come home drunk and act so obnoxious. It's to the point where they don't even know what they are saying or doing. They could go out and do something that they would never do when sober and they wouldn't even remember it in the morning. That to me is good enough reason to abstain from drinking. I'd much rather have control over my body and my emotions. And be able to remember the things I did throughout my college life. After all, my parents are paying a lot of money for me to go here and get a good education. I think the least I can do is remember what I did while I was here.

Here Jenny mentioned what many other women did—that is, that she did not want to harm her body, that she wanted to be "in control," and that she did not want to disappoint her parents who were paying "a lot of money" for her college education. Personal control and the ability to be independent and responsible as well as pleasing parents were often moral issues. Several women felt morally obligated to their parents to do well in school and not use drugs. Most of the women viewed, as Jenny did, academics and parents in the same sphere that was directly in opposition to drug use. They frequently used discourses of morality when describing their academic responsibility to their parents.

Health and Safety Concerns and the Acceptability Ranking

Fears about hurting oneself physically and perceptions about what different drugs could do physically, particularly if one was "out of control," were factored into many of the women's individualized drug acceptability rankings. Reflected in many of the women's individualized drug acceptability rankings were these women's perceptions of personal health and safety issues as they related to different drugs. Progression down one's personal drug acceptability ranking seemed to be directly related to what a woman perceived as increasingly more dangerous to her or her friends in her present life. In other words, drugs that were believed to have the power to kill a person right away (i.e., cocaine and heroin) were viewed as "hard-core," dangerous drugs and relegated to the end of the acceptability ranking, whereas drugs such as marijuana or alcohol which were perceived as not posing a direct and immediate threat were viewed as safer. Interestingly, alcohol was perceived as dangerous when combined with driving because it was believed to pose an immediate threat. However, cigarette smoking, which has received a great deal of negative press recently because of its health risks, was not viewed with as much concern (although some nonsmokers mentioned concerns over the health risks), unless it posed an immediate health risk, such as asthma or bronchitis. Even when faced with these threats, some women continued to smoke cigarettes. It seemed that most of these women were more concerned with the immediate risks associated with a drug than the long-term risks, and the likelihood of use increased as the perception of immediate risk or serious harm or death decreased.

Discourses of fear. Many women used discourses of fear when describing many of the drugs. Fear of harm was what kept many women from trying new drugs further down their acceptability ranking from where they had set their personal limits. Women who had used various illicit drugs tended to weigh fear of physical harm more than legality or morality when constructing their personal drug acceptability ranking. These women, who were fairly regular drug users, tended not to mention legal consequences or morality in their journals or acceptability rankings. Maggie was afraid to try cocaine, and Jude was afraid to try LSD. Neither was concerned with getting in legal trouble, as much as each was afraid of having a bad physical reaction.

Discourses of fear were also prevalent through the words of nonusers. Sometimes they feared that harm would come to their friends. Merry described her fears the first time she watched someone snort Ritilin: "They put the powder on the desk and separated it into lines. They then took a pen and took the front and back off so it was just a long thin tube. They then stuck one part in their nose and the other in the beginning of the line and snorted it. I was so scared, I have never seen that before. I will never do that, I'm too scared of it."

Fear of physical harm to oneself or others was factored into women's acceptability rankings of different drugs, and this fear that Merry mentioned is at least partly based on a fear of physical harm.

Frequently considered in one's fear of physical harm was the method of administering a particular drug (i.e., injecting, inhaling, smoking, drinking, ingesting orally), as Merry indicated in this passage. She had a brother who took Ritilin pills for his Attention Deficit Disorder and thought nothing of it but was horrified to see her friends snort it. Injecting a drug was often considered the most dangerous method, and most women seemed to share the sentiment that "I would never inject anything into my arm." When I would show videos of injecting heroin, most of the students would moan or cringe at the sight. For some of the more frequent drug-using women in this project, particularly those who had experimented with several different illegal drugs, injecting was seen as the point where they drew their personal line. For many of the women who were inexperienced with illegal drugs and the methods of administration, snorting was viewed as scary, as Merry described. Ingesting, as in the case with pills, alcohol, and any other drug that can be eaten (e.g., Psilocybin mushrooms on pizza), was seen as the safest or least frightening way to use a drug. Smoking, though perhaps the most physically harmful, was viewed by most women as safer than snorting or injecting.

A couple of the athletes mentioned the effect of different drugs on their bodies and their decisions to abstain for this reason. Maria was the only one who admitted she was a scholarship athlete, and she used only alcohol and very infrequently. Other athletes smoked cigarettes and drank alcohol, and only one of them mentioned using marijuana. Janet, who played field hockey, wrote, "when I run sometimes my lungs feel as if they're going to explode. I know its *[sic]* horrible for me and vow to stop smoking after college."

Cathy, who was not an athlete but exercised regularly, wrote about drinking excessively despite knowing its negative effects on her body: "The next morning we will all wake up with huge hangovers and dehydrated bodies. I will be unable to work out and will probably drive home half asleep. The funniest thing is that I plan and look forward to nights like this even though the next day is hell for my body."

Even though women would experience at first hand the physical dangers of alcohol such as blacking out (i.e., losing memory but still remaining conscious), passing out, or vomiting, they would often still continue to use it. They did so at least partly because alcohol's legal status for adults (and most women in this study, regardless of age, saw themselves as adults), and morally accepted status among their friends, most of their families, and their boyfriends, seemed to outweigh its potential for physical harm. Some women would abstain from drinking at least temporarily after experiencing profound physical problems from drinking (e.g., blacking out, repeated vomiting). For some, the abstinence period after a profoundly negative experience was short-lived. Cindy described her negative physical experiences from drinking, and these would not be enough to prevent her from drinking again: "I spent all day literally in bed feeling very sick I couldn't keep anything down and the thought of drinks made me more sick. The sad thing is, I bet I will still do this. Just a bad experience. I had fun, it was worth it even though, about that chart and how much I had this weekend, I don't know how I am still alive."

The "chart" Cindy wrote about was the Blood Alcohol height and weight chart in the textbook for the course. The lethal dose is given, and it seems as if she may have surpassed this limit and blacked out from excessive drinking. Most women who experienced negative physical consequences from a drug that was legal and morally acceptable found that these consequences were insufficient to make them stop using the drug. For example, Cindy enjoyed going to fraternity parties with her friends and being actively engaged in the culture of finding romance, and alcohol is legal (though not for her) and widely accepted in society. These positive associations outweighed occasional negative experiences such as the one she described.

Fear of physical harm and fear of the unknown effects of a drug on one's body did prevent women from trying some drugs. Mostly, however, this fear of physical harm was often seen with the hallucinogens, cocaine, and heroin.

Some women with diagnosed health problems did stop using different substances, particularly if they feared a dangerous physical reaction. Jackie mentioned her heart condition in her journal, and even though she had smoked marijuana for four years before college, she stopped when she had this condition diagnosed. She wrote: "After the bars we went to my friend's house and they smoked pot. I can't smoke pot because of my heart, but practicley *[sic]* all my friends do. It doesn't bother me that much even though I smoked pot for four years. Sometimes I get the urge but I resist because I know that it's not a good idea right now."

Existing medical conditions prevented some women, but not all, from using certain drugs. Some women mentioned friends who smoked marijuana despite heart conditions and drinking excessively despite being on several medications. In Jackie's case, she was using prescription tranquilizers that did not interact well with drugs like marijuana, cocaine, and alcohol, so she no longer used cocaine and marijuana, and she limited her alcohol intake severely.

Fear of psychological harm. Some of the women mentioned their fear of psychological harm such as "losing your mind." This fear was described most often with regard to the hallucinogens. Fear of "bugging out" or "tripping out" drove several women to set their limits at a point on their personal drug acceptability ranking that did not include the hallucinogens. This fear also prevented some women from experimenting with any other illegal drug that they thought would cause psychological harm.

Much of the language these women used when writing or speaking about the drugs further down their acceptability ranking focused on fear of harm to oneself, close friend, boyfriend, or loved one. Sometimes women said these fears prevented them from experimenting with certain drugs (i.e., drawing the line before these drugs on their acceptability ranking).

HOW AND WHY LIMITS WERE SET: PERSONAL AND VICARIOUS EXPERIENCES

Most of these women were concerned about knowing their personal limits and discovering how much they could use and still be "in control." Knowing limits and being in control was important so that one did not look foolish in front of friends or boyfriends, get in trouble with authorities or parents, or lose sight or their goals (e.g., becoming a teacher, doing well in school). Learning limits was based on personal and vicarious drug experiences.

Many of the women drew their own personal limits for the legal drugs based on their personal experiences with these drugs. Some of the women knew their limits for coffee drinking because they would get shaky or have difficulty sleeping, or have a profound crash after several nights of taking Vivarin to help study for exams. Some women learned their limits for smoking cigarettes because they began to have health problems, although some continued to smoke regardless of health problems that they knew were exacerbated by smoking. However, most did not have any immediate health problems and continued to smoke, while at the same time, they claimed they wanted to quit. Some women learned their personal limits of alcohol use through excessive drinking, resulting in blacking out or repeated vomiting. Some of the women learned their limits for marijuana smoking after doing poorly academically. Unlike their experiences with these drugs, most women learned their limits for illicit drugs (other than marijuana) by watching others, or through stories about others and/or the media.

Vicarious experiences were very important to most of these women in relation to their decisions about where to set their personal limits. Some women, through growing up in alcoholic homes, learned to be very cautious with their alcohol use. Some women learned through friends, community members, or boyfriends—particularly those who had problems with excessive use. For example, Merry described her reasons for not wanting to use Vivarin after having watched her friend's reaction: "I have always been scared of taking Vivarin and now I know why. After seeing how she reacted to the caffeine I will never try Vivarin. It scares me too much."

Many women's personal limits were strongly affected by vicarious experiences they had watching others' experiences with various drugs. (Several examples were described in the previous sections.) For example, if a woman tended to experience a positive vicarious drug experience, she would be more likely to try that drug. If a woman had a negative vicarious drug experience, she would be less likely to try the drug.

CONCLUSIONS: SOCIALLY CONSTRUCTING DRUGS AND COMPLEXITY OF THE DRUG ACCEPTABILITY RANKING

The women in my project socially constructed each of the drugs they encountered differently, drawing on personal and vicarious experiences with friends and boyfriends. These constructions were different for women within their racially segregated groups. Using these traditional discourses of morality, legality, and health/safety, women constructed drugs in hierarchical ways. This hierarchical and traditional way of thinking led most women to rank-order drugs factoring in not only the moral, legal, and health issues associated with each drug, but also the amount of and the way a drug was used. Each woman placed different emphases on these factors in various settings and within different relationships.

Women's constructed meaning about drugs and subsequent acceptability ranking seemed to serve as a guide to simplify the complex questions a woman had about each psychoactive drug, including her personal limits for each drug. Many women occasionally surpassed their limits for the drugs they used, and these events tended to reinforce what a woman's limit was, and where she should set it, and still maintain "control." Some women learned their limits by watching others.

The notion of the drug acceptability ranking should not simplify the understanding the reader gains about the decisions individuals make about drugs. Rather, this notion should complicate matters for those involved in drug education, prevention, and rehabilitation. Having an individual explore how she or he has come to rank different drugs and how one justifies using or avoiding drugs could be useful in some of the education, prevention, and rehabilitation models.

Conclusions and Implications

Women constructed meaning about drugs within the context of their important interpersonal relationships. Whether it be drinking at a bar, tripping on LSD, or smoking marijuana from a bong, these events were most often done with friends or boyfriends. It was not surprising that most of the major themes emerged around relationships—the role of drugs in relationships and the ways various drugs were socially constructed within these relationships. Although relationships with family, friends, and community prior to college were important to these women, and they drew on these relationships to help them construct meaning about various drugs, for my project, I focused on relationships with peers and romantic partners in college. Drawing on their experiences within these relationships, women constructed drugs hierarchically, using traditional discourses of morality, legality, and health/safety.

In this chapter, I describe some of the limitations of the study and make recommendations for future research in light of these limitations; discuss generalizability; and reexamine some of the issues associated with power and my relationships with these women. I also discuss some of the implications of the themes described in the previous chapters as well as some recommendations for drug education and prevention.

LIMITATIONS, CONCERNS, GENERALIZABILITY, AND POWER RELATIONSHIPS

Concerns may be raised about the generalizability of this study, but it is important to mention that the goal was to tell how these women constructed meaning about the role of drugs in their lives (specifically within their relationships) at college. Understanding the everyday drug experiences of the women involved in this study, analyzing the words these women used to construct meaning of the role of drugs in their relationships, and analyzing how drugs affected these women's relationships in college were the major goals of this study. It is inappropriate to overgeneralize one's experience to another's. It is also inappropriate to generalize to other college environments. The informants were all full-time students at a particular university. Was the culture at this university similar to other college cultures? This is a question to be answered by each individual college or university: How do students make meaning about drug use on *this* campus? How might these experiences be different on a campus that was not as racially segregated?

Another possible limitation was the relatively homogeneous population of women (mostly White, middle to upper class, heterosexual, with stated goals of becoming elementary school teachers) to whom I had access and with whom I had the opportunity to build rapport around topics of drug use. The women in this study were not representative of the population of the university. The women were students in my "Drug Education for Teachers" course, so the majority of them had a career goal of becoming an elementary school teacher. Whether these women tended to adopt more traditionally "feminine roles" than their non-School of Education counterparts is not known, for they had selected a college program leading to a "traditionally female" occupation. Nevertheless, I wanted to focus on women with whom I had built a rapport and a trust where they felt comfortable sharing personal information about drugs and their drug use. A very small minority of women in this study were from different racial groups because the class (and the teaching profession in general) has typically lacked this diversity. I feel it is important to mention this limitation because I would have preferred to hear the voices of women from more varied backgrounds. None of the women mentioned being anything but heterosexual and able-bodied. I mention these facts because the voices of lesbian women and disabled women also need to be heard. More non-White women, women from various geographical locations, and women from poorer social class backgrounds also need to be heard. These aspects of social location seemed to be important but need to be explored further using other methods such as interviewing and participant observation.

It is important to listen to as many different voices from as many different social locations as possible in the research process—all ages, all educational levels, all cultures, all religions, all abilities, and so on. This is difficult, but I think we need to challenge the positivist assumptions that underlie most re-search on drug use. This kind of positivist thinking has kept scientists (social scientists included) searching for "truth." Often, this "truth" is not "true" for people from different social locations. This has often resulted in the silencing of different groups of voices in research—or in certain types of research not being regarded as rigorous, useful, or even correct. Qualitative, feminist methods that allow for various women's voices to be heard provide ways to learn about different experiences and standpoints.

The women in my project had successfully completed high school and gone on to college. More work needs to be done with younger people who are not as successful in their educational pursuits to determine how they make meaning of the role of drugs in their lives. Also, researchers need to determine the influence of relationships prior to college in shaping views about drugs (e.g., relationships with family, friends, teachers, community members). Women in my project suggested that these relationships were important in shaping their views, but I did not focus on this aspect. More work needs to be done to determine how younger people make meaning about drugs as they are beginning to formulate their ideas about drugs and the role of relationships in this formulation.

In addition, more work needs to be directed to the matter of what happens to women after they leave college. Do they moderate their use of drugs as they proceed to their junior and senior years? Do they experience drug-related problems after they graduate? What happens to those who don't graduate or are academically dismissed? Do women who become teachers continue to use drugs? Do the heavier users actually become teachers? We need to hear the voices of women outside of college to examine how they make meaning of drugs in their postcollege lives.

More critical analyses of the words that various women used to describe substance use on campus need to be completed in order to begin to examine, describe, and deconstruct the discourses that shape one's understanding about issues of addiction and codependency. Although feminists have analyzed these engendered psychological paradigms (Van Den Bergh, 1991; Babcock & McKay, 1995, respectively), more exploration needs to be done to determine how individual women take up these particular discourses, and how these paradigms structure the ways women make meaning of drug use in their own lives.

The Tendency to Generalize

I worried about how my analysis might be misinterpreted, or that the subject positions of these women, and my own, would not be seen as *plural and shifting*. I knew of the tendency for those reading drug research to make generalizations quickly in an attempt to *fix* the *"drug problem"* in this country. For example, I gave a talk about my project on the campus where I conducted the research. The person responsible for drug education and prevention on campus asked, "Did you find a drug-abusing personality type?" I pictured in my mind the typical checklist of personality traits that frequently are used to label groups of people, lumping them into a category of "drug-abusing personality," instead of looking at the individual women as having subject positions that were plural and shifting. I replied that I did not think so and that I thought each woman involved in this project had complex reasons for using (sometimes abusing) or not using certain drugs, and that the situation of each woman today would not necessarily be her situation tomorrow. Drug use is part of a complex web of other social interactions. Each individual seemed to be affected differently by these interactions and to choose paths based on experiences within their relationships. These women modified their often traditional and hierarchical views about drugs as they had new drug-related experiences and as their relationships and contexts changed.

In my experience, most of my college friends who used illegal drugs frequently and excessively no longer use them. They drink alcohol only when they can fit it into their professional and personal lives. One of my college friends who had problems with his drinking quit drinking entirely after college. One of my best college friends, who was a regular drug user, has recently been battling leukemia. After college he was living a drug-free life, but now, within his hospital environment, he has a self-administered Demerol pump to reduce his pain, and he is frequently given steroids to increase his strength, increase his weight gain, and prevent him from scratching. Without drugs, his life would have ended years ago. Many of my college friends who were regular drug users are now positive contributors to society. The reality of their college drinking and illegal drug use shifted after they left college. Perhaps the same will be true for the women in my project who were regular drinkers and illegal drug users.

The comments of my parents, journal editors, and others who read early drafts of my work forced me to look more deeply at the issue of generalizability and predictability. I also needed to deal with my own, and others', tendency to seek validation, generalizability, and predictability in these women's words. My Psychology background had drilled into my head the quantitative essentials of reliability and validity. People, including myself at times, tended to search my written materials for answers to the complex questions that surround drug abuse. Readers wanted to make sweeping generalizations about these women's words, or they wanted me to make generalizations. Some readers wanted to know how generalizable this project was. Although I suspect that there are many college environments where women make meaning of the role of drugs in their lives in ways similar to these women, more work needs to be done to hear voices from other college campuses to confirm this notion.

Power and Relationships with the Women in This Project

In addition to the vexing question of generalizability, I also again questioned the imbalance of power in the relationship I had with the women in this project. Why would these women open up to me, their teacher, a person often thought to be in a position of power over them, about their illicit activity? This question led me to these others: "What did *they* get out of this?" versus "what did *I* get out of this?" research relationship. These women placed their trust in me. They confided in me about their illegal behaviors, intimate thoughts, and knowledge of their friends' and loved ones' illegal behaviors. They believed that I would not betray this trust by using their real names or their friends' names. I can only hope that in return the experience of talking about and writing about their personal experiences was somehow helpful in allowing them to examine and analyze their own lives. I also hope that the distance that might have arisen from taking a step back to engage in the process of speaking or writing allowed them to make some changes that improved their lives. I tend to doubt that much positive change occurred for most of them based on their relatively brief interactions with me. Certainly, those for whom drug use was a significant part of their lives would have had to make major life changes in personal relationships and social groups before they could have reduced their drug use. This kind of change would have taken more than a few interactions with me.

To answer the question of what I got out of my relationship with these women, I would say that I got volumes of information from them, a dissertation, potential for career advancement, and material for several articles and numerous other professional opportunities (e.g., speeches and conference presentations). I was able to gather more information about a topic of profound interest to me for over a decade by interrupting the personal lives of some of these women, and asking them what few people had likely never asked. I asked them to put into written and spoken words their experiences with drugs. This was not a simple task when the discourses available to them, as I see now, were so limited. Even more work needs to be done to examine these discourses.

I raise the issue of power imbalance again, not just of me as "teacher" but of me as "researcher" now speaking for this particular group of women. I want to emphasize again that these were the lives of a particular group of women, at a particular historical moment, at a particular place (a prestigious research university), at particular ages (aged 18 to 21 years), and at a particular stage in their academic lives. These findings cannot and should not be generalized to all college women. These stories belong to these women and cannot belong to other women. My project should be taken as an invitation to listen to the lives of as many people as possible about their experiences with drugs instead of simply generalizing from the statistics. We need to resist the tendency to generalize in an attempt to find quick remedies for an ill-defined national "drug problem," and open ourselves up to listen to individual voices telling us how this "problem" is experienced daily. We need to examine the issues of drug use and abuse from a postmodern perspective which, according to Rosenau (1992, p. 117) "presumes methods that multiply paradox, inventing ever more elaborate repertoires of questions, each of which encourages an infinity of answers, rather than methods that settle on solutions."

Most drug studies have focused on finding out the facts or truths about drug use and drug users. What my study did differently was to approach the question within a postmodern framework, assuming that there is not "one true and objective reality" that is unchanging and "universal" (Kvale, 1995, p. 24). In an attempt to examine the culture for each of the women in my project, I examined the language they used to make meaning of drugs in their daily lives. Language, as Kvale wrote, is "neither objective or universal nor subjective or individual, but intersubjective" (p. 27). In my project I engaged in dialogue as teacher and researcher, creating meaning with a language that was "intersubjective" with these women in the classroom, in the journals (although this was more of a one-sided telling of information), and in the interviews. This intersubjectivity was influenced by my role as teacher during much of the dialogue begging the question, "What were some of the implications of this project, including but not limited to those related to teacher-research?"

IMPLICATIONS AND RECOMMENDATIONS

Implications for Teacher Research

I am a firm believer in the notion that in studying something you are bound to change it. An important implication for teacher-researchers to consider is how students involved in a course might have changed during the course as a result of their participation in it. No doubt, the women in my project changed some of their views about drugs (though perhaps only temporarily) as a result of the seven-week course. I will give one example. In every class, one of the first things I flashed on my Powerpoint slideshow was a quote from Ray and Ksir (1993, p. 5): "Drugs, per se, are not good nor bad." I proceeded to ask, in my animated way, "what drugs do we tend to think are bad?" Students frequently shouted, "heroin" and "crack." I would reply by saying that it was not the chemical itself that was evil, but the physiological and psychological effects of chemical interactions, and how the resulting behaviors were socially constructed as good or evil.

I showed clips from the movie *Reefer Madness* (1937), which describes marijuana as a "deadly narcotic," "the real public enemy number one!" "our nation's scourge." Most of the students laughed at these clips, as if the descriptions were intended to be a joke. I described the atmosphere of the 1930s and emphasized that this was a very serious movie shown at Parent-Teacher meetings and Health classes in order to convince the American public that marijuana was deadly and should be illegal. Many people from 1930s through the 1950s believed that marijuana was evil, in much the same way that crack and heroin are viewed today. Many students in my class viewed this movie through the now popular lens that marijuana is harmless and that people who label marijuana as dangerous are simply wrong. Were these students changed by this particular class? Were they more open to examine how they had come to hold the beliefs they had about certain drugs? I do not know, but in one of the few mentions of the course in one of the women's journals, Sandy wrote: "I also saw marijuana during a superbowl party I was at and I have listened to my guy neighbor talk about shrooming this weekend, laugh about songs that have to do with acid trips and stuff like that. Drugs are everywhere. I saw a drug transaction while walking on my floor the other day. Pot. Nothing too bad I guess. Someone the other day said 'drugs are bad' and I said no drugs aren't good or bad when they are sitting there. They aren't anything until they get into your body. Then they can do good or bad things."

I am still uncertain about the ways these women might have changed their attitudes or behaviors about drugs as a result of their participation in the course and their interactions with me as their teacher. Few women specifically mentioned aspects of the course in their journals. Some wrote, as Sandy did, that this course increased their awareness of the amount of drugs around them. Nor did any of the women specifically mention the course in their interviews as having changed their behavior or their drug use. The fact that only a handful of women reflected on the course directly in their journals is interesting to me but does not necessarily provide evidence that these women were unchanged by the course. Lisa wrote about the impact of her group presentation on her thoughts about marijuana: "All my life I heard about how smoking cigarettes were bad to the lung, but no one ever told me how marijuana is ten times worst [sic]. I was also a firm believer in the legalization of marijuana since to me, it was a 'good drug.' It was only after my presentation that I realized that legalizing some drugs will only increase its [sic] use."

Several of the women mentioned the journal assignment as eye-opening to what had become a "fact of life" for them, that "drugs are everywhere." Many women wrote or said that they did not realize the extent of the role that drugs played in their lives until they had to write down their observations. Perhaps reflecting on the drugs they used caused these women to think about cutting down or modifying excessive use. Jude and others quit smoking cigarettes (at least during the course), but I do not know whether others were affected enough to reduce their use.

Earlier I raised the issue of studying sites where one is perceived as being in a position of power over those whom one is studying, as is the case in much teacher-research and was the case in my project. I attempted to downplay the power differential as much as possible by creating a climate of trust, openness, acceptance, respect, and listening in the classroom. Students would teach one another through group discussions and group presentations. I tried as much as possible to create an environment where all voices mattered. Some classes were better than others at creating this environment—partly, I think because of size. The larger classes (twenty to twenty-five students) were more impersonal. Students in them could hide from discussions, and a few of the more vocal students tended to dominate discussions. In the smaller classes (ten to fifteen students), discussions tended to be very personal, and students tended to be open about their own illegal activity. In the smaller classes, I tended to speak much less (unless to guide discussions, or on the rare occasions when I would lecture), allowing for students to learn more from one another. I wondered whether this kind of format could be used with younger students for drug education at the secondary level when they are beginning to be exposed to illicit drugs—that is, a seminar-style, open forum, with the person who is guiding the discussion being knowledgeable about the physiological and psychological effects of drugs, but nonjudgmental and considered a safe person to talk to about difficult drug-related issues. They could also be encouraged to write and speak about their personal experiences without fear of getting in trouble. Many of these women may have viewed me as a peer more than as a teacher because I am often mistakenly thought to be younger than my years, even though at the time of this project I was about nine or ten years older than most of the students. Perhaps they trusted me as a peer and did not think of me as an authority figure because I was able to "talk the talk" since I knew much of the drug slang. I was honest with them when they asked questions; and I genuinely cared (and demonstrated this in the classroom by listening carefully and attentively) for them and what they had to say.

Teachers can provide a wealth of information and insight into the issues facing young people in their classroom. If those in the research field begin to acknowledge this information as important and useful, we could begin to tap into what has to date remained a relatively untapped resource—teacher-research.

Implications of the Importance of Interpersonal Relationships

Drug use is a complex phenomenon. It is a complex interplay of the biological, psychological, and sociological. I asked a group of women to describe the role of drugs in their lives as college students. Sometimes women focused on how drugs affected them physiologically, and sometimes they described how drugs affected them personally and emotionally. Most often, however, women described the role of drugs within their relationships—particularly their friends and romantic partners.

The women in this project sought the love, acceptance, and respect of others. They wanted to have friends and most wanted to have boyfriends. They wanted the acceptance of their families when available. They did not typically use drugs simply for the sake of experiencing a drug's effect. Most viewed drugs as part of their relationships with others—partying. Whether or not they chose to use drugs themselves, drugs were often part of their relationships in one way or another. Some of the abstainers grew up in alcoholic families or drug-infested neighborhoods. Some of the more regular users experienced drugs as a daily part of their relationships.

Friends influenced each other's drug use. Groups of abstainers validated these decisions for one another, whereas groups of heavier users validated this behavior for one another. As important as friends were, perhaps even more significant in shaping many of the women's attitudes and decisions about drugs were boyfriends.

Women were not asked specifically to write or talk about their romantic relationships, yet nearly every woman mentioned a boyfriend or romantic relationship (only heterosexual) in some way. A great deal of emphasis was placed on romantic relationships, particularly by women who did not have boyfriends. A particularly disturbing aspect of the emphasis on romance was the fact that many women suffered because of a boyfriend's or a love interest's drug use or abuse.

To look critically at why rape all too often accompanies excessive drinking, we need to listen to both women's and men's words to determine what people are thinking when they are not using drugs. In many examples in my project, women reported that men were seeking sex and that the women were seeking boyfriends, but not necessarily sex. Women were not supposed to initiate a sexual encounter within this environment, nor were they supposed to express their sexuality openly. Drinking was a site where women had an excuse to be less sexually inhibited, but the ultimate decision to "hook up" was still the man's. The descriptor of "hookup" implies two active players mutually hooking or joining for an encounter when a man and a woman who have been drinking end up together in a sexual situation kissing, fondling, or having sexual intercourse in someone's bedroom. The term seems inaccurate based on what most women reported actually happened. Perhaps more accurately, these situations were a drunken *pickup* where women were picked up and men did the picking up. Most women did not report playing the active role suggested by the term of a mutual *hookup*.

Some negotiation takes place during the drunken hookup, which some women referred to as a form of verbal "tug of war." If we know that negotiations are consistently happening with women and men during the drunken hookup, perhaps we can begin to create some reasonable and realistic negotiation strategies that might help prevent the drunken hookup from becoming sexual assault or rape. Ideally, we should try to eliminate drunkenness as being such a significant part of coupling in college. However, until we create an environment where bars and parties are not the primary meeting place for "hooking up," we need to develop ways of talking about the expectations men and women have of the "hookup" and create strategies to prevent one person from winning the tug of war at the other's expense.

Alcohol played a major role in facilitating the often stressful hooking-up process, and if a woman did not enjoy drinking (for whatever reason), being on the sexual auction block was usually very uncomfortable. Perhaps this was why many of the women put so much energy into keeping their boyfriends, even when the relationship was not satisfying. Having a boyfriend could keep women off the sexual auction block where they needed to remain attractive and worthy of being picked up.

Many women seemed to place emphasis on getting coupled and staying coupled. It is unclear from the women's words how much emphasis the men placed on coupling, or whether men were more interested in sampling (as was the case of Richy's and Maria's male friends) than bidding for keeps (as was the case of Alana's boyfriend) in their college experience. More work needs to be done to listen to men's voices and how they make meaning of the process of romance in college and the role of alcohol and other drugs in this process.

There seems to be a great deal of pressure in American culture to be in a heterosexual couple relationship—if not in college, then shortly after graduating. This message came through loud and clear in both the narratives and the interviews. More research needs to be conducted to ascertain where women are receiving these messages, how they internalize or make meaning of them in their daily lives, and how they decide what treatment they are willing to accept from a mate. A great deal of time was spent on maintaining, or sometimes salvaging, romantic relationships with men who were abusing drugs (and sometimes abusing their girlfriends too). This time often took women away from their academic work, subtly derailing some of them from their goals.

In addition to trying to help or take care of their boyfriends, many women took care of one another in drug-using situations. Caretaking was another important theme that emerged for most women in this project. Regardless of their personal drug-use levels, almost all women in this study took care of another person and in some cases may have saved the life of that other person.

Knowing the importance of interpersonal relationships and some of the other individual factors associated with a person's social location (race, social class, geographic location), we can begin to create more targeted drug education and counseling that address these different factors. For example, education could include group education that addresses the important role of drugs in friendships and romantic relationships that offers safer alternatives for shared and pleasurable activities. It is insufficient simply to tell students about alternatives, but strategies should include providing these alternatives. Dances, athletic activities and events (including workout facilities), camping trips, and retreats are a few of these activities that educators could provide. Young people will often tell what they enjoy doing if they are asked. These pleasurable alternatives need to be offered at night and on weekends for youth starting at young ages as they are beginning to establish relationships with peers.

The generalized drug education that has existed to date, preaching the myths and horrors of drugs or telling young people not to question but to "just say 'no!,'" has been inconsistent with the pleasure and seemingly apparent risk-free experience that many young people associate with different drugs These past strategies have been insufficient for reaching these young people. Drug education curricula that have been "one size fits all" have not prevented the problems in this country associated with adolescent drug abuse. Drug education needs to address the role of drugs in friendships and romantic coupling and to examine realistic alternatives with young people for ways to meet friends and romantic partners and activities to do with them that do not center around drug use.

Importance of the Drug Acceptability Ranking

Each woman in this project seemed to take into consideration the legality, morality, and potential for harm of each drug; each method for using a drug (i.e., injecting, smoking, ingesting, inhaling); and their personal and vicarious experiences lived through close friends and boyfriends before rank-ordering or creating their own personal drug acceptability ranking, and making decisions about their own personal drug-use limits. Women placed different emphases on each of these factors when making their own decisions.

When the women in my study arrived at college, most of them sought friends who used drugs (or chose not to use drugs) at similar levels. When abstainers were in their groups of abstaining peers, they did not materially modify their individual acceptability rankings. The more regular drug users and experimenters found peers who used at similar levels, and within these groups, women tended to modify their personal acceptability ranking to accommodate the information from their friends' drug experiences and opinions. Personal acceptability rankings and drug-use decisions (including drug-using limits) were affected by new peer groups that these women were exposed to in college, that is, their male and female friends, and perhaps most importantly their romantic partners, or potential romantic partners.

One implication of having an individualized, internalized, but unarticulated ranking of drugs that is based, at least to some extent on fear (fear of legal ramifications, moral judgment, and health risks), is that once a drug has been shown to not be fear-worthy (i.e., friends try a drug and tell how great their experience was with it), then some women may call into question their fears about other drugs. According to Kirsh (1986), "ultimately, misinformation and outright lies have cost authority dearly. The price has been loss of credibility." For some of the women, fear was enough to prevent them from experimenting with illegal drugs. However, for some, the fear approach was insufficient. Instilling fear in young people is not necessarily effective for all. We need to examine the messages that underlie each drug—particularly the messages around morality, legality, and health/safety. We need to examine further how these messages are internalized and influence behavior. Perhaps determining the messages that young people internalize could be a built-in part of drug education.

IMPLICATIONS AND RECOMMENDATIONS FOR DRUG EDUCATION

The women in my study struggled to learn their limits and how to be responsible in their drug use. Defining what "responsible drug use" means is a problem that society at large continues to struggle with as well. Because there has been no definition of "responsible drug use" that has been acceptable to the majority of society, drug education, policies, and laws have been schizophrenic in nature and young people continue to search for their own definitions within their relationships with their friends and romantic partners.

School could be a place for young people to ask their questions about drugs and search for reasonable definitions. However, schools have not been successful sites for this. As Fine (1991, p. 44) observed in her ethnographic study of a public inner-city high school: "Conversations about these very conditions of life, about alcoholism, drug abuse, domestic violence, environmental hazards, gentrification, and poor health—to the extent that they happened at all—remained confined to individual sessions with counselors (for those lucky enough to gain hearing with a counselor in the 500 to 1 ratio, and gutsy enough to raise the issue), or if made academic, were raised in hygiene class (for those fortunate enough to have made it to the twelfth grade, when Hygiene was offered)."

Students who often suffer the most significant drug-related problems begin these problems early and are likely to fail to make it to twelfth grade health class, for they may drop out to work to support their habit, or they continue to fail courses because of chronic use and frequent tardiness. Fine continued that this "privatizing and psychologizing of public and political issues served to reinforce the alienation of students' lives from their educational experiences. . . an unwillingness to infuse these issues into the curriculum helps to partition them as artificially and purely psychological" (p. 44). Drug education has been "privatized and psychologized." Students with serious drug problems are removed from schools and rarely are able to get the help or rehabilitation needed to allow them to function in society. This "psychologizes" the problem, making it the individual's problem and fails to help the student or their peers learn more about the nature of drug dependence. The reality of drug abuse and dependence needs to be addressed throughout the curriculum—not simply as "add-on" programs that students rarely take seriously. This "reality" needs to be meaningful for young people in the environment in which they live. Students' experiences need to be brought into the classroom in safe ways where discussion and learning can take place without fear of punishment.

In college, many of the young people who drop out, or are dismissed for academic reasons, are likely to have drug-related problems, but they are frequently dismissed without any opportunity for help. And what kind of help or intervention is needed? Most of these young people do not believe they have any drug problem. There needs to be more individualized interventions to fill in the vast amount of gray area between Alcoholics Anonymous and Zero Tolerance for Drugs. Currently, little support is available for people who may not need or want to go to a rehabilitation or detoxification center, go to AA meetings regularly, or give up drinking alcohol or other drug use entirely to function in society. Some young people may have difficulties adjusting to their new social environments (particularly the sometimes awkward culture of romance), or finding a balance between their work and social lives—in short, a difficulty learning their limits. Some kind of nonpunitive help needs to be made available to these students to help them get back on track, if they have been derailed by a failure to learn their limits.

In an attempt to deal with national and local concerns about adolescent drug-related problems, education has been touted as the panacea. However, most forms of drug education to date have demonstrated little long-term impact in reducing drug abuse among our nation's youth.

Difficulty Defining the Goals of Drug Education: Abstinence or Responsible Use?

Exactly what is the purpose of the majority of drug education programs? Is it total abstinence from all mind-altering substances—a drug free life? Or is it educating students about what it means to live in a society where psychoactive substances are part of our culture, and how to make informed, responsible choices about these substances? If the latter, what is a *responsible* choice, who determines what is "a responsible choice," and how does one learn how to make it?

I was describing to my mother my frustrations teaching the "Drug Education" course. I said, "It is incredible the amount of incorrect information they have learned in high school. . . that drugs fry brain cells, that LSD causes chromosome damage, etc., and they seem unwilling to hear any other information."

"What's so bad about that?" She asked. "They need to be afraid, so they won't do drugs."

"But they still do drugs—they're just *afraid* when they *do* them, and they don't know the *real* effects they have on their bodies. . . and they sneak around and do it. . . they guzzle and binge drink, they're afraid to seek help from adults when they need it because they don't want to get into trouble, and they fear adults' wrath because they know the antidrug sentiment in adult society. They don't want to call for rides home when they are drunk because they don't want to get in trouble. They don't think they'll die, from anything, so they take chances, some more dangerous than others."

This anecdote describes two of the opposing viewpoints in the typical debate about drug education. On the one side, there is a fundamental belief that drugs are bad and that the way to prevent abuse is to convey myths and misinformation designed to scare kids from experimenting. Until the middle of the twentieth century, drug education programs used a one-sided, fear tactic approach to achieve the goal of abstinence, and because this approach was assumed effective, little was done to evaluate these programs (Ray & Ksir, 1993). My mother, like many others, believes that abstinence is the preferred option, and frightening young people is the best way to achieve it.

The other school of thought is that adolescence is a time of experimentation and a period when the prevailing feeling is that of invulnerability. This school would argue that experimentation with drugs is inevitable, that teachers (including parents) need to accept this fact and give students correct information about drugs, so that students can make informed, responsible choices about the substances they put into their bodies. Perhaps accepting experimentation as an effective way to learn one's limits and using this normal curiosity as a springboard into a discussion about how to live a healthy lifestyle, how various drugs affect one's body (the physiological effects), and how drugs can affect one's emotions (the psychological effects) might be more meaningful than telling students simply to say "no!" to drugs. As Goode (1993) stated "the truth is, as measured by harm to the user, most illicit drug users, like most drinkers of alcohol, use their drug or drugs of choice wisely, nonabusively, in moderation; with most, use does not escalate to abuse or compulsive use" (p. 335). This belief has not been widely accepted by drug policymakers or educators. Drug use is illegal (with the exception of caffeine, nicotine after age 18, and alcohol after age 21), and those who use drugs are treated as criminals. To date, the evaluations of drug education programs have been based more on students' use of illegal drugs and less on problems students have because of their drug use. Granted, the latter is more difficult to determine, but it would likely give a better assessment of the effectiveness of drug education programs.

The Need to Examine and Include the Context and
Norms of Use in Drug Education

Drug education approaches have consistently preached complete abstinence from any kind of mind-altering substance without addressing the culture in which these behaviors are learned. According to Goode (1993): "It is possible that this goal is unrealistic with current experimenters and users." Hanson and Venturelli (1995) suggested that "people have an innate need to alter their conscious state. This belief is based [partly] on the observation that, as a part of their normal play, preschoolers deliberately whirl themselves dizzy and even momentarily choke each other to lose consciousness" (Hanson & Venturelli, 1995). In addition, researchers such as Weng and Newcomb (1989) have found support for Brehm's (1966 in Weng & Newcomb, 1989) reactance theory and adolescent drug use—that is, adolescents will want to use drugs more and are more likely to act on that desire if it is something that is forbidden. In their study of 1,177 seventh, eighth, and ninth graders, "results indicated that, although students were legally and socially prohibited from engaging in drug-taking, some of them intended to use drugs" (Weng & Newcomb, p. 27). By striving for the unattainable goal of abstinence and preaching abstinence of forbidden fruits that many people use unproblematically, we set young people up to obey their natural curiosity, then punish them for it, and miss the opportunity to educate them about personal health and responsible use.

As long as the social norms of certain subcultures promote use of illicit substances (and in many cases abuse of these substances), a few hours of education in the form of a course on drugs, whether it be purely "factual" or fear-inducing propaganda, will not eliminate the use of them. Cookson and Persell (1985, p. 16) state that "learning certain social roles and behaviors is a central—and perhaps the only—purpose of education." Elementary and secondary schools accomplish this quite well and from a very early age. According to Dreeben, "To the question of what is learned in school, only a hypothetical answer can be offered at this point: pupils learn to accept social norms, or principles of conduct, and to act according to them" (1967, p. 63). I would argue that the "social norms" that students are learning in many schools are promoting social use and occasional misuse and abuse of substances.

Formal drug education alone is insufficient to remedy drug abuse among students and has to date merely provided a band-aid approach to the problem. The cultural norms within a larger societal context, as well as the ethos of each individual school, must be transformed through efforts involving families and communities before any significant reduction in drug abuse will occur. The norms must include a refusal to accept abuse, but offer adequate support and help for those who have a recognized drug problem. The norms must also recognize that some amount of experimentation and moderate use is likely. Creating a climate that addresses this issue and provides appropriate, meaningful help for substance abuse as well as a safe haven to discuss concerns about drugs is critical to combating the problems associated with drug abuse in schools.

Athletics and learning about one's body. Women who participated in athletics tended not to be involved in illicit drug use and were involved in subcultures where alcohol tended not to be used excessively. Promoting exercise and athletics for women accomplishes many things. First, exercise has been demonstrated physiologically to produce endorphins (i.e., the body's own pleasure chemicals), and endorphins are chemically very similar to the psychoactive elements in various drugs. Becoming fit takes advantage of one's own pleasure chemicals and may reduce the need for psychoactive substances to produce pleasure. Exercise may also lead people to become more in touch with their bodies in ways that might make them less likely to introduce elements harmful to them. In addition, a culture where fitness (and outdoor or healthy-lifestyle activities) are promoted may reduce the "downtime" or boredom that many women in this study referenced. Teaching young people about how to live a healthy lifestyle (e.g., through good nutrition, exercise, and stress reduction activities) needs to start early in school and be encouraged throughout one's lifetime.

Secretary of Health and Human Services Donna Shalala introduced a new program called "Girl Power" in November 1996. This program is attempting to create a more appropriate way to educate young girls (ages 9–14) about their health and their bodies while sending the message that "drugs are dangerous." By reaching girls at this "key transitional age when they are forming their values and attitudes," it is hoped that fewer young girls will take "dangerous chances with the only lives they will ever have" (quoted from Shalala, 1996 U.S. Department of Health and Human Services). Promoting women's athletics early in school through funding for quality physical education, weaving in health and wellness discussions with physical education, and giving children a choice of physical activities in which they can excel might be a way to start.

Most of the women in my project who used drugs regularly planned to quit after college. Most were high academic achievers (with a GPA of 3.0 or better). The only "problems" they noticed were occasional health problems from overindulging. They declared the benefits to outweigh the costs. The prevailing feeling was, "I'll quit before anything bad happens to me—and college is the place to do these things right?" Perhaps if these women were aware of the health risks of drugs, learned at an early age to place a top priority on their physical wellness, and found similar pleasure and opportunities for fun with friends and boyfriends through healthy activities, they would not be as drawn to drugs. Instead of drinking or using other illegal drugs, partying could mean dancing and listening to music, as it did for the Black and Latina women, or it could mean biking, hiking, jogging, skiing, and playing intramural sports. Sites for meeting potential romantic partners could be at structured sporting events, activities, or the gym instead of at bars and keg parties.

Drug Education in College

Many of the women in the study reported learning a great deal about drugs in college. They learned how various drugs affect people, and in some cases, some of the women learned how various drugs affected them personally. Most of these women learned how to take care of themselves, each other, and the men in their lives during episodes when one exceeded one's limits. Perhaps this care-taking was learned out of necessity, because so many felt it was necessary to keep quiet about illicit drug use and underage drinking because of a fear of be-ing "busted." This kind of silence can be dangerous and teaches young people to rely on one another, instead of seeking the professional help they might need. Most of these women also learned how to play the game of romance, and in some cases how to use certain drugs to facilitate this awkward and daunting initial meeting process or "hooking up." Most of these women learned how to balance and prioritize their academic (work) and social lives (partying/drug use). Most of all, they were learning their limits: What they could and could not do within this culture, and as their lives changed, they adjusted these limits ac-cordingly. These women were learning norms, consistent with what Dreeben (1967) thought was all that formal education could accomplish.

What remains unclear is how many of the women who were heavier drug us-ers were derailed from their originally intended goal of becoming teachers. Perhaps a study designed to follow a group of women throughout their college careers would shed some light on this question. Another question is how might women from different academic disciplines have made meaning about drugs in their lives. For a couple of women (Maggie and Lee), education was perceived as less academically rigorous than their previous majors, and changing their majors to education allowed them more time to party (use drugs). I received journals from only a couple of women who were doing their student teaching (which is often considered the most difficult and demanding part of the educa-tion major), and neither of them (Candy and Gilly) used any illicit drugs and they rarely drank alcohol.

IMPORTANCE OF THE PROJECT

College as a Place to Learn Limits

Most of the White women in this study described a culture where blackouts from excessive drinking were not uncommon, where people felt justified in dis-claiming personal responsibility when individuals used drugs (particularly drinking) to excess, and where women were expected to take care of others who had gone "beyond their limits." Nonusers or light users, including but not limited to Black and Latina women, were often placed in roles where they were expected to be the caretakers for their more regular or heavy-using friends. Caretaking was most clearly evident in situations where heavy drinking had occurred, but it was also evident in cases where people "freaked out" from other illicit substances (most frequently mentioned was marijuana). Men were rarely mentioned as caretakers in this culture, but the male role was defined as providing the supply of drugs (including alcohol), "bidding" on women on the "sexual auction block" at bars and parties, and initiating and carrying out the heterosexual pickup encounter. It is not surprising in this culture that domination and violence against women occurs; what is surprising is that it doesn't happen *more often.*

College is a place where many of these women were learning their drug-using limits based on their personal experiences and their experiences observing friends and boyfriends. Nearly all of the White women came to college expecting this to be the case. They also learned "how to act" under the influence. This was clearly demonstrated by one young woman who described when her younger sister (in high school) came to visit: "My younger sister (she's 16) came up to visit me this past weekend with her best friend. Let's just say we. . . celebrated. I've never drank *[sic]* with my sister, in fact she's only drank *[sic]* 1 or 2 times before. . . . My sister and her friend were hilarious. They didn't know quite how to handle themselves. They were really worried about 'making a scene.' I guess you get used to how you should act with experience."

The few women who before they came to college had made a conscious decision not to use any illicit drugs (this included athletes, Black and Latina women from poor urban "drug-infested" neighborhoods, women who had negative experiences within their alcoholic families) were instantly confronted with a culture where substances were readily available and abuse of these substances was the norm. The most popular substances reported were caffeine, nicotine, alcohol, marijuana, nitrous oxide, Psilocybin mushrooms, LSD, and Ecstasy (MDMA). Some mention was also made of opium, heroin, and cocaine, although most of these were not first-hand or even second-hand experiences. Although many of the women reported that they abstained from use of illicit drugs, they frequently reported feeling "surrounded by" various drugs, particularly marijuana.

Many of the White women involved in this project expected that the majority of people at college would experiment, use, and abuse substances (regardless of whether or not *they* used any substances). Many of the women of color (who also tended to have grown up in poor, urban communities) expected that they would go to college to avoid the drug use that was so prevalent in their neighborhoods. Nevertheless, college was the place where many students were learning their limits with alcohol and other substances. Some learned "the hard way" through personal experiences or experiences within an intimate relationship; some entered college having already learned; others learned by observing others; and still others never learned. For those involved in higher education, understanding the perceived cultural norms of drug use is critical. This is not to say that the cultural norms are uniform throughout college. There are different subcultures or pockets where different levels of use and abuse are tolerated.

The research on college student substance use that has examined gender and race differences has lacked the kind of *thick description* that qualitative, feminist analysis brings. To analyze critically the college culture in which abuse of psychoactive substances and abuse of women are widespread, we need to continue to engage in the kinds of in-depth analyses required within the context of qualitative research.

Qualitative, feminist methods describing the role of alcohol and other drugs from the point of view of college women (and men) continue to be lacking in the research literature. More work needs to be done to understand the college environment and how the social organization of college contributes to psychoactive substance experimentation, use, and abuse. I found it helpful to examine the role of drug use from the standpoint of women and their descriptions of drug use in their everyday worlds in order to uncover more pieces of the puzzle of why substance abuse and related problems have become so prevalent on college campuses. Clearly, more work needs to be done to include as many voices as possible to find out how people make meaning of the role of drugs in their lives before we can understand what motivates individuals to use drugs in ways that are harmful to themselves or others.

It is not enough to know why people use different drugs at one time in their lives, for these reasons are plural and shifting. However, individualized help for those who need it, and are willing to receive it, needs to be considered and developed. We need to rethink our existing, prevailing antidrug sentiments, and think about how we have come to construct the meaning we have about certain drugs, and how this leads us to vote or make policy, or treat those with drug-related problems.

Recently, I was speaking with one of my students, a poor African-American woman with whom I have worked for four years. While talking about her previous semester, she said that her cousin was found shot and killed in his car because of drugs and that her sister and her husband were in prison for selling drugs. She said, "Kim, my sister is a beautiful person. . . she told me, 'I tried the right way and I tried the wrong way and neither one worked, so we started selling drugs to be able to afford a roof over our baby's head.' My sister's truly a good person, she was just trying to do the best she could." We need to rethink how our society treats drug users, abusers, and dealers, and why those who are poor and non-White often receive harsher penalties from the legal system than wealthier Whites. We need to examine how racist beliefs factor into popular social constructions of drugs, particularly crack and heroin, and the harsher legal penalties that result. Stiffer fines and longer prison terms do not result in help for chemical dependency. By constructing and believing these particular drugs to be somehow more inherently evil than others, we depict the users (often people of color from inner-city poverty) as somehow more evil and worthy of harsh legal sanctions instead of emotional and physical help for substance abuse. By constructing drugs such as alcohol, nicotine, and to some extent marijuana (drugs that the wealthier White young people are using) not as drugs but as an essential part of college and of society after college, individuals with problems stemming from these substances are not criminalized or removed from the society, but instead are placed in hospitals, thirty-day treatment facilities, twelve-step programs with similar (i.e., often other White, middle-aged or older, White, heterosexual male) people. We need to examine the fundamental, socially constructed, sometimes racist, classist, and sexist beliefs that underlie much of our legal sanctions and treatment paradigms for various drugs. Most people are trying to do the best they can, and people with chemical dependency need to be helped, not criminalized. Most young people are seeking love and acceptance from others. Some find this love in their families, some in their communities, some in their peers (including gangs), and some in their intimate partners. When young people think they have found true love among their friends or an intimate partner, they generally do the best they can to be accepted by these people. If these people engage in criminal activities, often so too will the young person, in an attempt to gain acceptance. When people are poor, they will work in whatever way they can to provide food, clothing, and shelter for their families—even if this work is selling drugs. We need to begin to think about drug use within the context of relationships and the seeking of love and acceptance, and sometimes, as was the case with my student's sister, in difficult situations. However, as Bertram, Blachman, Sharpe, and Andreas (1996) suggested: "Change will only come when pressure mounts from citizens and organized groups demanding an end to the politics of denial and a new commitment to a politics of reason, care, and collective responsibility" (p. 263).

In an effort to change the existing research paradigm dominating the literature about college drug use, I examined the words college women used to describe the role of drugs in their lives. These women constructed meaning about drugs in hierarchical and traditional ways, including discourses of morality, legality, and health/safety. Using these traditional discourses, women ranked their acceptability of drugs in an effort to simplify the complex task of learning and setting personal drug-using limits. Women drew on their drug experiences within their intimate relationships in order to help them construct their acceptability rankings and set their personal limits.

A CALL FOR A PARADIGM SHIFT

These women's words suggested that drug-use decisions are more complicated and individualized than the previous literature has suggested. Studies attempting to find correlates of college student drug use, personality traits of drug abusers, gender differences, racial differences, parental influences, and educational influences continue to dominate the literature on college student drug use. Those working within the field of college student drug use are eager to find a solution to the complex problems associated with drug use, and I suspect the belief is that more "scientific" studies will bring us closer to finding the "answer" to end, or at least reduce, the problems associated with drug abuse. It has become like the search for the cure for cancer, and the reason is the same— to save people's lives. I hope my project will provide a starting point and an invitation to listen to more voices to determine other factors that influence one's drug-using decisions. I hope this project allows people to think differently about the issues of college student drug use and the less obvious problems that may accompany it.

APPENDICES

Appendix A
Selected Text from the Report of the Results from the University's Core Alcohol and Drug Survey, Spring 1996

With the Support of the Substance Abuse Prevention Program
Funded in part by the Division of Student Affairs, and the U.S. Department of
Education, Fund for the Improvement of Post-Secondary Education (FIPSE)
Spring 1996

INTRODUCTION

Methodology

In the spring of 1996, 10% of the university students were randomly selected by Testing Services to receive the survey. The sample parameters were all main-campus students 18 years of age or older, who were registered for the Spring of 1996 and had a campus, local, or New York mailing state address. Students from underrepresented groups were selected to participate at a higher rate to increase the stability of the requested information. Students received two separate mailings of the survey during the third and fourth weeks in February and the first week in March of 1996.

Surveys were mailed and returned through either U.S. mail, campus mail, or turned in at the student's residence hall main desk. Each student received a copy of the survey and a cover letter that explained the purpose of the survey, insured confidentiality of individual responses, and identified prizes for the core survey raffle for which all respondents were eligible. Students also received a postcard on which they were instructed to print their names and return separately from their completed survey to ensure their entry into the prize drawing. A total of 1,210 students received the survey. Four hundred and seven students returned completed questionnaires, for an overall response rate of 33.6%.

Core Survey

The development of the Core Alcohol and Drug Survey was undertaken by the U.S. Department of Education/Fund for the Improvement of Post-Secondary Education (FIPSE) to measure alcohol and other drug usage, attitudes, and perceptions among college students at two- and four-year institutions.

The Core instrument was developed using American Psychological Association standards for test development to ensure validity and reliability. The Core Institute continuously examines the psychometric properties of the survey for the sake of obtaining the most accurate data possible. The Core instrument consists of thirty-nine items; survey questions can be broken down into the following categories:

- Attitudes, perceptions, and opinions about alcohol and other drugs
- Patterns of alcohol and drug use and consequences of use
- Perceptions of campus climate and policy issues

Five items were added to the instrument to tap students' perceptions of drinking norms at the university.

Demographics

The following analyses are based on a subset of 334 respondents. A reduced set was necessary to randomly select out graduate/professional students who were overrepresented in the returned survey. Table 1 provides a breakdown of age, gender, ethnic origin, marital status, residence, and student status of this subset. It compares demographic characteristics of the 1996 sample to the 1995 sample. The 1996 sample consists of significantly more White, non-Hispanic students than the 1995 sample. Additionally, the 1996 sample consists of more Black, non-Hispanic students than the 1995 sample. Table 1 gives a more detailed comparison of sample demographics.

Table 1

1996 Core Sample Demographic and 1995 Core Sample Demographics

1996 Sample (N=406)	Percent	1995 Sample (N=447)	Percent
Gender		**Gender**	
Female	67.8	Female	63.7
Male	32.2	Male	36.3
Class		**Class**	
Freshman	18.9	Freshman	19.3
Sophomore	20.1	Sophomore	22.2
Junior	24.9	Junior	22.2
Senior	28.4	Senior	28.7
Graduate	7.2	Graduate	7.4
Age		**Age**	
18	15.3	18	15.6
19 or 20	40.8	19 or 20	42.0
21 or 22	33.6	21 or 22	30.4
23 or 24	3.3	23 or 24	5.7
25 to 30	4.5	25 to 30	3.8

Table 1 (cont.)

Ethnicity		Ethnicity	
Amer. Ind/Ak Nat.	0.3	Amer. Ind/Ak Nat.	0.2
Hispanic	4.6	Hispanic	4.1
Asian/Pac. Islander	11.7	Asian/Pac. Islander	5.7
White(non-Hispanic)	69.8	White(non-Hispanic)	84.7
Black (non-Hispanic)	11.7	Black (non-Hispanic)	4.1
Other	1.9	Other	1.1
Residence		**Residence**	
On-campus	63.0	On-campus	58.5
Off-campus	37.0	Off-campus	41.5
Grade Average		**Grade Average**	
A	37.7	A	40.0
B	53.0	B	50.1
C	8.6	C	9.6
D or F	0.6	D or F	0.2
Marital Status		**Marital Status**	
Single	96.4	Single	97.1
Married	3.0	Married	2.2
Separated	0.3	Separated	0.2
Divorced/Widowed	0.3	Divorced/Widowed	0.2

EXECUTIVE SUMMARY

Following are key findings on the quantity and frequency of use of alcohol.

1. 86% of students consumed alcohol in the past year ("annual prevalence").
2. 14% reported having never used alcohol in past year.
3. One third of students seldom or never drink alcohol (0– 6 times in the last year).
4. 75.5% of students currently use alcohol (at least once during the past 30 days); among current users, less than 1% used on a daily basis.
5. 36.7% of students consumed 1–5 drinks per week, 29% consumed 6 or more, and 34% did not drink on a weekly basis.
6. Weekly use was highest among male students. Five times more men than women drink 15 or more drinks a week. Significantly more women (8% more than men) reported having no drinks on a weekly basis.
7. Freshmen and seniors consume more drinks/week than sophomores and juniors and graduate/professional students. 27% of seniors and 24% of freshmen consume 10 or more drinks/week, whereas 13% of grad/prof, 18% sophomores, 22% juniors consume the same.
8. In terms of location of use, significantly fewer students living on-campus (43.1%) reported 0 drinks/per week than those living off-campus (23%). Students living off

campus were more likely to report consuming more than 15 drinks/week (15%) versus those living on-campus (5%).

Binge Drinking

1. Overall, 43% of students reported having binged in the two-week period prior to the administration of the survey. A binge is defined as consuming 5 or more drinks in one sitting.
2. The majority of bingers (54.8%) binged 1–2 times, 32.6 % binged 3–5 times, and 12.4 % binged 6 or more times in the previous two weeks.
3. Fewer females (43%) reported episodes of binge drinking than males (64%).

Following are some key findings on the use of other drugs.

1. 41.3% of students have used marijuana in the past year ("annual prevalence").
2. 24% of students currently use marijuana (at least once during the past 30 days); among current users, 2% used on a daily basis.
3. The top 6 most frequently reported illegal drugs used in the past year were: marijuana (41.0% pot, hash, hash oil); hallucinogens (8.8% LSD, PCP); amphetamines (8.2% diet pills, speed); designer drugs (6.1% Ecstasy, MDMA); inhalants (5.5% glue, solvents, gas); cocaine (4.0% crack, rock, freebase).
4. 97% did not use cocaine in the past 30 days (current use). Among those who currently use, 1.5% used 3 or more days during that 30-day period.
5. 97.5% did not use amphetamines in the past 30 days (current use). Among current users, 1.5% used more than 3 days during that 30-day period.
6. 98.8% did not use sedatives in the past 30 days (current use). Among current users, .3% used more than 3 days during that 30-day period.
7. 98.8% did not use hallucinogens in the past 30 days (current use).
8. Among current users, 1.2% used more than 3 days during that 30-day period.
9. 99.4% did not use opiates in the past 30 days (current use). Among current users, .3% used more than 3 days during that 30-day period.
10. 97.9% did not use inhalants in the past 30 days (current use). Among current users, .6% used more than 3 days during that 30-day period.
11. 98.5% did not use designer drugs in the past 30 days (current use). Among current users, .3% used more than 3 days during that 30-day period.

Age of first use of substances

1. On average, students first used alcohol between the ages of 14 and 17.
2. On average, pot users first used the drug between the ages of 16 and 20.
3. On average, students first used tobacco between the ages of 16 and 20.

Following are key findings on the consequences of alcohol and drug use.

1. More than 1 in 3 students (37.2%) said that other students' drinking **interrupts their studying** and **messes up their physical living space** (e.g., cleanliness, neatness, organization).
2. About 1 in 4 students (26.9%) said that other students drinking makes them **feel unsafe** and **prevents them from enjoying events** (e.g., concerts, sports, social activities).
3. 62 % of students said that other student drinking **interferes with their life**.

4. Among those who use alcohol, binge drinkers (once or twice) and frequent binger (binged 3 or more times) reported experiencing problems such as **public misconduct** (such as trouble with police, fighting/argument, vandalism) and **serious personal problems** (such as suicidality, being hurt or injured, trying unsuccessfully to stop, sexual assault) more frequently than nonbingers.

Following are key findings on opinions about the availability of alcohol and other drugs.

1. 73.3% of students said they would rather not have drugs available and used at parties they attend and around campus.
2. 26% of students said they would rather not have alcohol available and used at parties they attend and around campus.

Following are key findings on student perceptions of campus climate.

1. Overall, 89% of the students were aware of the university's alcohol and drug policies.
2. 53% of the students believed that the policies were enforced.
3. 51% of the students were aware of the existence of alcohol and other drug awareness programs.
4. 70% felt that the campus was concerned about the prevention of alcohol and other drug use; this represents an 8% increase over last year.
5. Students surveyed overestimate how much their peers tolerate excessive or unsafe drinking practices. Most students reported that they hold relatively responsible attitudes about drinking. However, most students are not aware that their peers also hold these attitudes.
6. Students consistently believed that usage is more excessive than is actually the case. For every substance, students perceived considerably more usage than is actually the case. For instance, students surveyed believed that an insignificant (.6%) number of students abstain from alcohol. Actually, nearly 14% of students report abstaining from alcohol in the last year.
7. More dramatic misperceptions are evident when examining perceptions about tobacco and marijuana usage.

PREVALENCE OF SUBSTANCE USE

Annual Prevalence of Alcohol

Alcohol continues to be the drug of choice for students. Of students responding to the survey, 86% reported that they had consumed alcohol at least once in the past year. The majority of drinkers (42.2%) drink 1–3 times a week, 19% drink 1–2 times a month, 19.9% drink 1–6 times a year, while only 5% drink five or more times a week (see Table 2).

Table 2
Percentage of Students Indicating Frequency of Alcohol Use

Frequency of Use	Percent of Students
Never	13.9
1x year	8.1
6x year	11.1
1x month	7.2
2x month	12.7
1x week	21.1
3x week	21.1
5x week	3.6
Daily	1.2

Quantity of Alcohol Consumed

A drink was defined as a bottle of beer, a glass of wine, a wine cooler, a shot glass of liquor, or a mixed drink. Table 3 demonstrates that 67% of students report drinking once a week or more. Among weekly drinkers, 36.7% consumed 1–5 drinks per week, 29 % consumed 6 or more, and 34% did not drink on a weekly basis. Almost 2 times as many males (32%) as females (18%) were reported consuming 10 or more drinks per week. More than 4 times as many males (19%) as females (4%) had over 15 drinks per week.

Among students who had the highest consumption (10 or more drinks per week) seniors (27%) and freshmen (24%) consumed the most, followed by juniors (22%), sophomores (19%), and graduate/professional (13%) students.

Students residing off-campus reported higher consumption than those living on campus. Among students living off-campus, 24% reported consuming 0 (zero) drinks per week and 32% reported consuming 10 or more drinks per week. Among those residing on campus, 43% had 0 drinks per week, while 16% had 10 or more drinks per week. Almost 4 times as many students living in Greek houses (72%) as those living in residence halls (16%) or approved housing (17%) consumed 10 or more drinks per week. Twenty-one percent of those living in a house/apartment reported consuming 10 or more drinks per week.

Table 3

Percentage of Students Reporting Number of Drinks Consumed per Week by Gender

Number of Drinks	Percent of Students		
	Male	Female	Totals
None	28.13	36.95	34.11
One	10.42	12.82	12.04
2–5	26.04	24.63	25.08
6–9	4.17	7.39	6.35
10–15	2.50	14.29	13.71
16 or more	18.75	3.94	8.70

Annual Prevalence of Other Drugs

Alcohol (86%), marijuana (41.3%), and tobacco (40.8%) remain the most frequently used substances in terms of annual prevalence. Hallucinogens (9%), amphetamines (8%), designer drugs (6.1%), and inhalants (5.5%) were used by a small percentage of students. Sedatives, "other" illegal drugs, opiates, and steroids were the least used drugs, with negligible use reported "in the last year." Of note is the fact that twice as many students use alcohol as use tobacco and almost as many students use tobacco as use marijuana.

More females (63%) than males (54%) report having never used tobacco and in the last year. Almost 3 times more men (19%) than women (7%) report having used tobacco 1–6 times a year. It is noteworthy that monthly to daily use is as common among women (29%) as it is among men (26%).

Although more women (61%) than men (55%) report having never used marijuana in the past year, almost as many women (21%) as men (19%) report having used 1–6 times in the past year.

30-Day Prevalence: Other Drugs

Table 4 presents detailed prevalence data regarding alcohol and other drug use "during the last 30 days." These data represent a more immediate pattern of student drug use than the annual prevalence data; the percentages are lower than the annual prevalence figures. Tobacco and marijuana remain the most commonly used substances, followed by hallucinogens, cocaine, amphetamines, inhalants, and designer drugs, respectively.

More students reported having currently used tobacco (30%) than reported having currently used marijuana (24%). Among students who reported current use, 7% reported using tobacco daily, whereas only 2% reported using marijuana daily. Significantly fewer students reported more frequent use of other drugs.

Table 4
Percent of Students Reporting Frequency of Drug Use "in the Last 30 Days"

	Percent of Students/Frequency of Use						
Substance	0	1–2	3–5	6–9	10–19	20–29	All
Alcohol	24.5	20.5	19.6	16.8	15.3	3.1	0.3
Tobacco	70.0	8.3	3.4	3.7	4.6	3.1	7.0
Marijuana	76.1	7.2	2.8	4.3	5.2	2.5	2.1
Cocaine	97.2	1.2	1.2	0.3	0	0	0
Amphetamine	97.5	1.2	1.2	0	0.3	0	0
Sedatives	98.8	0.9	0	0	0	0.3	0
Hallucinogens	96.6	3.1	0.3	0	0	0	0
Opiates	99.4	0.3	0.3	0	0	0	0
Inhalants	97.9	1.5	0.6	0	0	0	0
Designer	98.5	1.2	0.3	0	0	0	0

Age of First Use

While the most frequently reported "age of first use" for alcohol was 14–17 (51%), for other drugs (marijuana, hallucinogens, amphetamines, cocaine, opiates), the 18–20 age range had the highest percentages of reported first use.

Binge Drinking

Heavy drinking is frequently associated with injuries and other health complications, criminal victimization, including sexual and physical assault, vandalism, and impaired sleep and study time. Recent research literature on alcohol use has associated heavy episodic or binge drinking with serious personal and public health problems. The literature operationally defines binge drinking as the consumption of 5 or more drinks in one sitting.

Overall, 43% of students reported having binged in the two-week period prior to administration of the survey. The majority of bingers (54.8%) reported bingeing episodes 1–2 times. Thirty-three percent reported binge episodes 3–5 times, and 12% binged 6 or more times in the previous two weeks. Table 5 presents the number of binge drinking episodes reported by students in the two-week period prior to administration of the survey. Note that 6% of the students reported more than five binge episodes in the last two weeks. It is also noteworthy that a majority of students responding to the survey (57%) reported having not binged in the past two weeks.

Table 5
Frequency of Binge Drinking Episodes "in the Last Two Weeks"

Number of Binge Drinking Episodes	Percent of Students/Place of Residence		
	On-campus (189)	Off-campus (111)	Total (300)
None	60	51	57
One	15	14	15
Two	12	7	10
3 to 5	9	18	12
6 to 9	4	5	5
10 or more	0	4	1

As shown in Figure 1, fewer females (36%) reported episodes of binge drinking than males (57%). Bingeing 1–2 times was almost as common among women (20%) as it was among men (28%). Frequent bingeing (3 or more times) was more common among males (28%) than females (16%).

Figure 1
Percentage of Binge Drinkers by Gender

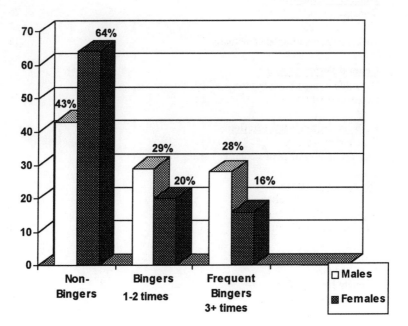

Consequences of Binge Drinking

As shown in Table 6, survey findings indicate that a higher percentage of binge drinkers experienced alcohol-related problems since the beginning of the school year than nonbinge drinkers. When asked how often they experienced problems due to drinking or drug use, students who binge drink reported experiencing problems more often than students who did not binge drink. Among binge drinkers, those who reported frequent binge drinking (i.e., 3 or more episodes in two weeks) consistently experienced problems more frequently than those who binged one or two times.

Table 6
Percentage of Students Experiencing Alcohol-related Problems by Binge Level

Alcohol-related Problem (N= 446)	Nonbinge Drinkers	Bingers	Frequent Bingers
Academic Performance			
Missed a class	16	38	87
Performed poorly on test or important project	8	22	52
Violence/Vandalism			
Damaged property, fire alarm	2	5	25
Argued or fought	9	36	62
Took advantage of another sexually	2	6	12
General Disorientation			
Did something later regretted	20	60	72
Had memory loss	13	54	76
Personal Injury/Victimization			
Was hurt or injured	5	20	45
Was taken advantage of sexually	5	22	25
Disciplinary Action			
Was in trouble w/ police, residence hall, or other campus authorities	4	17	26
Other			
Been criticized	15	40	57
Thought had a problem	2	18	27
Driven under the influence	11	41	59
Tried/Failed to stop	0	3	22
Thought about suicide	4	4	11
Tried to commit suicide	0	0	2

Academic Performance

With regards to academic performance, 2 times more "bingers," and 3 times more "frequent bingers" than nonbingers reported missing a class as a result of drinking or drug use. Three times more bingers and almost 7 times more "frequent bingers than nonbinger" reported performing poorly on a test or important class project.

Personal Injury/Victimization and Violence

Four times as many bingers and frequent bingers as nonbingers reported being taken advantage of sexually as a result of their drinking and drug use. Nine times as many frequent bingers than nonbingers reported having been hurt or injured. Two times as many bingers and 6 times as many frequent bingers reported having taken advantage of another sexually.

General Disorientation

As many as 3 in 4 frequent bingers and 3 in 5 bingers reported experiencing some form of disorientation, including memory loss, as a result of drinking or drug use.

Disciplinary Action and Drinking and Driving

Four times as many bingers and almost 7 times as many frequent bingers as nonbingers reported being in trouble with the police, and residence hall or other college authorities.

Significantly, 4 times more bingers and 5 times as many frequent bingers reported driving under the influence.

"Second-hand" Effects of Drinking

As demonstrated in Table 7, survey findings also demonstrate how students are adversely affected by other students' drinking. Specifically, students were asked if and how other students' drinking interfered with their studying, safety, living environment, involvement with athletic teams or other groups, and their enjoyment of social events.

A significant percentage of students responding to these questions reported having to deal with the negative outcomes of other students' drinking. More than 3 in 5 students reported that other students' drinking interferes with their life. More than one in three students reported having their study interrupted and their physical living space messed up by other students' drinking. Almost 2 in 5 had their study interrupted, and nearly 1 in 4 were prevented from enjoying an event including concerts, sports, and social activities.

Table 7
Percentage of Students Reporting Adverse Effects of Other Students' Drinking

Interrupted study	37 %
Felt unsafe	27 %
Messed up physical living space	36 %
Prevented from enjoying events	22 %
Interfered in other way(s)	43 %
Interfered with my life	62 %

Campus Environment

Campus culture regarding alcohol and other drugs can exert a strong influence on the social choices students make while in the campus environment. The Campus culture and overall social milieu are influenced by perceptions of use, perceptions of campus climate (levels of tolerance) with respect to alcohol and drug use, the accessibility of alcohol, the availability of nonalcoholic-focused social options, and perceptions of campus policies and enforcement. The following findings address many of these factors and the potential impact they may exert on the curricular and co-curricular aspects of students' experience at the university.

Perceptions of Behavioral Norms

When asked about their perceptions of students' drinking and drug usage, respondents consistently believed that usage was more excessive than was actually the case. It is particularly noteworthy that for every substance, students perceived considerably more usage than was actually the case. For instance, students surveyed believed that an insignificant (.6%) number of students abstained from alcohol. Actually, nearly 14% of students reported abstaining from alcohol in the last year.

More dramatic misperceptions are evident when examining perceptions about tobacco and marijuana usage. Students mistakenly perceived that only 1.3% of The university students abstained from tobacco use. In actuality, almost 3 in 5 percent of students reported that they never used tobacco in the last year. Likewise, students perceived that an insignificant percent (1.6%) of students abstain from using marijuana. Again, 59% of the students reported that they never used marijuana in the last year. Table 8 summarizes students' perceptions of how often other students drink and use drugs.

Not only did respondents overestimate the number of their peers who used alcohol, but they also overestimated how often alcohol was used. For example, when asked how often they believed the average student used alcohol, students believed that 96% of students used alcohol once a week or more. Significantly fewer students 47% reported using alcohol this frequently (see Figure 2).

Of interest was the finding that students perceived that 2 in 3 students binge drink (drink 5 + drinks) when they party. Only 1 in 3 students reported doing the same.

Table 8
Percentage of Students Indicating Perception of Use by the "Average" Student

| Use last year | Percent of Students | |
	Personal Use (Actual Campus Norm)	Perceived Use (Perceived Campus Norm)
Alcohol (n =321)		
Never used	14%	0.6%
Used less than once a week	39%	2.2%
Used once a week or more	47%	96.3%
Tobacco (n=318)		
Never Used	59%	1.3%
Used less than once a week	20%	9.5%
Used once a week or more	21%	89.0%
Marijuana (n= 312)		
Never Used	59%	1.6%
Used less than once a week	25%	33.0%
Used once a week or more	16%	34.0%

Figure 2
Perceived Weekly Drinking for Self (Actual Use) and Other Students (Perceived Use)

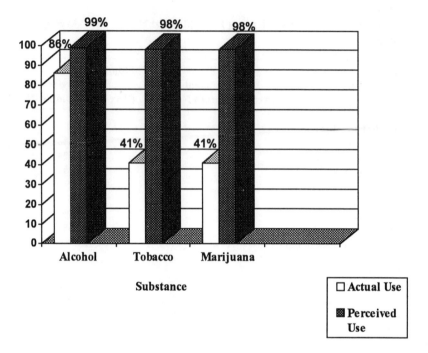

Substance

☐ Actual Use

▧ Perceived Use

Perception of Attitudinal Norms

As Table 9 shows, students also overestimate how much their peers tolerate excessive or unsafe drinking practices. Most students reported that they hold relatively responsible attitudes about drinking. The majority of students (69%) believe that "it is OK to drink occasionally as long as it does not interfere with academic or other responsibilities." However, most students are not aware that their peers also hold these attitudes.

When asked about their perceptions of the most common attitude among students, many students (40%) believed that the most common attitude was more permissive (i.e., "it is okay to get drunk occasionally even if it does interfere with academic and other responsibilities") than was actually the case. Only 7% of the students held the view that occasional drunkenness was okay even if it interfered with academic and other responsibilities. Table 9 presents the percentage distribution of personal attitudes and perceived campus norms for alcohol use among students (n = 332).

Table 9

Student Perception of "Most Common" Student Attitude about Alcohol Use

Items N=332	Percent of Student	
	Personal Attitudes	Perceived Campus Norm
1. "Drinking is never a good thing to do."	11%	.6 %
2. "It is OK to drink as long as you don't get drunk."	9 %	1.0 %
3. "It is OK to drink occasionally as long as it does not interfere with academic or other responsibilities."	**69%**	33%
4. "It is OK to get drunk occasionally even if it does sometimes interfere with academic or other responsibilities."	7 %	**40%**
5. "It is OK to get drunk frequently if that's what an individual wants to do."	4%	**26%**

Perceptions of Campus Climate Towards Use

The survey assessed students' perceptions about the university policies and climate with respect to alcohol and other drugs. Overall, 89% of the students were aware that the university had alcohol and drug policies. Fifty-three percent of the students believed that the policies were enforced. Fifty-one percent of the students were aware of the existence of alcohol and other drug awareness programs. The level of awareness about these issues remained unchanged over the past year. Seventy percent felt that the campus was concerned about the prevention of alcohol and other drug use; this represents an 8% increase over last year.

Preference for Availability of Alcohol and Other Drugs

It is often assumed that college students drink or want to drink and are willing to try drugs. Some prevention efforts that currently exist at the university assume that there is a critical mass of students who want to live in an environment that is free from the negative influences resulting from alcohol and other drug abuse. This survey explored student interest in having such an environment by asking students their preference for the availability of alcohol and other drugs around campus and at parties they attend. Overall, more than 1 in 4 students preferred an alcohol-free environment. A significant majority (74%) of the students preferred a drug-free environment.

Overview of Drug Use Trends

Percentage of students who believe that people risk harming themselves with drug use:

Cocaine

- 79% believe there is moderate to great risk in trying cocaine infrequently (once or twice).
- 95% believe there is moderate to great risk in trying cocaine regularly.

LSD

- 72% believe there is moderate to great risk in trying LSD infrequently.
- 91% believe there is moderate to great risk in trying LSD regularly.

Amphetamines

- 65% believe there is moderate to great risk in trying infrequently.
- 87% believe there is moderate to great risk in trying regularly.

Marijuana

- 19% believe there is moderate to great risk in trying infrequently.
- 43% believe there is moderate to great risk in trying occasionally.
- 74% believe there is moderate to great risk in trying regularly.
- 28% have driven under the influence.

Percentage of students who had a negative or harmful experience as a result of their own drinking or drug use:

- 13% have been taken advantage of sexually as a result of their drinking or drug use.
- 11% have been in trouble w/ the police as a result of their drinking or drug.
- 17% have been hurt or injured as a result of their drinking or drug.
- 20% performed poorly on a test as a result of their drinking or drug.
- 26% got into an argument or fight as a result of their drinking or drug.
- 40% did something they later regretted as a result of their drinking or drug.

Alcohol and Other Drug Trends

Annual Prevalence

	1996	1995	Ref. 91–93*
Alcohol	86.0	89.0	85.0
Tobacco	41.0	46.0	39.0
Marijuana	41.3	41.0	25.0
Cocaine	4.2	2.6	3.6
Amphetamines	8.2	6.7	5.6
Sedatives	3.3	2.0	2.2
Hallucinogens	8.8	9.8	5.5
Opiates	1.5	.2	.5
Inhalants	5.5	3.3	1.9
Designer	6.1	1.7	1.8

30-day Prevalence

	1996	1995	Ref. 91–93*
Alcohol	75.5		72.0
Tobacco	30.0		29.0
Marijuana	24.0		13.0
Cocaine	2.8		1.1
Amphetamines	2.5		2.2
Sedatives	2.5		.9
Hallucinogens	3.4		1.8
Opiates	.6		0.2
Inhalants	2.1		0.5
Designer	1.5		0.6

* = Reference group of 38,715 college students completing the same questionnaire in 1991–93

Appendix B
Informed Consent Letter

Dear Student,

I am inviting you to participate in a research study which will help my work toward completion of my Ph.D. degree at Syracuse University. Involvement in this study is voluntary, so you may choose to participate or not. This form will explain what the study is about, but if you have any additional questions, please feel free to ask me.

I am interested in learning more about drug use on college campuses. You will be asked to keep a written account of your personal exposure to drug use (including drugs such as nicotine, caffeine, alcohol, prescription medication, etc.). This will include making observations of your own drug use as well as any observations of others with whom you have contact. Please make these observations at least weekly (although daily would be helpful) for the next seven weeks.

I would like to use this information as a part of a larger study to determine the drugs to which students are frequently exposed, and where this exposure takes place. The journals will be kept in a locked drawer which will be locked in an office. You will be anonymous (i.e., your names and names of any individuals mentioned will be changed in any written or published material). Also, if you are interested in being contacted to engage in an interview with me in an attempt to gather more in-depth information please put your campus phone number at the bottom of this letter.

The benefit of this research is that you will be helping us better understand the extent and frequency of drug use on college campuses. The risk to you of participating in this study is minimal. If you no longer wish to continue, you have the right to withdraw from the study, without penalty, at any time. If you feel at any time that you may need to seek professional help for a drug-related problem please contact either the University Counseling Center at 443-4715 or the University's Health Services office at 443-2666. The researcher is not immune to legal subpoena about subjects' drug use or information they have about others' use of illicit drugs.

I understand that all information will be kept anonymous; my name will not appear anywhere and no one will know about my specific journal entries except the researcher. All of my questions have been answered and I wish to participate in this research study.

This is to certify that I am 18 years or older having been born on _____.

(date of birth)

_____ _____
Signature of participant   Date

_____ _____
Signature of investigator   Date

_____(Phone number if interested in being interviewed)

Appendix C
The Drug Acceptability Ranking Composite

The Drug Acceptability Ranking Composite developed using informants' narratives—reconciling and ranking the moral, the legal, and the health consequences of different drugs

Note: The ranking progresses downward from the drugs that most of the women in the study felt were "morally okay" and "safe" and had fewest legal consequences to use to drugs that were perceived as less so (i.e., referred to as "hardcore" drugs). Most of the women in the study tended to progress down their own personal ranking until they reached the point where they set their personal limit. These women also set their personal limits for each drug as well. The composite ranking would look similar to many of the women's individual rankings. Most drew their line after alcohol. Caffeine and nicotine were the only drugs that all of the women could legally use. After each drug included in the ranking are some of the women's thoughts that went into setting their personal limits for each drug.

The drugs included in the women's rankings and some of the thoughts that went into setting limits for each drug:

1. Caffeine. "The problems arose the day after taking Vivarin I would just crash, then I would be unbelievably fatigued. At around five o'clock the day after taking Vivarin, I would be so tired I would hardly be able to go to the dining hall or even some of my evening classes." (Paula)

2. Alcohol. "I wasn't planning on drinking an excessive amount. I just wanted a slight buzz from the alcohol. I had promised my boyfriend (who is back home) that I wouldn't go over my personal limit of six. After that, I never know what will happen. I mean I've only drank more than that 2 or 3 times. Usually, I'm 'all set' at 5 or 6. I'm in, what I would call control." (Kathy)

The Drug Acceptability Ranking Composite (cont.)

3. Nicotine. "Unfortunately, at college there are more occasions to smoke. So my smoking habits have increased. I even see the results. For instance, I play field hockey and when I run sometimes my lungs feel as if they're going to explode. I know it's horrible for me and I vow to quit when I graduate." (Janet)

4. Marijuana. "This past week I had been smoking marijuana more often than usual. I found that it was becoming a daily habit therefore I am going to begin to cut back. I have watched too many people let it rule their lives, and I would never let that happen to me." (Erin)

5. Nitrous Oxide. "I tried it and I thought it was scary, it was kind of cool because I really felt high and in another world for only a few seconds, and then I was fine, so I did it a few more times. When I told my friends about it, they told me what whippits could do to you so I stopped." (Dana)

6. Codeine. "I had to take codeine after I had an operation. It knocked me out in a matter of minutes. I would only stay up like 4 hours a day. I felt like I was getting addicted, then they ran out. It seemed like I had to have it." (Tara)

7. Opium smoking. "There was actually opium here this week. This guy kept packing bowls and putting a small chunk in with the weed. Only those who have smoked it before knew what the taste was." (Jude)

8. Psilocybin mushrooms. "I personally will never do any chemical stuff. What I mean by that is acid, cocaine, etc. If I could get really pure—100% pure ecstasy then maybe I would try that but right now I'm sticking to shrooms and weed." (Jude)

9. LSD. "I see nothing wrong with it [LSD] in this setting [a Rave]. I don't see LSD as bad unless abused. The effects made me skeptical to use it, but then again alcohol has risks and I drink." (Cathy)

The Drug Acceptability Ranking Composite (cont.)

10. Ritilin (snorted). "When I snorted the ritilin it burned. I only did two lines after that. I didn't really feel anything except a little more awake and buzzed. . . They do ritilin a lot at my friend's house. Mainly when everyone is already pretty drunk or high."
(Maggie)

11. MDMA (Ecstasy). "Joanie wants me to do ecstasy with her this weekend and I'm way too nervous. I have never done it before and she's not sure what it's cut with. It all sounds way too sketchy to me." (Jude)

12. Special K. "When I got to the Rave I snorted some Special K and when I got inside I bought a pill of E [Ecstasy]. I felt incredible. I can't even describe how it felt. I was so content with everything."
(Darla)

13. Cocaine (snorted). "This was my first exposure to cocaine. My boyfriend and his three friends were high and they brought some with them. This was a very hard situation for me. I do not think I was pressured in a direct way, but sort of indirectly. Maybe it was me, but it was too hard to say no. Maybe it was because I liked him a lot, I really do not know." (Christine)

14. Cocaine (smoked). "I am really concerned about one of my friends who smokes up [smokes marijuana] a lot. She's been smoking a while and now she is experimenting with other substances. Nothing like Crack Cocaine because she would never do anything like that, but she's thinking about dropping acid, and I don't know what to tell her." (Jill)

15. Heroin. "The movie ["The Gift"] was gory and horrifying. The message that heroine *[sic]* is a really desperate, dirty and horrible drug was sent across effectively in this film." (Hetty)

Appendix D
An Example of an Individual Drug Acceptability Ranking

An Example of Maggie's Individual Drug Acceptability Ranking

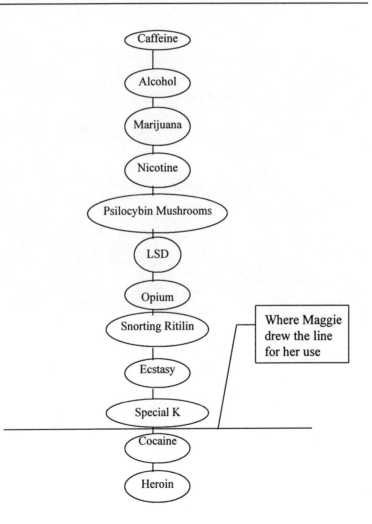

Appendix E
An Example of an Individual Drug Acceptability Ranking

An Example of Darla's Individual Drug Acceptability Ranking

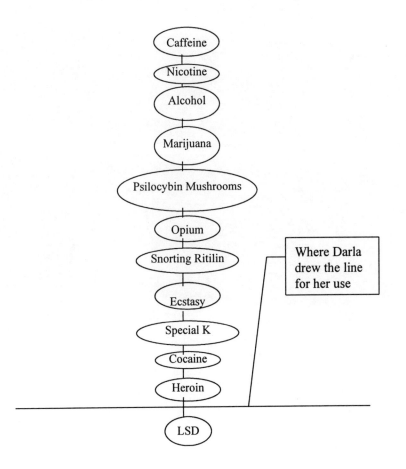

References

Alcoff, L. (1994). The problem of speaking for others. In S.O. Weisser & J. Fleischer (eds.), *Feminist Nightmares: Women at Odds*. New York: New York University Press.

Arafat, I., & Yorburg, B. (1973). Drug use and the sexual behavior of college women. *Journal of Sex Research, 9*(1), 21–29.

Babcock, M., & McKay, C. (1995). *Challenging Codependency: Feminist Critiques*. Toronto: University of Toronto Press.

Bannerji, H. (1995). *Thinking Through: Essays on Feminism, Marxism, and Anti-Racism*. Toronto: Women's Press.

Barker, G., & Musick, J. S. (1994). Rebuilding nests of survival: A comparative analysis of needs of at-risk adolescent women and adolescent mothers in the US, Latin America, Asia, and Africa. *Childhood, 2*(3), 152–163.

Bell, S. G., & Yalom, M. (1990). *Revealing Lives: Autobiography, Biography, and Gender*. Albany: State University of New York Press.

Ben-Yehuda, N. (1990). *The Politics and Morality of Deviance: Moral Panics, Drug Abuse, Deviant Science and Reversed Stigmatization*. Albany, NY: State of New York Press.

Bertram, E., Blachman, M., Sharpe, K., & Andreas, P. (1996). *Drug War Politics*. Berkeley: University of California Press.

Birrell, S. (1987). The woman athlete's college experience: Knowns and unknowns. *Journal of Sport and Social Issues, 11*(1–2), 82–96.

Blacks are unfairly targeted for crack cocaine charges, Supreme Court is told. (1996, February 26). *Nando Times* [On-line]. Available: www.nandotimes.com/newsroom/ntn/nation/022696/nation10-258.html.

Blumer, H. (1969). *Symbolic Interaction*. Englewood Cliffs, NJ: Prentice-Hall.

Bordin, R. (1981). *Women and Temperance*. Philadelphia, PA: Temple University Press.

Bowker, L. H. (1974). Student drug use and the perceived peer drug environment. *International Journal of Addictions, 9*(6), 851–861.

Bowker, L. H. (1977). *Drug Use Among American Women, Old and Young: Sexual Oppression and Other Themes*. San Francisco: R. & E. Research Associates.

Bowles, G., & Duelli-Klein, R. (eds.) (1983). *Theories of Women's Studies*. London: Routelege & Kegan Paul.

Bushman, G. (1996). Alcohol and drug use at university parallels national figures. *Syracuse Record, 27*(9), p. 1–7.

Caetano, R., & Kaskutas, L. A. (1995). Changes in drinking patterns among whites, blacks, and Hispanics, 1984–1992. *Journal of Studies on Alcohol, 56*, 558–565.

Chase, S. (1995). *Ambiguous Empowerment: The Work Narratives of Women School Superintendents.* Amherst: University of Massachusetts.

Cheung, Y. W. (1990). Ethnicity and alcohol/drug use revisited: A framework for future research. *International Journal of the Addictions, 25*(5–6), 581–605.

Cheung, Y. W. (1993). Approaches to ethnicity: Clearing roadblocks in the study of ethnicity and substance use. *International Journal of the Addictions, 28*(12), 1209–1226

Collins, P. H. (1991). *Black Feminist Thought: Knowledge, Consciousness, and the Politics of Empowerment.* London: Harper Collins Academic.

Cookson, P. W., Jr., & Persell, C. (1985). Privilege and the importance of elite education. *Preparing for Power: America's Elite Boarding Schools.* New York: Basic Books.

Courtwright, D., Joseph, H., & Des Jarlais, D. (1989). *Addicts Who Survived: An Oral History of Narcotic Use in America, 1923–1965.* Knoxville: University of Tennessee Press.

Currie, E. (1993). *Reckoning: Drugs, the Cities, and the American Future.* New York: Hill & Wang.

DeVault, M. (1987). Women's talk: Feminist strategies for analyzing research interviews. *Women and Language, 10*(2), 33–36.

DeVault, M. (1990). Talking and listening from women's standpoint: Feminist strategies for interviewing and analysis. *Social Problems, 37*(1), 701–721.

DeVault, M. (1991). *Feeding the Family: The Social Organization of Caring as Gendered Work.* Chicago: University of Chicago Press

DeVault, M. (1996). Talking back to sociology: Distinctive contributions of feminist methodology. *Annual Review of Sociology, 22*, 29–50.

Dreeben, R. (1967). The contribution of schooling to the learning of norms. *Harvard Educational Review, 37*, 211–237.

Duster, T. (1970). *The Legislation of Morality: Law Drugs and Moral Judgment.* New York: Free Press.

Ellis, G. J., & Stone, L. H. (1979). Marijuana use in college: An evaluation of a modeling explanation. *Youth and Society, 10*(4), 323–334.

Fago, D. P., & Sedlacek, W. E. (1973). *Trends in university student attitudes and behavior toward drugs.* Maryland University, College Park, Counseling Center. (ERIC Document Reproduction Service No. ED089174)

Felmee, D., Sprecher, S., & Bassin, E. (1990). The dissolution of intimate relationships: A hazard model. *Social Psychology Quarterly, 53* (1), 13–30.

Fidler, P. P., & Bucy, E. M. (1976). *The scope of entering freshman drug use at the University of South Carolina: A report of the annual entering freshman drug survey conducted during summer orientation 1973.* South Carolina University. (ERIC Document Reproduction Service No. ED124085)

Fine, M. (1988). Sexuality, schooling and adolescent females: The missing discourse of desire. *Harvard Educational Review, 58*(1), 29–53.

Fine, M. (1991). *Framing Dropouts: Notes on the Politics of an Urban Public High School.* Albany, NY: SUNY Press.

Fine, M. (1994). Over dinner: Feminism and adolescent female bodies. In L. Radke & H. J. Stam (eds.), *Power/Gender: Social Relations in Theory and Practice* (pp. 219–246). London: Sage Publications, Ltd.

Fisher, B. S., & Sloan, J. J. (1995). *Campus Crime*. Springfield, IL: Charles C. Thomas, Publisher.

Fleischer, C. (1995). *Composing Teacher Research*. Albany: State of New York Press.

Frintner, M. P., & Rubinson, L. (1993). Acquaintance rape: The influence of alcohol, fraternity membership and sports team membership. *Journal of Sex Education, 19*(4), 272–284.

Gilligan, C. (1993). *In a Different Voice: Psychological Theory and Women's Development*. Cambridge, MA: Harvard University Press.

Girdano, D. D., & Girdano, D. A. (1976). College drugs use—A five year study. *Journal of the American College Health Association, 25*(2), 117–119.

Goldberg, R. (1997). *Drugs across the Spectrum*. Englewood, CO: Morton Publishing Co.

Goode, E. (1993). *Drugs in American Society*. New York: McGraw-Hill.

Graham, H. (1984). Surveying through stories. In Bell and Roberts (eds.), *Social Researching: Politics, Problems, Practice*. London: Routledge & Kegan Paul.

Hafner, S. (1991). *Nice Girls Don't Drink: Stories of Recovery*. Westport, CT: Bergin & Garvey.

Handler, L. (1995). In the fraternal sisterhood: Sororities as gender strategy. *Gender-and-Society, 9*(2), 236–255.

Hanson, D. J. (1975). College students' reasons for drinking: Twenty year trends. *College Student Journal, 9*(3), 256–257.

Hanson, G., & Venturelli, P. J. (1995). *Drugs and Society*. Boston: Jones & Bartlett.

Heath, D. B. (1990). Uses and misuses of the concept of ethnicity in alcohol studies: An essay in deconstruction. *International Journal of the Addictions, 25*(5–6), 607–628.

Herd, D. (1989). The epidemiology of drinking patterns and alcohol-related problems among U.S. blacks. In D. Spiegler (ed.), *The Epidemiology of Alcohol Use and Abuse among U.S. Minorities* (NIAAA Monograph No. 18). Washington, DC: Government Printing Office.

Heritage, J., & West, B. W. (1993, October). *Fifteen year study of drug and alcohol use on a college campus*. Paper presented at the Meeting of the Southeastern Conference of Counseling Center Personnel, Mobile, AL.

Holland, D. C. & Eisenhart, M. A. (1990). *Educated in Romance: Women, Achievement and College Culture*. Chicago: University of Chicago Press.

Horowitz, H. L. (1987). *Campus Life: Undergraduate Cultures from the End of the Eighteenth Century to the Present*. New York: Alfred A. Knopf.

Huba, G. J. (1977a). Organization of needs in male and female drug and alcohol users. *Journal of Consulting and Clinical Psychology, 45*(1), 34–43.

Huba, G. J. (1977b). Consistency of daydreaming styles across samples of college male and female drug and alcohol users. *Journal of Abnormal Psychology, 86*(1), 99–102.

Hunter, G. T. (1990). A survey of the social context of drinking among college women. *Journal of Alcohol and Drug Education, 35*(3), 73–80.

Inaba, D. S., & Cohen, W. E. (1996). *Uppers, Downers, and All Arounders: Physical and Mental Effects of Psychoactive Drugs* (6th ed.). Ashland, OR: CNS Productions.

Jessor, R. (1968). Expectations of need satisfaction and drinking patterns of college students. *Quarterly Journal of Studies on Alcohol, 29*(1), 101–116.

Johnson, P. B. (1988). Personality correlates of heavy and light drinking female college students. *Journal of Alcohol and Drug Education, 34*(2), 33–37.

Johnson, P. B., & Gallo-Treacy, C. (1993). Alcohol expectancies and ethnic drinking differences. *Journal of Alcohol and Drug Education, 38*(3), 80–88.

Johnston, L. D., O'Malley, P., & Bachman, J. G. (1993*). National Survey Results from the Monitoring the Future study, 1975–1992*. Rockville, MD: National Institute on Drug Abuse.

Johnstone, B. M. (1994). Sociodemographic, environmental, and cultural influences on adolescent drinking behavior. In R. A. Zucker, G. M. Boyd, & J. Howard (eds.), *The Development of Alcohol Problems: Exploring the Biopsychosocial Matrix of Risk*. Rockville, MD: National Institute on Alcohol Abuse and Alcoholism.

Julian, T. W., & McHenry, P. C. (1993). Mediators of male violence toward female intimates. *Journal of Family Violence, 8*(1), 39–56.

Kalof, L. (1993). Rape-supportive attitudes and sexual victimization experiences of sorority and non-sorority women. *Sex Roles, 29*(11–12), 767–780.

Kirsch, M. M. (1986). *Designer Drugs*. Minneapolis, MN: CompCare Publications.

Kreutzer, J. S. (1980). *An assessment of expectancies for sexual and aggressive behaviors of male and female drinkers*. Paper presented at the Annual Meeting of the Midwestern Psychological Association, St. Louis, MO.

Kvale, S. (1995). Social construction of validity. *Qualitative Inquiry, 1*(1), 19–40.

LeJeune, C., & Follette, V. (1994). Taking responsibility: Sex differences in reporting dating violence. *Journal of Interpersonal Violence, 9*(1), 133–140.

Lester, L. F. (1983). College student behavior: A ten year look. *Journal of American College Health, 31*(5), 209–213.

Lex, B. W. (1990). Prevention of substance abuse problems in women. In Watson (ed.), *Drug and Alcohol Abuse Reviews*. Clifton, NJ: Humana Press.

Lo, C. C., & Globetti, G. (1993). A partial analysis of the campus influence on drinking behavior: Students who enter college as nondrinkers. *Journal of Drug Issues, 23* (4), 715–725.

Lott, B. (1988). Separate spheres revisited. *Contemporary Social Psychology, 13*(2), 55–62.

Marin, G., Posner, S. F., & Kinyon, J. B. (1993). Alcohol expectancies among Hispanics and non-Hispanic whites: Role of drinking status and acculturation. *Hispanic Journal of Behavioral Sciences, 15*(3), 373–381.

Martin, P. Y., & Hummer, R. A. (1989). Fraternities and rape on campus. *Gender and Society, 3*(4), 457–473.

McGee, Z. T. (1992). Social class differences in parental and peer influence on adolescent drug use. *Deviant Behavior, 13*(4), 349–372.

Mies, M. (1983). Towards a methodology for feminist research. In Bowles & Duelli-Klein (eds.), *Theories of Women's Studies*. London: Routelege & Kegan Paul.

Minh-ha, T. (1989). *Woman, Native, Other: Writing Postcoloniality and Feminism*. Bloomington: Indiana University Press.

Moffatt, M. (1989). *Coming of Age in New Jersey: College and American Culture*. New Brunswick, NJ: Rutgers University Press.

Mohanty, C. T. (1991). Under Western eyes: Feminist scholarship and colonial discourses. In Mohanty, Russo, & Torres (eds.), *Third World Women and the Politics of Feminism*. Bloomington: Indiana University Press.

Morgan, H. W. (1981). *Drugs in America: A Social History 1800–1980*. Syracuse, NY: Syracuse University Press.

Myers, P. N., & Biocca, F. A. (1992). The elastic body image: The effect of television advertising and programming on body image distortions in young women. *Journal of Communication, 42*(3), 108–133.

Nechas, E., & Foley, D. (1994). *Unequal Treatment: What You Don't Know about How Women Are Mistreated by the Medical Community*. New York: Simon & Schuster.

Neff, J. A., & Hoppe, S. K. (1992). Acculturation and drinking patterns among U.S. Anglos, Blacks and Mexican Americans. *Alcohol and Alcoholism, 27*(3), 293–308.

Noddings, N. (1992). *The Challenge to Care in Schools*. New York: Teachers College Press.

Oakley, A. (1981). Interviewing women. In H. Roberts (ed.), *Doing Feminist Research*. New York: Routledge & Kegan Paul.

O'Hare, T. M. (1990). Drinking in college: Consumption patterns, problems, sex differences and legal drinking age. *Journal of Studies on Alcohol, 51*(6), 536–541.

Padilla, A. M., Duran, D., & Nobles, W. W. (1995). Inner-city youth. In Coombs & Ziedonis (eds.), *Handbook for Drug Abuse Prevention*. Boston, MA: Allyn & Bacon.

Palmer, C., & Horowitz, M. (1982). *Shaman Woman, Mainline Lady: Women's Writings on the Drug Experience*. New York: William Morrow & Co.

Ray, O., & Ksir, C. (1993). *Drugs, Society and Behavior*. St. Louis, MO: Mosby Year-Book.

Rebstock, J., & Young, S. (1978). Drug use among community college students. *Community College Social Science Journal, 2*(1), 29–34.

Reefer Madness [Film]. (Available from United American Video Corporation, 976 Murfreesboro Road, Nashville, TN 37217).

Reinharz, S. (1983). Phenomenology as a dynamic process. *Phenomenology and Pedagogy, 1*(1), 77–79.

Reinharz, S. (1992). *Feminist Methods in Social Research*. New York: Oxford University Press.

Ribbens, J. (1989). Interviewing—An "Unnatural Situation"? *Women's-Studies-International-Forum, 12*(6), 579–592.

Ritzer, G. (1996). *Sociological Theory* (4th ed.). New York: McGraw-Hill.

Rosenau, P. M. (1992). *Postmodernism and the Social Sciences*. Princeton, NJ: Princeton University Press.

Sandmaier, M. (1980). *The Invisible Alcoholics: Women and Alcohol Abuse in America*. New York: McGraw-Hill.

Schaef, A. W. (1987). *When Society Becomes an Addict*. San Francisco: Harper & Row.

Segal, B. (1975). Self-concept and drug and alcohol use in female college students. *Journal of Alcohol and Drug Education, 20*(3), 17–22.

Shields, E. W. (1995). Sociodemographic analysis of drug use among adolescent athletes: Observations–perceptions of athletic directors and coaches. *Adolescence, 30*, 839–861.

Slade, P. D. (1994). What is body image? *Behavior Research and Therapy, 32*(5), 497–502.

Smith, D. (1987). *The Everyday World as Problematic: A Feminist Sociology*. Boston: Northeastern University Press.

Spellman, E. V. (1988). *Inessential Woman: Problems of Exclusion in Feminist Thought*. Boston: Beacon Press.

Spreitzer, E. (1994). Does participation in intrascholastic athletics affect adult development? A longitudinal analysis of an 18–24 age cohort. *Youth in Society, 25*, 368–387.

Stammer, M. E. (1991). *Women and Alcohol*. New York: Gardner Press.

Strimbu, J., Schoenfeldt, L. F., Sims, O., & Suthern, J. (1973). Drug usage in college students as a function of racial classification and minority group status. *Research in Higher Education*, 1(3), 263–272.

Swaim, R., Beauvais, F., Edwards, R. W., & Oetting, E. R. (1986). Adolescent drug use in three small rural communities in the Rocky Mountain region. *Journal of Drug Education, 16*(1), 57–73.

Takaki, R. (ed.). (1994). *From Different Shores: Perspectives on Race and Ethnicity in America.* New York: Oxford University Press.

Taylor, J. M., Gilligan, C., & Sullivan, A. M. (1995). *Between Voice and Silence: Women and Girls, Race and Relationship.* Cambridge, MA: Harvard University Press.

Traub, S. H. (1983). Characteristics of female college student drug use. *Journal of Drug Education, 13*(2), 177–186.

United States of America v. Booker, 64 USLW 2367 (N.D. Ind. 1995) *aff'd*, 70 F. 3d 488 (7th Cir. 1995).

U.S. Department of Education, Fund for the Improvement of Post-Secondary Education (FIPSE) and Division of Student Affairs (1996). *Core Alcohol and Drug Survey Spring 1996: Report and Recommendations to the University Community.* Unpublished manuscript.

U.S. Department of Health and Human Services. (1996, November 21). Secretary Shalala launched Girl Power! at APHA Annual Meeting. *Join Together* [On-line]. Available: http://www.jointogether.org.

Van Den Bergh, N. (1991). *Feminist Perspectives on Addictions.* New York: Springer Publishing Co.

Wallace, J. M., & Bachman, J. G. (1991). Explaining racial/ethnic differences in adolescent drug use: The impact of background and lifestyle. *Social Problems, 38*(3), 333–357.

Weis, L. (1985). *Between Two Worlds: Black Students in an Urban Community College.* Boston: Routledge & Kegan Paul.

Weng, L., & Newcomb, M. D. (1989). Predicting changes in teenage drug use: The role of intention-behavior discrepancy. *Genetic, Social and General Psychology Monographs, 115*(1), 27–48.

White, J. (1993). Feminist contributions to social psychology. *Contemporary Social Psychology*, 73, 74–78.

Willie, C. V. (1989). *The Caste/Class Controversy on Race and Poverty: Round Two of the Wilson/Willie Debate.* Dix Hills, NY: General Hall.

Winslow, R. W., & Gay, P. T. (1993). The moral minorities: A self report study of low-consensus deviance. *International Journal of Offender Therapy and Comparative Criminology, 37*(1), 17–27.

Index

About the Author

KIMBERLY M. WILLIAMS is Assistant Director of the Violence Prevention Project and Adjunct Professor in the School of Education at Syracuse University.

ISBN 0-89789-556-8